ROUTLEDGE LIBRARY EDITIONS: PRISON AND PRISONERS

Volume 3

THE MODERN ENGLISH PRISON

THE MODERN ENGLISH PRISON

L. W. FOX

Routledge
Taylor & Francis Group

LONDON AND NEW YORK

First published in 1934 by George Routledge & Sons Ltd

This edition first published in 2024
by Routledge
4 Park Square, Milton Park, Abingdon, Oxon OX14 4RN

and by Routledge
605 Third Avenue, New York, NY 10158

Routledge is an imprint of the Taylor & Francis Group, an informa business

British Library Cataloguing in Publication Data
A catalogue record for this book is available from the British Library

ISBN: 978-1-032-55549-2 (Set)
ISBN: 978-1-032-56411-1 (Volume 3) (hbk)
ISBN: 978-1-032-56420-3 (Volume 3) (pbk)
ISBN: 978-1-003-43544-0 (Volume 3) (ebk)

DOI: 10.4324/9781003435440

Publisher's Note
The publisher has gone to great lengths to ensure the quality of this reprint but points out that some imperfections in the original copies may be apparent.

Disclaimer
The publisher has made every effort to trace copyright holders and would welcome correspondence from those they have been unable to trace.

THE MODERN ENGLISH PRISON

By

L. W. FOX

M.C., ASSISTANT COMMISSIONER AND INSPECTOR OF
PRISONS, SECRETARY OF THE PRISON COMMISSION

LONDON
GEORGE ROUTLEDGE & SONS, LTD.
BROADWAY HOUSE, CARTER LANE, E.C.

First Edition, 1934
Reprinted,   1936

Made and Printed in Great Britain at
The Mayflower Press, Plymouth.   William Brendon & Son, Ltd.

CONTENTS

CONTENTS

CONTENTS

APPENDICES

CONTENTS

ILLUSTRATIONS

PREFACE

THIS book was prepared in the belief that, among the growing literature of crime and the treatment of crime, there should be room for some account of the English prison system as it stands to-day. Its first aim is to give an objective and comprehensive view of the system as it is, rather than as it has been or ought to be : the historical matter is therefore limited to what is necessary for proper understanding of present practice, and no attempt is made to trespass on the ground of the " penologist."

I am indebted to the Prison Commissoners and the Permanent Under-Secretary of State for the Home Department for permission to publish this book, but it must be understood that while the facts and figures are derived almost entirely from published official documents, the responsibility for their accurate presentation and for any inferences drawn from them rests solely with myself.

My grateful thanks are due to my colleagues in the Prison Commission and the Home Office, without whose encouragement and advice I could neither have begun nor finished my task.

L. W. F.

December, 1933.

BIBLIOGRAPHY

THE following is not a bibliography of the subject, but a list of the principal works quoted or used in the text, with one or two others of general interest, together with a list of certain official publications of relevant interest. The words in brackets after the note on each book are those used for short reference in the text.

The State of the Prisons, John Howard, can now be obtained in Everyman's Library.

The Prison Chaplain, a Memoir of the Rev. John Clay, Chaplain of Preston Prison. By the Rev. W. Clay. (Macmillan, 1861.) Though primarily devoted to the work of the Rev. J. Clay at Preston, this is an invaluable source-book of information on early nineteenth-century opinion and developments, and contains much useful historical matter. [Clay.]

English Prisons under Local Government. Sidney and Beatrice Webb. (Longmans, 1922. 15s.) The standard history of our prison system up to 1898, of which any subsequent historical work must be to some extent a summary. A stimulating preface by G. B. S. on crime, punishment, and prisons in general. [Webb.]

The Punishment and Prevention of Crime. Sir Edmund du Cane. (Macmillan, 1885.) The first Chairman of the Prison Commission here describes and explains the system for which he was responsible for over twenty years. [du Cane.]

The English Prison System. Sir Evelyn Ruggles-Brise. (Macmillan, 1921. 7s. 6d.) Sir E. du Cane's successor takes the story up to 1921. [Ruggles-Brise.]

The Home Office. Sir Edward Troup. (Putnam (Whitehall Series) 5s., 1925.) A short account of the Home Office, its functions, and the way it works, with a history of the development of the office of Secretary of State. Sir E. Troup was Permanent Under-Secretary of State in the Home Office, 1908–1922.

Boys in Trouble. Lilian le Mesurier. (John Murray, 1931. 6s.)
A valuable contribution to the understanding of the problems of the young offender by Mrs. le Mesurier, who was
the creator and for many years the leader of the team of
Woman Visitors at the Boys' Prison, Wormwood Scrubs.

The Lawbreaker. E. Roy Calvert and Theodora Calvert. (Routledge, 1933. 7s. 6d.)
The late Mr. Calvert was, and Mrs. Calvert is, a member
of the Committee of the Howard League for Penal Reform,
and their book may profitably be read as an introduction
to the general problems of crime and punishment in England
to-day written from an unofficial and " reformist " standpoint.

STATIONERY OFFICE PUBLICATIONS

Notes on Imprisonment, Borstal Detention, etc. (1928. Price 2d.)
A short pamphlet issued under the authority of the Home
Office giving concise information about the different forms
of detention, classification, etc.

*Reports of the Commissioners of Prisons and Directors of Convict
Prisons.* Published annually. Price usually 1s. 6d.

Criminal Statistics, England and Wales. Published annually.
Price usually 3s. 6d. or 4s.

*Report from the Select Committee of the House of Lords on the
Present State of Discipline in Gaols and Houses of Correction,*
1863.

Report from the Departmental Committee on Prisons, 1895.

*Report from the Select Committee of the House of Commons on
Debtors (Imprisonment),* 1908.

*Report from the Departmental Committee on the Treatment of Young
Offenders,* 1927. Price 2s. 6d.

Report from the Departmental Committee on Persistent Offenders,
1932. Price 1s. 6d.

*Report from the Departmental Committee on the Employment of
Prisoners.* Part I. 1933. Price 1s. 6d.

THE
MODERN ENGLISH PRISON

CHAPTER I

HISTORICAL OUTLINE

1. *Primitive—to* 1774

RIGHT into the nineteenth century the system of criminal justice in England was so chaotic as to defy reduction to a short statement of any accuracy. But it is clear that at any rate before the seventeenth century imprisonment was not used as a form of punishment in itself. The punishment for treasons and for all felonies was death, and at the end of the eighteenth century there were over two hundred capital felonies—though owing to the curious complications of " benefit of clergy " a considerable proportion of convicted felons escaped with fines, burnings in the hand, and so forth. It was not till 1827 that " clergy " was abolished, and the death sentence limited to treason and the " non-clergyable " felonies, and not till 1861 that the capital felonies were reduced to murder, piracy, and the burning of dockyards. In the seventeenth century, when territory had been acquired in America, the further practice grew up of granting Crown Pardons to condemned felons conditionally on their agreeing to be " transported beyond the seas " : this practice received statutory recognition in 1679,[1] and in 1767[2] the Judges were empowered to order transportation as a form of sentence.

For misdemeanours, the punishments were fines, whipping, or exposure in stocks or pillory : and though imprisonment

---

[1] 31 C. II, cap. 2.   [2] 8 G. III, cap. 15.

1

was recognised at Common Law as a lawful punishment for misdemeanours, it was used not for its own sake but to assist the Crown to exact its fines. At Common Law imprisonment means no more than deprivation of liberty, and our subject is the story of the statutory modification of this simple conception into the complicated system of to-day, together with the substitution for the capital penalty of various forms of punishment involving imprisonment.

The earliest lawful place of detention was the Common Gaol, and in 1403 it was provided by statute[1] that Justices should commit only to the Common Gaol. In legal theory all these gaols were the King's, but in practice the only gaol in which the Sheriff, who was the King's Officer, had authority was the County Gaol, and there were innumerable other small gaols kept by municipal corporations, or by nobles and bishops under franchise. Few of the gaols were specially provided buildings—anything from the cellar of a public house to the gate-house of an abbey was made to serve—and there was no clear responsibility on the Sheriff or Justices for their upkeep or for the maintenance of the prisoners. The keeping of the gaol was farmed out to private individuals who made what profit they could out of it, by the charging of fees, legal and illegal, to the prisoners,[2] by the hiring of rooms and sale of food (the only official provision was a pennyworth of bread per diem for convicted felons), and by the tap and brothel side of the business—this last perhaps the most lucrative of all. The public duty of the gaoler was limited to the safe-custody of persons committed to his charge, whether committed for debt, or to await trial at Assizes or Sessions, or subsequently, in the case of convicted felons, to await transportation ; and as safe buildings and staff were expensive, irons and chains were used instead—both ironing and the removal of irons being made the subject of a fee.

The Elizabethan Poor Law produced a second type of institution : in order to provide work for the unemployed poor, and that able-bodied vagrants, harlots, idle apprentices

---

[1] 5 H. IV, cap. 10.
[2] " Every incident in the prison life, from admission to discharge, was made the occasion for a fee." Webb, p. 5.

and the like might be corrected in their habits by laborious discipline, the Justices of every county were required to provide Houses of Correction, which came later to be known as Bridewells, or Working Houses. These institutions were under the direct control of the Justices, who appointed and paid the Master, and were responsible for finding work for the inmates, who were kept out of the proceeds of their labour.

At the outset, therefore, the gaol and the bridewell embodied two quite distinct sets of ideas. The gaol had only two objects, safe-custody and the exaction of money, and no question arose either of deterrence or reform—it was the gaoler's business to make the gaol as jolly as possible for those who could pay, and as unpleasant as possible for those who could not or would not pay : the deterrent power of the law was entrusted to the gallows. The bridewell, on the other hand, imported the ideas both of reform and of deterrence, though no doubt the Justices were more concerned to protect the rates by frightening vagrants out of their districts than to " correct them in their habits." This distinction, however, did not last very long : as early as 1609 the Justices were authorised to institute " hard labour " as a penal rather than reformatory measure,[1] and during the century it became common to commit all sorts of minor offenders to the bridewells, though this practice seems not to have been definitely legalised till 1719.[2] During the eighteenth century the two types of institution became almost completely assimilated, and were commonly under the same roof and the same master or keeper—a position which was given statutory recognition in 1823, though the Gaol Act of that year, while recognising that the two might be " in united or contiguous buildings," still provided that debtors should be confined only in that part " ascertained to be the Gaol," and vagrants only in the House of Correction. This Act did, however, give the Justices a definite responsibility for the whole building, though it was not till 1865 that the distinction was finally abolished. The combined establishment, under the name of prison, was then placed under the jurisdiction of the Justices in Quarter

[1] 7 J. I, cap. 4.   [2] 6 G. I, cap. 19.

Sessions, the jurisdiction of the Sheriff being limited to prisoners under sentence of death.[1]

It is unnecessary to dwell in detail on the conditions which existed throughout the eighteenth century, and often well into the nineteenth, in the reeking bestiality of these filthy dens, where felons and debtors, convicted and untried, young and old, with no more distinction of age, condition, or sex than they could afford to buy from the gaoler, were herded together, chained, starving, and half naked, in the most pestilential conditions of disease, debauchery, lechery, brutality, and extortion. One can only wonder how any at all resisted the gaol-fever by which one quarter of the prisoners were, it was computed, annually swept away. Yet it was not till John Howard, on his appointment to be High Sheriff of Bedford in 1773, began his exposure of the " state of the prisons " that any criticism at once influential and effective was directed towards these conditions in public life.

2. *Development from* 1774 *to* 1877

Howard. 1774–1791. The immediate effect of Howard's work was a series of statutes, from 1774 to 1791,[2] directed to securing a decent level of cleanliness and sanitation, with a view to preventing the gaol-fever ; to the provision of work for prisoners to assist in their maintenance ; the separation of the sexes ; and the effective supervision of the gaols by the Justices. They also gave approval to the principle of confining prisoners in separate cells. But though these statutes are historically interesting as indicating the movement of instructed opinion, their immediate effect was inconsiderable : they were permissive, not mandatory, and in any case there was no machinery to ensure that they were enforced, or even to see whether they were being enforced or not. In a few counties exceptionally progressive Justices got something done, but reforms cost money, and local authorities were not generally disposed to spend money for the benefit of prisoners. In the year of

---

[1] This Act did not apply to the Borough Gaols.
[2] The full titles of these and other important statutes are given in Appendix A.

Waterloo, the Aldermen of the City of London, in whose prisons a debtor had recently died of starvation, and two women prisoners were shortly to be found with only a rug to hide their joint nakedness, declared that " their prisoners had all they ought to have, unless gentlemen thought they should be indulged with Turkey carpets "[1]—perhaps the first public protest of common sense against the pampering of prisoners. Nevertheless, a general improvement in sanitation and cleanliness resulted, though this must be ascribed less to the suggestions of Parliament than to the malice of the gaol-fever, which, no longer content with its annual quota of prisoners, began to sweep away Bench and Bar as well as juries at the Assizes, and to spread virulent epidemics in the county towns.

The efforts of Howard and his friends were not, however, directed solely to the material standards of the gaols ; their real motive power was concern for the moral standards of the prisoners—they wished to bring back the long-forgotten notion that the Houses of Correction should correct. And this correction, in their belief, was to be attained primarily through the influences of religion : for this reason the main planks in their platform, after the elementary decencies had been secured, were the appointment of chaplains, and the introduction of separate cells for the prisoners, firstly because this was the only evident method of breaking down the contamination of the gaol-yard, and secondly because they sincerely believed in the reformative effect of solitary meditation.

These were the principles underlying the first group of Gaol Acts, but they were not the only principles in the field : the interest of Jeremy Bentham had been caught, and he became the mouthpiece of another school of thought —a philosophic rather than a religious school—which, while aiming no less sincerely at the reform of the prisoners, believed that this was to be achieved principally by industry, and produced various elaborate schemes for turning prisons into " hives of profitable industry." Bentham even succeeded in persuading Parliament to accept his fantastic scheme of a Panopticon Prison, but though this got no

[1] Clay, page 91.

further than the purchase of a site at Millbank, the notion
of prisons made not only self-supporting but profitable was
not unattractive to Justices, and made considerable head-
way. Separate confinement, on the other hand, was not
only regarded as a cranky reformist idea but did present a
real difficulty in that it required complete and costly
rebuilding. Nevertheless, in a few counties the experiment
was begun.

Peel's Gaol Act, 1823. Howard died in 1791, and for twenty
years very little more was heard or done about prison
reform : but the ferment was working, and when the matter
came to a head again both the religious and the utilitarian
schools were still in action. Now the Evangelical successors
of Howard were strengthened by the accession of the
Quakers, and notably of Mrs. Elizabeth Fry, while the
Benthamites brought prison reform within the ambit of
that great movement for reform of the whole system of
criminal justice and police which was to come to fruition
when Sir Robert Peel became Home Secretary in 1822.

Peel's Gaol Act of 1823 took its place among a series of
historic statutes which swept away the old, chaotic gibbet-
justice of the Middle Ages, reformed the procedure of the
Courts, and established a system of police for the Metropolis.
It consolidated the twenty-three pre-existing statutes on the
subject of gaols and houses of correction, took the first step
towards assimilating these institutions, and " for the first
time it made it peremptorily the duty of Justices to organise
their prisons on a prescribed plan, and to furnish quarterly
reports to the Home Secretary upon every department of
their prison administration. They were expressly required
to adopt, as the basis, Howard's four principles of the
adoption of sufficient secure and sanitary accommodation
for all prisoners, the transformation of the gaoler or master
from an independent profit-maker into the salaried servant
of the local authority, the subjection of all criminals to a
reformatory regimen, and the systematic inspection of every
part of the prison by visiting justices."[1] The nature of the
reformatory regimen, however, was something of a compromise between the religious and the utilitarian schools,

[1] Webb, page 74.

for while copious provision was made both for religious and for educational instruction, the principle of separate confinement was specifically rejected and its place was taken by the Benthamite idea of classified association in five groups, viz. debtors (or, in the bridewells, vagrants), unconvicted felons, unconvicted misdemeanants, convicted felons, and convicted misdemeanants. Each group was to be associated in productive employment, from the profits of which the prisoners were to be maintained. All the worst abuses of the old system were now swept away, including irons and chains, fees, taps, unauthorised punishments, and the supervision of women by men, and the Act prescribed a Code of Rules of which many survive, in whole or in part, to this day.

It was no fault of this admirable statute or its sponsors that the constitution lacked the machinery to secure its enforcement : indeed, the major problem throughout this " transitional " period was not so much to decide what should be done as to bring the various Benches and Corporations to do what was decided, or, indeed, to do anything at all. Nevertheless, although in a large number of counties and most of the small-town and franchise gaols the Act was only enforced partially, or not at all, it did act as a tremendous stimulus to the more progressive, and a considerable number of the more important prisons were rebuilt under its influence.

The Problem of the Convict. We must now diverge from the history of the local gaols to consider what was at the time an even more pressing, difficult, and alarming problem— the treatment of those convicted felons (hereafter known as " convicts "), who were not executed. This was effectively the central problem of criminal justice as distinct from prison administration, since almost every offence which we should to-day call a crime was then a capital felony : it is also of central importance to our subject, since from its solution derived those curious distinctions between imprisonment with and without " hard labour," and between imprisonment and penal servitude, which still complicate our prison system.

We have seen that in fact a considerable proportion of convicts, during the seventeenth and eighteenth centuries, were not executed but transported to the plantations. When, therefore, they were faced with the loss of their American Colonies, the Government also found themselves faced with the fact, as stated in the preamble of the Act of 1775, that the transportation of felons was " attended by divers difficulties and inconveniences." Accordingly this Act provided that convicted felons, instead of being transported, might be set to " hard labour " for various terms, either in dredging the River Thames, or other such "laborious service," or in " any proper place of confinement," and Justices were directed to prepare their Houses of Correction for setting convicts to hard labour. A later Act of 1824 further provided that it should be lawful to keep to hard labour any offender under sentence of transportation while he remained in the Gaol or House of Correction.

These arrangements were only intended to be temporary, and the intentions of the Government for the future were embodied in an Act of 1778, which provided for the building of two Penitentiary Houses in which convicts sentenced to imprisonment with hard labour were to be detained : the Penitentiaries under this Act were, in fact, never built, but the Act is interesting as giving some idea of what was then intended by " hard labour," viz. " Labour of the hardest and most servile kind, in which drudgery is chiefly required . . . such as treading in a wheel or drawing in a capstern for turning a mill or other machine, sawing stone, etc., etc., or any other hard and laborious service," with " other less laborious employment " according to age and sex for those unfitted for the heavier work. In a later Act of 1791 regulating Gaols and Houses of Correction, Justices were required to have regard to the provisions of this Penitentiary Act in making Rules for Hard Labour in their establishments.

It is not clear how far this theory of Hard Labour was applied in practice in the local gaols. The Gaol Act of 1823, while specifically retaining in force the provisions of the Act of 1791 relative to Hard Labour, and requiring Justices to make due provision for its enforcement, adds nothing fresh. It is however interesting to find that it emphasises the distinction, already clearly drawn in the Act of 1782 regulating Houses of Correction, between Hard Labour on the one hand and the employment of prisoners not so sentenced on the other. Section 38 provides that " whereas persons convicted of offences are frequently sentenced to imprisonment without being sentenced to Hard Labour, all such persons, except such persons as shall maintain themselves, shall be set to some work or labour not severe," and further provides that such persons shall maintain themselves and have " no claim to be supported at the expense of the County." It would seem, then, that even at this stage Hard Labour was conceived as a merely penal discipline, as distinct from the employment which was provided for others in order that they might maintain themselves.

However that may be, the Government soon found that it could not shuffle off its responsibility on to the local authorities, whose gaols and houses of correction were, as we have seen, quite unfit for the detention of large numbers of convicts, and who were by no means prepared to go to any expense or trouble to make them so. The Act of 1775 had further authorised the imprisonment of convicts sentenced to Hard Labour in disused ships known as " hulks," and these soon became the main receptacles of these prisoners : they were placed at Woolwich and in various harbours where the convicts could be usefully employed on dredging or other public works. In 1778 imprisonment in the hulks was made a separate form of legal sentence in place of transportation, though like the other expedients this was only intended to be used till the National Penitentiaries were built. However, it was not till 1816, following still another statute, that the Government actually began to build, on the site of Bentham's abandoned Panopticon at Millbank, a Penitentiary which was completed in 1821.

Meanwhile the discovery of Australia had given the transportation system a fresh start. The original intention had been to substitute imprisonment in the Penitentiary, like imprisonment in the hulks, for sentences of transportation, but the position now arose that some convicts served their whole sentences in Millbank or the hulks, while others were merely confined in them till they could be removed to

Australia. Here they were kept for a time either in Government employment in the penal settlements, or " on assignment " to private employers, and then, if well-conducted released on " ticket-of-leave " to be at large in the colony, though under police supervision, until the sentence had expired or a pardon was granted. It should be added that convicts who were not transported, though they were rarely required to serve the whole of their long terms of 7 or 14 years or Life in the hulks or at Millbank, were not at this stage released on " ticket-of-leave," but were granted Pardons after varying periods.

The Reaction against Reform, 1824–1839. The years following the Napoleonic Wars were marked in England by a terrible increase in crime, both real and apparent, and in the numbers of persons committed to prison. It was a period of serious social and industrial unrest, marked by political disturbances and acute distress, with a rapidly increasing population rotten with drunkenness and pauperism. At the same time the abolition of the death penalty for a large number of felonies had resulted in a vastly increased number of convictions, owing to the greater willingness of juries to find a verdict of guilty, while improvements in the police and in the procedure of courts of summary jurisdiction swept a much larger number of offenders within the net.

The old system had to some extent checked crime by removing the criminal population, whether by the gallows, the gaol-fever, or the transports. But now the thousand or so convicts who should have been transported each year were dammed up in the gaols and hulks, and the local prisons had been made reasonably healthy. In many counties, too, " reform by industry " had so attracted the Justices that their prisons had become busy workshops, concentrating solely on the profitable employment of the prisoners— profitable not only to the Justices but to the prisoners themselves, for in some counties they were able to earn substantial sums over and above their cost of maintenance. It was not therefore surprising that there should be a reaction of opinion, and that more and more strongly a call should be made for methods of deterrence which should tend to repress rather than, as was alleged against the " reformed " prisons, to encourage crime.

Now began that " battle of the systems " in which the last word was not said until 1931. " Classification " had failed, and the " separate system " began to look up again. But now the separate system itself subdivided into at least three schools, and both in England and the United States experiments under first one influence and then another were eagerly watched and discussed. The most extreme school, which for a time found some favour in America, advocated completely Solitary Confinement in separate cells by day and by night, the food and the Gospel being purveyed alike through the gratings of the cell doors. In England a modified version of this, the Separate System, permitted of intercourse with officers and instructors of the prison, and the leaving of the cell for chapel and exercise, though as between prisoners complete non-intercourse was to be enforced— at exercise by the provision of separate " airing-yards " for each prisoner, and at chapel by the division of the benches into separate compartments, from which only the chaplain and the altar were visible. A third version, the Silent System, following more closely the intention of Howard and the reformers, required the separate cells for use only by night and for meals, with association for labour in workshops or day-rooms under a strict rule of silence : this system, which permitted the continuance of useful industry, and suited the construction of the prisons rebuilt after the Act of 1823, found a good deal of support, and in a number of prisons " Silent Systems " were introduced of varying value and efficacy.

Meanwhile the question of employment of prisoners was also exciting experiment and dispute. Although of course in a number of gaols there was still no attempt to provide any work at all, the principle that prisoners should work was now generally accepted, though more as a means of covering their maintenance than on the Benthamite principles of reform. But now a further element appeared in the problem —the use of labour neither for profit nor for reformation, but simply for deterrence. The use of the tread-wheel had already been suggested in connection with " hard labour " in certain statutes, and the hint had been eagerly taken by some few Benches, who found the letting-out of man power to local millers profitable to themselves, while the actual labour of treading in the wheel was unquestionably obnoxious to the prisoners. As the notion of deterrence gained in influence, so the popularity of the tread-wheel spread with it, though now it was no longer considered necessary that it should " turn a mill or other engine "—labour was only fully deterrent, it was held, when the prisoner knew it to be perfectly useless ; all that was necessary was to find something as severe, irksome, and monotonous as possible, the sole object being " to plague the prisoner " ; it was therefore held to be much better that the prisoners in the wheel should treadle empty air. For these reasons the tread-wheel itself was shortly ousted from favour by the crank, an engine more severe, more futile, more capable of simple measurement, and more easily adapted for use in separate cells or compartments.

This stage of the Battle of the Systems may be said to have ended when the Government of the day, in spite of the general prejudice against the Separate System, and the success attained by many prisons with an intelligent use of the Silent System, allowed itself to be convinced by the advocates of the former, and by the Act of 1839 repealed so much of the Act of 1823 as related to Classification, and made it permissible for justices to adopt the " Separate System."

The Development of " Penal Servitude " to 1853. In the general alarm created by the increase of crime in the years following Peel's Gaol Act, the Government's arrangements for dealing with convicts had not escaped attack : and on this aspect of the problem the call for more sharply deterrent measures was seconded by revelations of the revolting conditions which prevailed in the hulks, and of alarming reports from the penal settlements. The general dissatisfaction was strongly expressed in the report of the Parliamentary Committee of 1837, which condemned the whole system. The Government made a considerable effort to put it on a proper basis : the period spent abroad was divided into the Probation Period, during which the convicts were employed in gangs on public works ; the Probation Pass Period, during which they might be assigned to private employment ; then the Ticket-of-Leave. For selected convicts believed to be susceptible to " reform " a preliminary period was added, not exceeding 18 months, of separate confinement in a Penitentiary, according to their conduct in which was decided the Stage into which they would pass in Australia. Millbank being inadequate, the Government, in 1842, built a large prison at Pentonville, not only to serve as a Penitentiary for convicts, but to provide local authorities with a " model prison " in which they could see how the Separate System, which they were now being urged to adopt, ought to work in proper conditions. It served this latter purpose so well that " in six years after Pentonville was built 54 new prisons were built after its model, affording 11,000 separate cells."[1]

The success of the Pentonville experiment enabled the Government, when (in 1846) it became necessary for the time being to suspend transportation, to formulate a definite system for the treatment of convicts without transportation to penal settlements. The first 15–18 months of the sentence were to be spent in separate confinement, with hard labour, in Millbank or Pentonville, or in cells rented by the Government in the county gaols : then followed a period of employment in association on public works, for which the convict was removed to a " Public Works Prison " at such harbours as Portland or Chatham, or (in the earlier stages) Gibraltar or Bermuda : some of these prisons were, in fact, the old hulks,[2] but large and expensive prisons of the cellular type were built at Portland (1848), Dartmoor (1850), and Chatham (1856), while in 1853 Brixton Prison was taken over for the reception of the female convicts.

In order to encourage good conduct and industry a daily record was kept, and a well-behaved convict could, in due course, earn a ticket-of-leave entitling him to removal to one of the Australian Colonies, where he was at large, though under police supervision, during the remainder of the sentence.

[1] Du Cane, page 56.
[2] The last hulk in this country was destroyed in 1857.

When the Australian Colonies[1] finally made effective their long-continued protests against receiving convicts on whatever conditions, it became necessary to substitute for ticket-of-leave in Australia ticket-of-leave in this country, and so was developed that tripartite system of (1) separate confinement ; (2) public works prison ; (3) conditional release on ticket-of-leave[2] under police supervision, which was regularised and given legal force, under the name of Penal Servitude, by the Penal Servitude Act, 1853. This Act limited transportation to sentences of 14 years and upwards, substituting appropriate periods of penal servitude for the shorter sentences, but by a further Act of 1857 sentences of penal servitude were legalised for all offences punishable by transportation.

The subsequent developments of penal servitude will be traced in Chapter XIV, but it may be added here that an Act of 1850 had placed the control of all " Convict Prisons " (which included the remaining hulks, the Penitentiaries of Millbank and Pentonville, the special prison for young convicts established at Parkhurst in 1838, and the new Public Works Prisons), under a new body corporate of Directors of Convict Prisons, to be appointed by the Secretary of State. In them were vested the powers and duties of the Superintendent of Hulks, and of the various bodies which had been created to manage Millbank, Parkhurst, and Pentonville. So for the first time the control of a considerable part of the prison system was brought under one permanent body of administrators responsible to the Home Secretary.

The Triumph of Deterrence, 1840–1865. Notwithstanding the Act of 1839, the adoption of separate confinement and the purely penal conception of " hard labour " was neither complete nor undisputed. Different authorities continued to take their own line, and the dispute boiled up again in the late '40s with a violent press campaign against the

---

[1] With the exception of Western Australia, to which transportation was continued until 1867. There were still a few " transports " in Australia as late as 1894 ! Bermuda was also used till 1867.

[2] Release on ticket-of-leave in this country was first authorised by the Act of 1853 ; the ticket-of-leave was there described as a " licence to be at large," and " licence " has been the correct term since that date, though an old convict will still talk of his " ticket."

separate system and "reformatory discipline" generally :
this resulted in 1850 in another Parliamentary Committee,
which, while supporting the separate system, gave general
satisfaction by coming out strongly in favour of hard labour
in individual separation, with crank or tread-wheel, instead
of "useful industry." The day of the Silent System was
now nearly over : by 1857 there were only two prisons in
the South and West which had not adopted Separate
Confinement,[1] while a return made to Parliament in 1856
showed that "in about one third of the prisons in England
the system was fully carried out ; in another third partially ;
while the rest were either on the Silent System or in the
old disorderly state."[2]

The question was finally settled by a Committee of the
House of Lords of 1863, which laid it down with no uncertain
voice that the object of imprisonment was deterrence—
"hard labour, hard fare, and a hard bed" were the proper
elements of a prison régime, and the foundations of such a
system must be separate confinement and the crank.[3] In
this view they had the undoubted support of a considerable
body of public opinion, including, it would seem, the Church,
since Archbishop Whately had pronounced that "we cannot
admit that the reformation of the convict is an essential
part of the punishment ; it may be joined incidentally,
but cannot necessarily belong to a penal system" ; and
including certainly the Bench, which in 1847 had definitely
declared "reform and imprisonment to be a contradiction
in terms and utterly irreconcilable. They expressed a doubt
as to the possibility of such a system of imprisonment as
would reform the offender, and yet leave the dread of
imprisonment unimpaired."[4]

To these principles Parliament gave approval by the
important Prison Act of 1865, which revised and consolidated previous Acts, amalgamated the Gaols and Houses
of Correction into what were henceforth to be known as
"Local Prisons" as distinct from "Convict Prisons," and
took the first definite and peremptory steps to secure uniform

---

[1] Webb, page 131.   [2] Clay, page 264.
[3] For the views of this Committee, see Appendix B.
[4] Ruggles-Brise, page 89.

compliance by all the Justices. The provisions of this Act were not permissive but mandatory, and effect was given to them by a detailed code of regulations which were enacted as a schedule to the Act and given the force of law. Every prison was henceforth to provide separate cells for the confinement of all its prisoners, and for the first time precise definition was given to the term " imprisonment with hard labour." For at least three months of his sentence the offender serving a sentence " with hard labour " was to be kept to First-Class Hard Labour, which included the heavier forms of exercise (tread-wheel, crank, shot drill, etc.) duly set out in detail ; but thereafter he might, at the discretion of the Justices, be employed on Second Class Hard Labour, which was defined as " such other description of bodily labour as might be appointed by the Justices." It is interesting to note that the liability of the County to maintain all criminal prisoners having been established, prisoners not sentenced to hard labour were now required to work without pay,[1] but there was still so much delicacy about forcing them to work, that they might not be punished for neglect of work save by alteration of diet.

Meanwhile, it may be added, " imprisonment with hard labour " had become the standard punishment prescribed by statute not only for felonies not punishable by death or transportation, but for many misdemeanours as well.

The Development of Central Control, 1835–1877. It has been evident throughout our story that the continuing inefficiency of the prison system in the nineteenth century was due less to the unwillingness of Parliament to put it right, according to its lights, than to its constitutional inability to make the responsible local authorities take notice of its statutory enactments. An early gesture was made by Peel in his Gaol Act of 1823, which required Justices to make quarterly reports to the Home Secretary, but that Minister had no power to do anything but receive the reports. In the agitation about prison matters that led eventually to the Act of 1839, this aspect of the problem received special attention, and as the matter fell to be dealt with by the

---

[1] The Act of 1782 had provided that they should on discharge receive half the profits of their labour.

Reformed Parliament, and a Whig Ministry " dominated by
two leading assumptions . . . namely . . . uniformity of
administration . . . and the impossibility of attaining that
uniformity without a large increase in the activity of the
central government,"[1] it was dealt with at once by a method
that was to have immediate and continuing effect. The
Home Secretary was, by an Act of 1835, empowered to
appoint persons to inspect prisons on his behalf and to report
to him, and by the same Act Justices were required to make
Rules for the Government of their prisons and to submit
them to the Home Secretary. By a later Act of 1844 the
Home Secretary was also empowered to appoint a Surveyor-
General of prisons, to advise the Home Office and the local
authorities on all matters concerning the construction of
prisons. The first holder of this post was Colonel (later Sir
Joshua) Jebb, R.E., the architect of the model prison at
Pentonville, who in 1850 became in addition first Chairman
of the Directors of Convict Prisons.

With these appointments a new administrative era began.
There was now at the Home Office a permanent body of
administrators, active and pertinacious, whose published
reports exercised a growing influence on official and parliamentary opinion, and played a considerable part not only
in framing policy but in forcing its adoption on local
authorities. The new Inspectors took an active part—not
all on the same side—in the Battle of the Systems, and those
(notably Mr. Crawford) who favoured the Separate System,
with the active collaboration of Sir Joshua Jebb, must
receive most of the credit—or blame—for the final triumph
of that system and its concomitant hard labour. The
influence of the Home Office was further increased by the
establishment of the Penal Servitude system, with its
permanent body of administrators, in which and by whom
the latest ideas could be tried out and presented as object-
lessons to Parliament and the public. To the persistent
pressure of the Home Office for uniform administration, and
its devotion to the ideals of separate confinement and
rigidly applied deterrent hard labour, must also be ascribed
the drastic nature of the Act of 1865, which finally stripped

---

[1] Webb, page 110.

c

the local authorities of almost the last vestige of discretion in the management of their prisons, and even gave the Secretary of State power to enforce compliance by withholding the Grant in Aid to recalcitrant prison authorities. But even the Act of 1865 was not enough. Although it had one desirable result in securing the closing of a large number of the smaller prisons, there were still too many local prisons : they were already expensive, and to put them all into a state to comply with the law and satisfy the Inspectors was not only in many cases a waste of money, but would have imposed an intolerable burden on the county rates. Further, there was still a lamentable lack of uniformity in the methods of enforcing the statutory code.

It was at this stage that " the General Election of 1874 brought into power a government pledged not to increase but actually to relieve the burden of rates upon the rural districts "[1] ; the opportunity seemed a fitting one to revive a proposal already made by the Committee of 1850, but never seriously entertained, to transfer the whole administration of local prisons to a Central Board ; and in 1877 Parliament took the plunge.

By the Prison Act of that year the ownership and control of all local prisons, with all the powers and duties of the Justices relative thereto, were vested in the Secretary of State, and the cost of their maintenance was transferred to public funds. Their general superintendence, subject to the control of the Home Secretary, was vested in a board of Prison Commissioners, assisted by Inspectors appointed by the Home Secretary, and a departmental staff. The rule-making power of Justices having passed to the Secretary of State, a new code of rules was issued in 1878, and as from the 1st April of that year all the Local Prisons came for the first time under one central control and a single code of Rules. The first Chairman of the Commissioners was Sir Edmund du Cane, R.E., who had succeeded Sir Joshua Jebb as Surveyor-General and Chairman of Directors of Convict Prisons : in effect therefore the whole of the prisons, convict and local, were now brought under one administration.

---

[1] Webb, page 198.

3. *Transition to Modern*, 1878–1898

The Du Cane Régime, 1878–1894. In its basic ideas, this phase of the prison system belongs rather to the period that it succeeded than to the system as it stands to-day : but in so far as it marks the first stage of central as distinct from local control, and in many important respects laid the foundations on which the present system stands, it is difficult to dissociate it from the period that followed.

In necessary reaction against the wasteful chaos of earlier years, the Prison Commissioners set themselves as their primary task to secure strict economy, sound administration, and rigid uniformity ; of the 113 prisons handed over, 38 were closed forthwith, and by 1894 only 56 remained open. The success of the measures taken to secure these important ends, which were the main objects of the Act of 1877, was unquestioned, and formed a rock on which their successors could confidently build.

If in their treatment of the prisoners the Commissioners would seem to have advanced little from the conceptions of the Act of 1865, it must be remembered that the Regulations of that Act were still to be observed, nor could the Secretary of State make Rules which were in conflict with them. It is nevertheless sufficiently clear that the new administration was in substantial agreement with the House of Lords Committee of 1863 as to the spirit in which the statutory code should be enforced. Sir Edmund du Cane, who was Chairman of the Prison Commission and of the Directors of Convict Prisons throughout this period, says[1] " According to the principles which have long been accepted in England, these methods must be founded on a combination of penal and reformatory elements applied . . . in their due proportions. The object of the penal element is more to deter others than for the effect on the individual subjected to the punishment." But it is evident that deterrence by severity was the first aim—" if you are going to punish, you must find something that does punish, and is disagreeable "[2] —and that while sight was never lost of the desirability of

[1] Du Cane, pages 1 and 2.
[2] Evidence before Departmental Committee on Prisons, 1895, Q. 10832.

" reformatory elements," these were only introduced to the extent that they were compatible with the needs of deterrence. Indeed, Sir Godfrey Lushington, who was for nine years Permanent Under-Secretary of State at the Home Office, expressed the opinion that in its nature a prison could not be reformatory, that it was not possible to introduce into it reformatory influences, and that therefore the prison system should be simply punitive and deterrent. " I consider a mediæval thief who had his right hand chopped off was much more likely to turn over a new leaf than a convict who has had ten years' penal servitude."[1]

For the deterrent aspect of a sentence reliance was placed on " the punishment of hard, dull, useless, uninteresting, monotonous labour "[2] with rigid enforcement of separate confinement and the rule of silence—though these latter still continued, apparently, to be regarded as the necessary basis of the " reformatory influences." The theory was that the more deterrent part of the sentence should come first, and accordingly prisoners sentenced to Hard Labour were placed on " penal labour " (standardised as so many revolutions per diem on the tread-wheel) for at least the first[3] month of the sentence. Thereafter a prisoner by good conduct might, as a reward, earn the " privilege " of being placed on " useful " labour, which the Commissioners regarded as " one of the principal reformatory influences in the prison system."[4] This " useful labour " (the Second-Class Hard Labour of the Act of 1865) was, however, limited to such processes as could be carried out in cellular confinement, and it would seem that, except for prisoners in the later stages of long sentences who might be brought out to work in the domestic services about the prison, separate confinement (except at exercise and chapel) was rigidly enforced throughout the sentence. Prisoners not sentenced to hard labour were placed on " useful labour " from the beginning.

[1] Evidence before Departmental Committee on Prisons, 1895, Q. 11480–11485.
[2] Du Cane, page 175.
[3] The minimum period of 3 months on First-Class Hard Labour had been reduced to 1 month by the Act of 1877.
[4] Evidence before Departmental Committee on Prisons, 1895, page 617, Appendix IX B.

This advancement from "penal labour" to "useful labour" formed the initial stage of what was perhaps the most definite contribution of this period to "reformatory influences," viz. the Progressive Stage System of "managing the prisoners by appealing to their better qualities" instead of "governing by mere fear of punishment," which had for some time been in use in the convict prisons. This is described by Sir E. du Cane as follows :

"The principle on which this system is founded is that of setting before prisoners the advantages of good conduct and industry by enabling them to gain certain privileges or modifications of the penal character of the sentence by the exertion of these qualities. Commencing with severe penal labour—hard fare and a hard bed—he can gradually advance to more interesting employment, somewhat more material comfort, full use of library books, privilege of communication by letter and word with his friends, finally the advantage of a moderate sum of money to start again on his discharge, so that he may not have the temptation or the excuse that want of means might afford for falling again into crime. His daily progress towards these objects is recorded by the award of marks, and any failure in industry or conduct is in the same way visited on him by forfeiture of marks and consequent postponement or diminution of the prescribed privileges."

It is, however, to be remembered that this progress was achieved by emphasising rather the rigours of the earlier stages than the "comfort" of the later stages. In the first stage no mattress was allowed, and no books of any sort ; in the second and third stages school books were allowed and a mattress on certain nights ; it was not till the fourth and last stage that the full "material comfort" of a mattress every night was achieved, with the "full use of library books and privilege of communication with friends." It may be that there was here some confusion of thought between "reformation" and maintenance of discipline.

Apart from separation and such habits of industry as a prisoner with a long enough sentence might form from employment on useful labour, it appears that the only other

reformatory influences to which any importance was attached
were " religious instruction "—the value of which Sir
Godfrey Lushington put down as " very little indeed "[1]—
and " literary education," which Sir E. du Cane confessed
had " not the reformatory influence on prisoners which was
once expected of it."[2] Nevertheless it is clear that devoted
work was done by many Chaplains, and there was a useful
educational organisation : if its efforts were limited to
elementary instruction in the " three R's " it must be
remembered that such instruction, at a time when public
elementary education was in its infancy, was the only form
of education possible for the large majority of the prison
population—and it was perhaps too much to expect any
" reformatory influence " from even Standard III of the
National Society's Reading Book. But it was always
difficult to satisfy the really earnest exponent of deterrence,
and even Sir E. du Cane was required to defend his
administration against the suspicion of " exaggerated
sentimentality."

For nearly twenty years the new machine was allowed to
run without interference either by Committee or by statute.
But thoughtful people had not ceased to think about prisons,
and in time the question began to be asked whether in the
pride of its sanitation, statistics, and standardisation the
administration had not lost sight of the prisoner ; and even
whether penal labour, silence, and separation were after all
the best and only basis of a sound prison régime. When
" in magazines and in the newspapers a sweeping indictment
had been laid against the whole of the prison administration,"[3] it became necessary to answer these questions, and
in 1894 Mr. Asquith, the Home Secretary, appointed a
Departmental Committee, under the Chairmanship of Mr.
Herbert Gladstone, to enquire into certain aspects of the
prison system.

Courageously exceeding its terms of reference, this Committee produced a wise and far-sighted report on the whole
system ; and its recommendations, with the consequential

---

[1] Evidence before the Departmental Committee on Prisons, 1895,
Q. 11480.
[2] Du Cane, page 79.
[3] Report of the Departmental Committee on Prisons, 1895, paragraph 5.

Prison Act of 1898 and the new Rules made thereunder, not only brought to an end the nineteenth-century system, but still form the substantial basis of the system of to-day. *The Gladstone Committee, 1895.* The Gladstone Committee acquitted the administration of many of the charges brought against it ; they emphasised the success with which it had achieved the objects for which it was set up ; and pointed out—a truth of permanent validity—that while " it is easy to find fault, to form ideal views, and to enunciate lofty speculations as if they were principles arrived at by experience," yet " nothing is more common than to find persons whose attention has been attracted only to some disadvantage in the system finally decided on discussing it without being aware that any alternative would produce still greater evils " ; but on the central questions their findings amounted to an indictment of the whole ideology of the Du Cane régime.

Their fundamental conclusion was that " the prisoners have been treated too much as a hopeless or worthless element of the community, and the moral as well as the legal responsibility of the prison authorities has been held to cease when they pass outside the prison gates." In the Committee's view it was the duty of the administration to emphasise all those elements of prison life which might make for the reclamation of the prisoner, and mitigate whatever elements made for degradation and deterioration.

They condemned the one unquestionable achievement of the administration—so far as it had concerned itself with prisoners and not with prisons—uniformity of treatment. " To Sir Edmund du Cane a prisoner was a prisoner, and practically nothing else "[1] ; but " we think," said the Committee, " that the system should be made more elastic, more capable of being adapted to the special cases of individual prisoners ; that prison discipline and treatment should be more effectually designed to maintain, stimulate, or awaken the higher susceptibilities of prisoners, to develop their moral instincts, to train them in orderly and industrial habits, and whenever possible, to turn them out of prison

[1] Webb, page 204.

better men and women physically and mentally than when they came in."

This emphasis on reclamation, they believed, was not incompatible with the maintenance of the deterrent aspect of imprisonment, and they were at pains to shatter the belief that the pursuit of deterrence as an end in itself had even achieved its own ends. " The diminution in the average prison population which had been so triumphantly adduced as a proof of the success of the Du Cane régime was shown to be almost entirely accounted for by a reduction in the average length of sentence awarded . . . The recidivism[1] was as great as ever."[2]

They condemned absolutely unproductive penal labour, and recommended the employment of all prisoners on useful industrial work. They did not, however, quite succeed in shaking off the conception of labour as " deterrent." " We start from the principle," they said, " that prison treatment should have as its primary and concurrent objects deterrence and reformation. It follows therefore that it is desirable to provide labour which, in conjunction with the general prison discipline, does not impair the one and which does not preclude the other "—a pronouncement which, one may perhaps feel, suggests more of compromise than of clear thinking.

They even laid hands on the separate system, " swept aside the old-fashioned idea that separate confinement was desirable on the ground that it enables a prisoner to meditate on his misdeeds " and " held that association for industrial labour under proper conditions could be productive of no harm, and this view was supported by the fact that association for work on a large scale had always been the practice at Convict Prisons."[3] In short, they held that separate confinement (except, of course, by night) was simply a deterrent instrument which they clearly viewed with grave mistrust, in the light of the known facts as to its effect on the physical and mental condition of prisoners ; but they did not feel able to condemn it absolutely, contenting themselves with the hope that it would prove possible to

---

[1] "The habit of relapsing into crime." (N.E.D.)
[2] Webb, page 222.   [3] Ruggles-Brise, page 137.

reduce the periods. The " Rule of Silence " received equal condemnation.

Among the constructive suggestions of the Committee which have since borne fruit may be noted those relative to the better organisation of Discharged Prisoners' Aid Societies, the co-operation of extra-official organisations and individuals in education and visiting, the extension of facilities for education and the use of library books, the special treatment of younger prisoners, and the special treatment of " professional criminals."

The Prison Act, 1898, and the Statutory Rules, 1899. The Report of the Gladstone Committee was accepted by the Home Secretary as a fresh basis of departure in prison administration, and Sir E. Ruggles-Brise, who succeeded Sir E. du Cane at this time, relates that " Mr. Asquith, in conferring this appointment upon him, expressed the strong desire of the Government that the views of the Committee should, as far as practicable, be carried into execution."[1] Some time was necessary for preparation, but in 1898 was passed the Prison Act which remains the last expression of parliamentary opinion on the subject, and forms, with the unrepealed portions of the Acts of 1865 and 1877, the substantial legal basis of the present régime.

Not the least important provisions of the Act were those which repealed the statutory regulations of 1865, and left the whole of the detailed regulation of the system to the Secretary of State, who was given power to make all rules[2] necessary for the government of both local and convict prisons. The code of rules made in 1899, with such amendments as have from time to time proved necessary, has remained in force until this present year. The value of this more elastic procedure, which made it possible for changes to be effected without fresh legislation on each occasion, is indicated by the fact that under it the natural development of over thirty years has proceeded without further intervention by Parliament.

The most important change in the system effected by the

---

[1] Ruggles-Brise, page 77.
[2] Rules under the Prison Acts 1865–1898 must lie on the Table of the House of Commons for thirty days before they can be made.

Act and Rules was the abolition of First-Class Hard Labour, and the requirement that all prisoners should from the beginning of their sentences be employed on useful industrial work, " such as will fit the prisoner to earn his livelihood on release." The unfortunate hedging of the Committee on this question was, however, reflected in the curious provision that a prisoner sentenced to hard labour " shall for 28 days be employed in strict separation on hard bodily or hard manual labour . . . after that period he shall, provided his conduct and industry are good, be employed on labour of a less hard description in association if practicable."

This clinging to the shadow of " hard labour " and " separate confinement " long after the substance had escaped them led the Commissioners into a somewhat illogical position.

" The practical difficulties raised by the requirements (1) that work shall be productive, (2) that for the first month the work shall be ' hard bodily or hard manual labour,' and (3) that subsequently it shall be labour of ' a less hard description ' are obvious. To find various useful employments suitable for various types of prisoners is a standing difficulty of prison administration, and it was a baffling problem to find for every prisoner sentenced to hard labour two kinds of work—one harder than the other but nevertheless of such a character that it could be carried on for a month by a prisoner confined to a cell.

" Moreover, the conception that a prisoner who behaves and works well shall be rewarded by being allowed to work less hard is irreconcilable with the conception that the period of imprisonment is to be utilised as a period of training. If training is effective, a prisoner should in the second month of his sentence be working harder, i.e. with more aptitude and more concentration, than in the first month.

" Oakum picking was originally the task for the first month of a man's hard labour sentence, but when this work was given up, little could be done to render effective the distinction in the Rule between ' hard bodily or hard manual labour,' and ' labour of a less hard description,' and the distinctive character of a hard labour sentence lay—not in the nature of the prisoner's work—but in the fact that for the preliminary part of his sentence he was liable to be kept in separate confinement, i.e. to be employed in his cell and not in an associated working party."[1]

In fact, what this provision did was to ensure that for 28 days a hard labour prisoner worked less hard than an ordinary prisoner, and the restriction to prisoners so sentenced of the vestige of separate confinement that was retained was presumably intended simply to preserve in another way the aspect of greater deterrence implied in sentences to Hard Labour.

Except for these Hard Labour prisoners[2] during the first 28 days of their sentences, all work during the day was henceforth done in association in workshops or outdoor parties. The Separate System from now onwards means only separate cells for sleeping and meals, all other activities being in associated parties under strict supervision : in effect the Silent System had again come into favour, though with the modification that absolute silence was less rigidly required, and " the privilege of talking " recommended by the Gladstone Committee might be earned by long sentence prisoners in their later stages.

As a corollary of this step it was necessary to elaborate the system of classification. Hitherto this had been limited to the separation, under special Rules, of Prisoners Awaiting Trial, Debtors, and prisoners ordered by the Courts under Section 67 of the Act of 1865 to be treated as Misdemeanants of the First Division. Arrangements were now made for the classification of convicted prisoners as well, by placing in separate parties those under 21 years of age, and those who had not been in prison before, or were not of depraved character.

A further important change authorised by Section 8 of the Act was that provision might be made by the Rules for enabling a local prisoner to earn by special industry and

---

[1] Annual Report of the Prison Commissioners, 1930, page 23.
[2] For separate confinement of *convicts* see Chapter XIV.

good conduct a remission of a portion of his imprisonment, and that on his discharge his sentence should be deemed to have expired. The Rules fixed the maximum period of remission to be earned at one-sixth of the sentence, and the system of awarding daily marks for industry, already operating in connection with the Progressive Stage System, was applied also to the earning of remission. The award and forfeiture of Stage and Remission Marks have remained the basis of prison discipline to the present time.

CHAPTER II

THE MODERN PRISON SYSTEM

1. *The Nature of the Problem*

THE definite re-orientation of policy at the end of the nineteenth century makes it necessary, before considering the development of the system in the twentieth century, to consider more closely the nature of the problem set before the new administration, of the principles governing the solutions attempted, and of the conditions which in practice limit their application.

Since the middle of the nineteenth century the prison régime had been designed simply and solely to inspire " a wholesome dread " : the duty of the prison was to deter potential offenders by fear of what would happen to them if they were sent to prison, and to deter those who had been in prison from further offence by painful recollection. True, the possibility of " reformative elements " was not excluded, but they were admitted only to the extent that they did not detract from the primary functions of deterrence and punishment.

After 30 years' experience of this policy, in the most favourable circumstances, it had been shown that, in a practical sense, it did not work. The prison population, which had at first fallen, was steadily rising, and careful inquiry had shown that recidivism had not been reduced but was increasing. It was held that the prisoner subjected for long, or often, to this régime was sent out of prison brutalised, embittered, anti-social, and unfit to take a decent place in society. This experience, indeed, confirmed what had already been suggested in other directions—as on the abolition of the death penalty for felony in general, or of corporal punishment in the fighting services—that the

29

volume of crime will not be favourably affected by severity of punishment—punishment, that is to say, conceived in the sense of physical or mental severities and degradations ; and that to increase the severity of punishment in this sense is likely to lead to a progressive hardening of the class against which it is directed, till measures of still greater severity are called for, and finally the " vicious circle " has to be broken by a fresh start from some new principle.

The new principle accepted as a fresh point of departure in 1895 was that " prison treatment should have as its primary and concurrent objects deterrence and reformation " and should be " effectually designed to maintain, stimulate or awaken the higher susceptibilities of prisoners . . . and turn them out of prison better men and women, both physically and morally, than when they came in."[1] From now on reformation was no longer to be regarded as " all very well so long as it did not interfere "—it was to be one of the two primary ends to which the system as a whole was to be directed. This new principle, with the general indications of the Committee as to the spirit and methods in and by which it was to be applied, was fully accepted by the Government, and under the direction of successive Secretaries of State has been followed by the Prison Commissioners for the past 35 years.

On any view of the functions of a prison which had been held up to that time the new policy was an attempt to reconcile the evidently irreconcilable. We have already noted the definite pronouncements by both Church and Bench that reform was not compatible with a régime directed to deterrence, and this view was again forcibly presented to the Committee by a distinguished official witness, Sir Godfrey Lushington, in these words :

" I regard as unfavourable to reformation the status of a prisoner throughout his whole career ; the crushing of self-respect, the starving of all moral instinct he may possess, the absence of all opportunity to do and receive a kindness, the continual association with none but criminals, and that only as a separate item among other

---

[1] Gladstone Committee, paragraphs 25 and 47.

items also separate ; the forced labour and the denial of liberty. I believe the true mode of reforming a man or restoring him to society is exactly in the opposite direction of all these. But of course this is a mere idea ; it is quite impracticable in a prison. In fact the unfavourable features I have mentioned are inseparable from prison life."

The Committee added : " As a broad description of prison life we think this is accurate ; we do not agree that all of these unfavourable features are irremovable." The subsequent policy of the administration has been a confident attempt to justify the optimism of the Committee against Sir Godfrey's pessimism, but Sir Godfrey's " mere idea " must remain uncomfortably in the back of our minds.

If then we are to understand this policy, it is necessary to examine a little further the implications both of deterrence and of reformation.

Society, we may assume, must protect itself against those who commit such anti-social acts as society from time to time deems to be " crimes " against itself, and unless on a full circle of the Erewhonian wheel society decides that all crimes are matters for the medical profession, its protective measures must be based primarily on deterrence. Experience goes to suggest that this deterrent power lies fundamentally not in *severity* of punishment, but in *certainty* of detection and punishment ; an efficient police and the swift and certain administration of justice are its first-line weapons.

Next in importance, so far as the deterrence is directed to potential offenders at large, come the shame, hardship, and social stigma attendant on arrest, public trial, and conviction. These exercise their effect without regard to the possible sentence, which must always be something of a gamble— there are many ways of dealing with offenders besides imprisonment, though the prison stands behind them all as the ultimate resort and sanction. And, so far as concerns prison, does not the effective deterrence for the person who has never been there lie in the dread of the unknown and the associations of the idea of imprisonment, and not in any notion of the particular régime in force at the time—as to which, in any case, the average man is in general quite ignorant ?

This assumption that the deterrent weapons of society are *inherent* in its police and judicial systems and in the *fact* of imprisonment is an important step towards the solution of the problem which the prison administration was required to solve : for it then becomes possible, without impairment of the principle of deterrence, to remove from the prison régime any features introduced to emphasise its deterrent aspect which prove to be incompatible with the concurrent duty " to turn the prisoners out of prison better men and women than when they came in." And if the end of reformation can thus be effectively furthered, the end of deterrence is also reached by another road : for deterrence has never been an end in itself—the object of the prison is to protect society against the criminal, and it has never been questioned that, quite apart from any moral obligation of society towards those whom it deprives of their liberty as a punishment, the most effective method of protection, *if it can be done*, is to reform the offender.

This conception of the inherent deterrence of imprisonment, however, applies with less effect, or none, to the person who has already served a sentence of imprisonment, and one of the strongest reasons for delaying recourse to imprisonment is the progressive weakening of its deterrent effect. A special problem is therefore presented by that small proportion, which may be estimated at 10–15%, of persons who are neither reformed nor deterred by their first sentence of imprisonment. The difficulties attendant on this problem have recently been examined by a Departmental Committee,[1] from whose Report it would seem that a satisfactory solution must lie less in methods of treatment within the existing prison system than in an extension of the powers of the Courts and the prisons in dealing with such offenders.

There are obvious difficulties in devising, within the framework of a system compatible with the application of the Gladstone Report, a régime which can effectively be directed *in terrorem* against " the criminal class." We may perhaps assume that no responsible person to-day desires a return

---

[1] Departmental Committee on Persistent Offenders, 1932.

to mere physical brutalities—the chain-gang, the tread-mill, or the dark cell. Nor would it be generally desired that the standards of diet, clothing, accommodation, and humanity of treatment should fall below certain established and recognised levels. But it is not always remembered that these standards, even at their minimum levels, remain in certain respects higher than those which many prisoners are able to secure when at liberty.

And these standards, at whatever level fixed, must be applied rigidly and impartially to all alike. Inflexibility and impartiality are of the essence of a prison system : a prison cannot make the punishment fit either the crime or the criminal. The sentence is meted out by the Court according to an established scale of time-lengths, which may be some measure of the offence but can be no measure of the effect upon the offender. Once in prison each has for his appointed term to tread the same road, at the same step, and in the same standard shoe—some it may pinch in one place, some in another ; some it may fit pretty well, others it may painfully crush ; many are already hardened to it, but of the others few will escape without bruises and callosities.

Yet the contrast between the standardisation of the punishment and the variety of the offender grows progressively greater. In the last hundred years the increasing complexity of society has brought with it a proportionately complex increase in the number of offences against society, and in the kinds of people who are convicted of such offences. The prison population to-day shows a vertical section through society from peer to vagrant : and to all these people their punishment must mean something quite different according to the differences in temperament, mental and moral calibre, education, and previous social circumstances and training.

The Gladstone Committee considered that the prison system should be made " more elastic, more capable of being adapted to the special cases of individual prisoners," and the modern conception of classification has enabled some progress in this direction : but this conception involves no mitigation for any special class of prisoner of those conditions of a prison sentence which, whatever the orientation

D

of the régime, constitute alike for recidivist and first offender the true deterrence of a sentence. For the least that a prison must mean to any prisoner, under any system compatible with contemporary opinion, is loss of liberty ; to live under lock and key behind a twenty-foot wall, in a bleak atmosphere of discomfort and disgrace, under rigid discipline and constant supervision ; to lack the smallest luxury or comfort ; to be subject to forced labour ; and to be cut off from family and friends, from the society of the other sex, and from all natural human intercourse.

But if the reconciliation of reform with deterrence may thus appear to present less difficulty to-day than in the nineteenth century, the difficulty does not disappear. One might still hesitate to give a confident answer to the question whether in any circumstances a prison system, rigid and standardised as it must be, and inevitably associated with the idea of punishment, is capable of bringing effectively to bear such influences as will bring about that change of mind or heart, that repentance, re-education, re-orientation, or whatever we understand by " reform." For this of all things is a matter for a rather delicate individual touch : reform will come to the offender in different shapes and by different methods of approach, but it must come from something inside the man—it is not a panacea which can be prescribed by the chaplain from the prayer-book or by the medical officer from the pharmacopœia. One man is reached by the message of the Gospel, another needs only a friendly hint, a sympathetic touch : in one case it is necessary to prick a bladder of conceit, in another patiently to build up self-respect : for some the mere withdrawal for a time from the circumstances leading to the offence will serve, for others complete re-education is required.

And this difficult duty laid on our administration must be performed under conditions which necessarily handicap its performance, over and above the difficulties which we have seen to be inherent. In the first place the Courts, in passing sentence, are not necessarily or usually concerned in the first instance with the reformative effect on the offender. Thus the prisons receive on the one hand a number of persons who stand in no need of reform—

" accidental " offenders who would be neither more nor less likely to offend again whether they were sent to prison or not, and on the other a number of whom it is safe to predict, after an experience of years, that they are not amenable to the reformative influences of prison. The residuum is not large, and in respect of these there is often the further difficulty that the length of the sentence is not calculated to promote their reformation, either because it is too short in the case of one who needs prolonged training, or so long as to neutralise the benefit in a case where a moderate period might have done good.

Thus even of the criminal population the proportion who may be regarded as proper subjects for reformative influences is small ; and it is not always realised that a prison serves two separate purposes over and above its central function as a place of imprisonment for convicted criminals—first as a place of detention and examination for untried prisoners, second as a place of detention for debtors and other " civil " prisoners. A very considerable proportion of the effort of a prison is therefore devoted to duties quite extraneous to its central purpose : indeed it may be said that from 80–90% of the persons who come to prison in any year are extraneous to that purpose. Of every 100 men committed to prison in 1931 only 26 were criminals in the ordinary sense of the word, i.e. persons convicted of indictable offences, and of these only 15 had sentences which implied any probability of reformative treatment, i.e. over 3 months ; the corresponding figure for women was 9. Of the other 74 men, no less than 41 were committed to enforce payment of sums of money (24 debts and 17 fines), 14 were untried, and most of the remainder were drunks, vagrants, and other committers of petty nuisances.

The whole of this miscellaneous collection of social nuisances has to be handled in one building of rigid design, dating usually from the middle of last century and designed for a system based on quite different principles and circumstances, and by one staff of fallible human beings working in circumstances of unusual difficulty and pressure. Improvements both of buildings and of staff are necessarily limited by considerations of public economy ; and finally, every detail of prison administration must be regulated by considerations of security and the safe-custody of prisoners.

We shall follow in later chapters the course which the prison system to-day steers among these difficulties and dilemmas. The purpose of these introductory chapters is to suggest that our prison system presents very strikingly that common characteristic of English institutions—" it never was born, it just growed," and that what we see to-day is not the result of any consistent and comprehensive code, but the contemporary phase of a long historical process with its roots still in the Middle Ages. Further, that the system is in the early stages of a comparatively new policy, and that the pursuance of that policy still presents problems calling for time, patience, and constructive thought.

2. *Development Before the War*

The change over of the prison system from deterrence and unproductive " hard labour " to reformation and useful productive labour involved considerable changes in the machinery of administration and the construction of the prisons, and broadly speaking one may say that the years before the War were devoted to building up the necessary framework for the full implementing of the new policy of the government. The difficult task of changing over from the tread-mill and crank to useful industries which no longer existed was the main concern of the new administration, and the introduction of associated labour and the new system of classification in local prisons were other important changes successfully accomplished. At the same time the system of earning marks for remission had to be worked out in the local prisons, and considerable progress was made in the improvement of prison libraries and especially in the organisation of the Discharged Prisoners' Aid Societies : it was now recognised that the true test of a prison system is what happens to the prisoner after discharge, and that an efficient Aid Society is not less important than an efficient security wall. Above all, special attention was devoted to the problems of young prisoners which we shall consider in the following section.

But in retrospect the significant contribution of the early years of this century to penal problems would seem to lie less in its administration of prisons, so far at any rate as concerned the ordinary adult prisoner, than in its realisation that a prison was in any case a *pis aller*, and that the more offenders, and particularly young offenders, could be kept out of it, the better.

There followed an important body of legislation which has had the effect, by keeping out of prison large classes of offenders for whom imprisonment is both unnecessary and unsuitable, not only of reducing very considerably the prison population, but of providing a more effective instrument of " classification " than could ever be devised inside a prison. First among these beneficent statutes stands the Probation Act of 1907,[1] but hardly less important in their effects were the provisions of the Criminal Justice Administration Act, 1914, under which Courts are required in all proper cases to allow reasonable time for the payment of fines. Prior to this provision over 50% of the population of local prisons had consisted of persons—usually quite minor offenders—committed because they were unable to pay their fines forthwith. The operation of the Mental Deficiency Act, 1913, was also instrumental in keeping out of, or in removing from, prison a large number of unfortunate people for whom punishment by imprisonment would now be regarded as indefensible. The abortive attempt to remove the " professional criminals " from the ordinary prisons by the method of Preventive Detention is described in Chapter XV.

The Problem of the Young Offender. To the special problem of saving the young from the taint and injury of prison life, a most important contribution was made by the Prison Commissioners, which remains as a notable monument to their administration and to the name of their Chairman, Sir Evelyn Ruggles-Brise. This was the institution of the Borstal system of treating young offenders. During the

---

[1] For an account of the Probation System to-day see the *Directory of Probation Officers, Home Office Schools, etc.* : Stationery Office, price 2s. 6d.

nineteenth century little had been done to differentiate the treatment of children and adults once they had offended against the law. In 1838 the Government had opened Parkhurst Prison for young convicts, and the Secretary of State had power to pardon young persons sentenced to transportation on condition of their placing themselves under the care of a Benevolent Association. It was not till 1854 that a Reformatory Schools Act provided any alternative to transportation or imprisonment for children under 16, and not till 1894 that a progressive Prison Governor ventured to tell the Gladstone Committee that " he entirely disapproved of children under the age of 13 being sent to prison, and would even raise the limit to 14 years."[1]

The Gladstone Committee had reported that " The age when the majority of habitual criminals are made lies between 16 and 21. It appears to us that the most determined effort should be made to lay hold of these incipient criminals and to prevent them by strong restraint and rational treatment from recruiting the habitual class." They did not feel that prison provided the best method to this end, and recommended the raising of the maximum age for admission to a reformatory school from 16 to 18, and the establishment as an experiment of a " penal reformatory," under Government management, to which courts might commit offenders between the ages of 16–23.

From this hint the Borstal system developed. Sir Evelyn Ruggles-Brise set himself, with humanity and insight beyond the common, to seek a solution of the problem of reclaiming the youthful offender by methods other than those of the prison ; and as a result of the experience gained in the special treatment of a group of selected prisoners under 21, who were collected in a disused convict prison at Borstal, near Rochester, the Home Secretary was, in 1908, enabled to ask Parliament to sanction an entirely new method of treating offenders between 16 and 21 in special institutions, known as Borstal Institutions. This system, which was set up by Part I of the Prevention of Crime Act, 1908, is fully described in Chapter XVI.

[1] Evidence before the Departmental Committee on Prisons, page 610.

In the same year was passed the Children Act, 1908,[1] which prohibited the imprisonment in any circumstances of children under 14, and strictly limited the imprisonment of " young persons " under 16.[1] It is perhaps well to make it clear that this still left a considerable number of young people between 16 and 21 in prison, for the intention of the Borstal System was not to provide a simple alternative to imprisonment, but to provide a special system of training for the " incipient criminals " of the Gladstone Report. " Our object was to deal with . . . the young hooligan advanced in crime, perhaps with many previous convictions, who appeared to be inevitably doomed to a life of habitual crime."[2] To deal with young people in the prisons a special system was established, which provided for their segregation from adults and for the application " as far as practicable, having regard to the length of the sentence, of the methods followed at Borstal Institutions."[3] It was unfortunate that an optimistic view of what could be done in a prison in this way led to this system being called, not the " Modified Prison System," but the " Modified Borstal System " ; and it was no doubt due to the misleading implication of this phrase that Courts of Justice sent—and often still send— to prison young people, who ought either to have been placed on probation or sent to Borstal, under the mistaken impression that they would there get " Borstal treatment." The system was substantially that under which the Young Prisoners Class is treated to-day (see Chapter XII).

3. Development Since the War

The War forms a convenient point of separation for two phases of the modern system, but such a division is in a sense arbitrary : the post-war phase derives from no fresh inquiry or specific point of departure, and introduces no fresh policy. Nothing is done to-day which is not implicit in the Gladstone Report, and many departures which may have been regarded as innovations have been no more than the

---

[1] Now revised and consolidated with later Acts in the Children and Young Persons Act, 1933, which raises to 17 the age for " young persons."

[2] Ruggles-Brise, page 92.

[3] *Ibid.*, page 96.

carrying into effect of specific recommendations of the Committee. The position would seem to be that the general change from a pre-war to a post-war habit of mind, with the natural development of thought on penal questions, created an atmosphere which facilitated the animation of the carefully constructed pre-war framework with something more of the true spirit of the Report in its application to the ordinary prisoner.

The standpoint of the Commissioners after the War was clearly explained in their Annual Report for 1923, page 16— " Since the offender has to return to ordinary life, take his place as a citizen, and earn his living, at some time in the future which is usually not far distant, our object is to fit him for those duties. The means to this end are fairly long hours of hard and steady work at an occupation which shall, if possible, give such industrial training as will enable him to earn a living ; the removal of needless degradations and the encouragement of self-respect ; and, in the evenings, well-considered education suitable for backward or unbalanced adults. To these are added visiting by voluntary workers of a strong character and personal influence ; and, wherever possible, such measures of trust as will awaken a sense of personal responsibility. The prison day should be hard, but the object is not mere severity. It should be interesting, but the object is not to make it pleasant. The aim is to make a citizen by quickening and directing the activities of both mind and body." Again in their Report for 1925, pages 17 and 18, they say : " Prisons exist to protect Society, and they can only give efficient protection in one of two ways, either (a) by removing the anti-social person from the community altogether, or for a very long period ; or (b) by bringing about some change in him. Any general application of the first method would not be supported by public opinion. The prison administration must therefore do its utmost to apply the second ; that is to say, to restore the man who has been imprisoned to ordinary standards of citizenship so far as this can be done within the limits of his sentence. Unless some use can be made of the period of imprisonment to change the anti-social outlook of the offender and to bring him into a more healthy frame

of mind towards his fellow citizens, he will, on leaving the
prison gates after a few weeks or months again become a
danger, or at any rate a nuisance. He may, indeed, be
worse than before, if the only result has been to add a
vindictive desire for revenge on society to the selfish care-
lessness of the rights of others which he brought into prison
with him."

From these statements of policy it is to be inferred that
the Commissioners to-day, once the offender has been convicted and sentenced to deprivation of liberty by imprisonment, conceive it to be the duty of the prison not to " rub
it into him " but to " rub it out of him." It may also be
noted that there is no word of " reform "—" training for
citizenship " is the new keynote. This change of phraseology may not be without significance—it does seem to
connote something rather more strenuous, more positive,
and more practical than the earlier ideal of " reformation,"
though no aspect of this ideal is excluded. Training does
not suggest more comfort in the prison, it suggests more
effort by the prisoner. It suggests the emphasising of every
positive and formative influence, of all that may build up
character and self-respect, and the mitigation of any element
that makes for degradation of spirit and deterioration of
body and mind : it is the fight against the physical and
mental deterioration, almost inseparable from a long prison
sentence, that is the hardest part of the duty laid on the
prison authorities " to turn their prisoners out better men
and women than when they came in." Nor does training
suggest any relaxation of discipline, though it does imply
the substitution of a positive and constructive discipline for
one based on purely negative repression.

How this works out in practice we shall see in the following chapters, but before we pass to them there are certain
general aspects to which attention may be drawn.

Perhaps the most interesting of these historically is the
final disappearance of " separate system," " silent system,"
and " hard labour " with all they connote of historic con-
troversy. We have seen how, following the Gladstone
Report, " hard labour " disappeared as a fact, but remained
as a legal fiction, to which some sort of colour was lent by

the practice of confining " hard labour " prisoners to their
cells for 28 days (during which, following tradition, they
were not allowed a mattress). As a consequence of the war
it became necessary for " hard labour " prisoners to work as
hard as their fellows, and in 1919 the period of separate
confinement was, with the approval of he Secretary of
State, reduced to 14 days. In 1931 new Statutory Rules
were made regulating the employment of prisoners, and the
period of separate confinement was then abolished altogether.
These Rules also formally put an end to the preliminary
period of separate confinement for convicts, although this
had stopped in practice as long ago as 1922. Thus ended
the " separate system," while " hard labour " is quaintly
represented by the provision, still preserved in the Statutory
Rules of 1933, that a prisoner so sentenced (unless he is under
16 or over 60, or the Medical Officer otherwise orders) shall
be deprived of his mattress for the first 14 days of the
sentence. This does not apply to women, for whom since
1899 there has been no distinction of any sort between
sentences with and without " hard labour." No doubt on
the next occasion for legislation we shall finally lose this
curious survival. With the new idea that prisoners should
be got out of their cells and into association for exercise,
work, education, and recreation, for as many hours as
practicable during the day, it was impossible to reconcile
the old idea of " non-intercourse " ; it followed that, though
the question of talking among prisoners still presents difficulties which are discussed in a later chapter, the " silent
system " has now followed the " separate " into history.

It is worth placing on record that the " silent system " of
the administration has also been abolished. As recently
as 1922 it was possible for our prisons to be described as " a
silent world, shrouded, so far as the public is concerned, in
almost complete darkness."[1] This is certainly not true
to-day ; indeed, so continuous is the publicity under which
the prisons carry out their work, that it is difficult to understand why evident ignorance of the elementary facts of
prison life and policy should still distinguish so much
comment thereon. Not only do the Commissioners year by

[1] Webb, page 235.

year outline their policy and give full details of their activities in their Annual Reports, but they freely grant permission to representatives of leading newspapers with a serious interest to visit and write about all types of penal establishment, and any reputable person actuated by a serious public interest—not mere curiosity—may hope to obtain permission to visit a prison or Borstal Institution.

Of such visitors it can of course be said that they see only what they are shown, and one would not wish to attach too much importance to these visits as a means of throwing light on dark places. But this cannot be said of the many hundreds of voluntary workers whose co-operation with the prison staffs in the work of education, visiting prisoners in their cells, and assisting them on discharge, has provided perhaps the most striking and fruitful development of the post-war administration. Of recent years this development has been taken a step further, and by means of annual conferences with the Commissioners all these voluntary bodies are enabled not only to facilitate and improve their own work but to exercise their influence on the policy of the administration. If further check on any sinister secrets were needed, it would be provided by the powers of the Visiting Justices, which are discussed in the following chapter. It is interesting to note in this connection that following the mutinous outbreak at Dartmoor in 1932 the inquiries were conducted by an independent Commissioner appointed by the Home Secretary, whose report was at once published as a White Paper.

Although since 1895 there has been no general inquiry into the prison system by Parliamentary or Departmental Committee, the subject has not been left quite alone. We have already noted the important effects of the Prevention of Crime Act, 1908, in setting up the systems of Borstal Detention and Preventive Detention, and of the Statutory Rules of 1931 in putting an end to Separate Confinement. There have in addition been four Departmental Committees each bearing on some special aspect of the problem. The first of these, the Young Offenders' Committee of 1927, dealt principally with matters outside the scope of the prison system, but made certain suggestions of detail affecting the Borstal System. In 1931 there followed the Committee on Persistent Offenders, which registered the failure of the Preventive Detention system,[1] and made important suggestions for alternative methods of dealing with offenders of this class. The third Committee, which is considering the centrally important problem of prison industries and their relation to the reinstatement of the prisoner in industry, has not yet presented its Report.[2] The fourth, which is considering the problems connected with the commitment to prison by Courts of Summary Jurisdiction of persons who fail to pay fines or sums due under maintenance orders, has only recently begun its work. As legislative effect has not yet been given to the Report of the Persistent Offenders Committee, or to that of the Young Offenders Committee so far as it relates to prisons and Borstal Institutions, the practical effect of these inquiries on the system is still a matter for the future.

It remains to be added that in 1933 the Statutory Rules of 1899 and all the subsequent Rules made under the Prison Acts and the Prevention of Crime Act were repealed, and a consolidated, simplified, and revised code was substituted. The revisions, however, were mainly in matters of detail, and were designed to bring the Rules into line with more recent developments and provide greater elasticity. No fresh principles of importance were introduced, and no detailed comment is necessary.

This is not the place, nor has the time yet come, to attempt an estimate of the success of the policy initiated by the Gladstone Committee. It would not, in any case, be easy to formulate the criteria of "success" in a prison system, and if they could be formulated it is difficult to see how they could be used in practice separately from relative criteria as to the standards and practice of courts committing to prison. Nor are adequate comparative statistics available. But it is not irrelevant to note, for what it is worth, that recent inquiry has shown reason to suppose that of persons

---

[1] This is fully discussed in Chapter XV.
[2] Part I of this Report, dealing with Employment, has now been presented.

committed to prison for the first time some 85–90% do not
return to prison. (See p. 207).

"We suspect," concluded Mr. and Mrs. Webb,[1] "that
it passes the wit of man to contrive a prison which shall not
be gravely injurious to the minds of the vast majority of
the prisoners, if not also to their bodies. So far as can be
seen at present, the most practical and the most hopeful of
prison reforms is to keep people out of prison altogether."
Perhaps it would not be too much to claim that under
present conditions imprisonment to the majority is no longer
gravely injurious, and to some there may be hope of definite
benefit. Few, however, would be unwilling to endorse the
latter part of Mr. and Mrs. Webb's conclusion, and sufficient
has been said to suggest that for the major developments of
the future in our prison system we must look not to the
Prison Commissioners but to Parliament and the Courts.

It may be helpful here, before we pass to the descriptive
chapters, to delimit the scope of the "prison system" in
England[2] to-day. It *is* concerned with 31 establishments
known as prisons, and 7 known as Borstal Institutions.
It is *not* concerned with the Approved Schools under the
Children Acts (formerly known as Reformatory and Industrial Schools) to which are committed young offenders
under 17 years of age,[3] nor with the cells in police stations in
which persons charged by the police, if they are not released
on bail, are detained over night till they can be brought
before a magistrate.[4]

---

[1] Webb, page 248.

[2] By "England" is meant the system in England and Wales : those
for Scotland and Northern Ireland come under separate jurisdictions.

[3] A full account of these schools will be found in the *Directory of Probation Officers, Home Office Schools, etc.*, published by the Stationery Office,
price 2s. 6d.

[4] Offenders may also be committed by the Justices to police cells
certified by the Secretary of State, for periods of not more than four days,
either on remand or as a form of punishment on conviction.

CHAPTER III

ADMINISTRATION AND STAFF

1. *The Prison Commission*

PRIOR to the Prison Act, 1877, the Justices in Quarter Sessions, subject to the direction of Parliament on matters of policy, not only owned but through the Visiting Justices administered in detail all the Local Prisons : the duties of the Secretary of State were limited to seeing that the directions of Parliament were given proper effect. For this purpose, as we have seen, the Home Secretary had powers to certify the Rules made by Justices, to have their prisons inspected and to publish his Inspectors' Reports, and (after 1865) to withhold the Grant in Aid from authorities whose prisons were unsatisfactory. These are substantially the principles on which other public services (e.g. Education and Police) are still administered, but the peculiar problems of the prison service led Parliament to adopt the principle of centralisation both of ownership and control, and in 1878, following a complicated statutory financial settlement, all the Local Prisons were vested in the Secretary of State. By the Prison Act, 1898, Parliament also, in effect, transferred to the Secretary of State the direct control of policy which it had previously kept in its own hands.

Subject to the control of the Home Secretary in matters of policy, the general superintendence, control, and inspection of the prisons was vested in the Prison Commissioners and their Inspectors. This central control was not however left absolute : the disciplinary powers of the Visiting Justices in regard to prisoners (but not in regard to staff) were transferred to Visiting Committees appointed by the Benches committing to the prisons, and these bodies were given concurrent rights to inspect and report to the Home

Secretary. The powers of Visiting Committees and the working of this interesting system of dual control are discussed in a later section.

The Prison Commission is a body corporate, with a common seal and power to hold land. Its first Chairman, Sir E. du Cane, was Chairman of the pre-existing Board oɩ Directors of Convict Prisons, and there was from the first a practical fusion of the two Boards to which legal effect was given by the Act of 1898, which provided that the Prison Commissioners should be *ex officio* the Directors of Convict Prisons. " The Directors " still have a legally separate existence, but they serve little more practical purpose to-day than to sustain the somewhat *ancien régime* tradition of the Convict Prisons by a differential touch in correspondence with the Department. Sir Maurice L. Waller, C.B., who succeeded Sir E. Ruggles-Brise in 1922, was only the third Chairman of the Commission, and but for his untimely retirement through ill health in 1927 might have carried on this remarkable continuity of administration for many more years. Sir Maurice, like his predecessor, became a Commissioner after considerable administrative experience in the Home Office, and was subsequently appointed to the Chairmanship : his successor, Mr. Alexander Maxwell, C.B., was appointed to the Chairmanship direct from the Home Office, as was the present Chairman, Mr. Harold R. Scott, C.B., who succeeded Mr. Maxwell in 1932 on the appointment of the latter to be Deputy Under-Secretary of State in the Home Office.

Commissioners have normally been appointed in part from experienced administrators of the Home Office staff, and in part from the Inspectorate, which in turn is recruited from the Prison Governors. Sometimes however men with other experience have been appointed, as in the case of the first Medical Commissioner, or again when Mr. Alexander Paterson, M.C., who had had a considerable experience in social and educational work in many fields, was appointed in 1922. Prior to 1930, the Board consisted of a Chairman and three Commissioners, one of whom was the Medical Commissioner, assisted by two Inspectors and a Medical Inspector appointed under the Prison Acts, and a Secretary who ranked as an Inspector. In that year, following a reorganisation of the administration, the Commissioners were reduced to two (including the Medical Commissioner), the post of Medical Inspector was abolished, and in place of the Inspectors four posts of " Assistant Commissioner and Inspector " were created : three of these posts are now filled by promoted Inspectors or Governors and one by the Secretary, who was appointed from the administrative staff of the Home Office. The present Commissioners are Messrs. H. R. Scott, C.B. (Chairman) ; Alexander Paterson, M.C., and W. Norwood East, M.D., etc. (Medical Commissioner). Both Commissioners and Assistant Commissioners are full-time pensionable Civil Servants : Commissioners are appointed by the Crown under the Sign Manual, Assistant Commissioners by the Secretary of State.

The Prison Commission, though housed in the Home Office,[1] is for accounting purposes a separate department, with its own Vote, for which the Chairman is the Accounting Officer. The Department is organised in four Branches— the Secretariat, under the Chief Clerk ; the Accounts Branch, under the Clerk of Accounts ; the Stores and Manufactures Branch, under its Controller ; and the Works Branch, under the Surveyor of Prisons. The total head-quarters staff, exclusive of Commissioners, Assistant Commissioners, and Heads of Branches, numbers about eighty.

Although the tendency to-day is towards greater elasticity and freedom of experiment, the method of administration is still based on the older ideal of rigid uniformity. All decisions of policy are taken at meetings of the Board, at which the Assistant Commissioners normally attend, and the day to day working of the prisons is regulated in the closest detail by a comprehensive body of Standing Orders issued by the Commissioners, from which no Governor is authorised to depart. Each Assistant Commissioner (other than the Secretary) is responsible to the Board for the administration and inspection of his own block of prisons or Borstal Institutions, which he visits as often as may be necessary (and usually at least twice a year), in addition to

---

[1] There is a separate Prison Department for Scotland, under the control of the Secretary of State for Scotland, with offices in Edinburgh.

the visits of the Commissioners themselves. The accounts of the establishments are audited annually, and the work of their clerical staffs is inspected, by members of the Prison Department staff : test audits are also carried out at one or two prisons each year by the Controller and Auditor General's Department.

The Commissioners present to Parliament an Annual Report[1] in which may be found all the published statistical matter relative to the nature and composition of prison populations (including certain tables formerly included in the Criminal Statistics), with explanatory comments by the Commissioners. Since the preparation and examination of the statistics is a lengthy matter, the Annual Report in respect of—say—1931 cannot be ready much before the end of 1932, so the practice has been adopted of publishing the Report early in 1933, in order that it may include, in addition to the statistics for 1931, a full review of all developments and matters of interest during 1932.

2. The Staff of a Prison

The staff of a prison consists of " superior " and " subordinate " officers, the superior officers (i.e. Governor, Chaplain, and Medical Officer), being appointed by the Secretary of State, the subordinates by the Prison Commissioners. All full-time officers (with minor exceptions to be specified later) are pensionable civil servants, whose appointments are subject to the issue in their favour of Certificates of Qualification by the Civil Service Commissioners, in accordance with the Orders in Council regulating admission to the Civil Service. Their powers and duties are prescribed by the Statutory Prison Rules, supplemented by the Commissioners' Standing Orders.

The responsible head of each establishment is the Governor : in the larger establishments he is assisted by one or more Deputy Governors who are also superior officers with statutory powers and duties. Where there is a Deputy

---

[1] Published by H.M. Stationery Office, Kingsway, W.C. 2, from whom, or through any bookseller, it may be obtained at a small charge (usually 1s. 6d.).

E

Governor he takes charge in the absence of the Governor with all the Governor's powers and responsibilities : where there is no Deputy Governor the charge devolves on the Chief Officer, or in a Borstal Institution[1] on the senior Housemaster.

The duties of the Chaplain in the majority of establishments are performed by local clergymen appointed on a part-time basis at a remuneration appropriate to the size of the prison. At the larger establishments where a full-time post is necessary it was formerly the practice to appoint the Chaplains as permanent pensionable civil servants : the Commissioners, however, now hold the view that it is better that a clergyman should after a period of work in prisons be free to return to parochial or other duties, and full-time chaplains at present are appointed in the first instance for a period of five years only : subsequently their services may or may not be renewed for a further period.

The Chaplain must by statute be a priest of the Established Church, but by the Prison Ministers Act, 1863, provision is made for spiritual ministration to prisoners who are not members of that church by Prison Ministers, who are appointed by the Prison Commissioners on the recommendation of the Bishop of the Diocese in the case of the Roman Catholic Church, or of the governing body in the case of one of the Protestant Free Churches. There are at every establishment a Roman Catholic Priest and a Methodist Minister, and Ministers of other denominations are appointed or specially called in as occasion arises. Prison Ministers are appointed on a part-time[2] basis and may be remunerated either by fixed salaries or by fees fixed on a capitation basis, according to the numbers of their congregations.

The Medical Officers of the larger establishments are full-time officers, and where the volume of work requires they are assisted by one or more Deputy Medical Officers, who may be either full-time or part-time officers. At the smaller prisons the duties are carried out by local practitioners engaged on a part-time basis.

---

[1] For the staff at a Borstal Institution see Chapter XVI, page 190.

[2] At one or two prisons with large Roman Catholic populations the Roman Catholic Priest is a full-time pensionable officer.

The Matron is the woman officer in charge, under the Governor, of the women's wing of a mixed prison.[1] In one or two of the largest mixed prisons the title of Lady Superintendent is given, and these ladies have the status of superior officers.

The subordinate officers, men and women, engaged in the normal duties of supervision and control of prisoners, were formerly known as Warders and Wardresses. In 1919 these terms were abolished, and the term Prison Officer substituted. Officers are divided into three grades : the Chief Officer is the head of the subordinate staff, and in the largest prisons is assisted by one or more Deputy Chief Officers : Principal Officers are in charge of " halls " and " districts " of the prison and grounds, and fill specially responsible posts in the larger prisons. The ordinary " officer " grade contains its own subdivisions of specialists : of these special mention may be made of the hospital staff, works staff, and trade instructors.

More will be said of the hospital staff in Chapter IX : it is sufficient to say here that in every prison for men there are one or more trained male nurses, known as Hospital Officers, and in every prison for women, or women's wing of a mixed prison, one or more trained and certificated Nursing Sisters of the Prison Nursing Service. At the largest prisons a qualified Pharmacist is employed on a full-time basis as dispenser to the Hospital.

The " works " staff, under the direction of the Works Department of the Prison Commission, is responsible for the maintenance of the prison premises, including the officers' quarters, and for new construction. The Foremen of Works and Engineers are recruited from the ranks of the service by competitive examination, and there is careful provision for their subsequent training in their specialist duties. Skilled workmen are employed at local rates of wages as and when necessary, for any special jobs that cannot be carried out by prison labour.

The training and supervision of prisoners in industrial

[1] Only two prisons, Holloway and Aylesbury, receive women only. The Governor, Deputy Governor and Medical Officer of Aylesbury are women : the Governor of Holloway is a medical man, with a woman Deputy Governor. The Deputy Medical Officers at Holloway are women.

work is in the main carried out by selected prison officers who receive allowances for acting as Trade Instructors, but for some of the more important industries requiring special skill qualified men are engaged from outside : some of these specialists, e.g. the Superintendents of Printing and Weaving, and the Farm Bailiffs—may be engaged on a permanent and pensionable basis, but the majority are engaged as " Civilian Instructors " on a weekly wage basis.

The clerical work is carried out by a staff of Clerical Officers recruited through the competitions held for the General Clerical Class by the Civil Service Commissioners. The Steward is responsible to the Governor for the efficiency of the clerical staff, for the cash and accounts, and the control of the stores and manufactures.

The established (i.e. permanent and pensionable) staff is not required to do night patrol duty, or such tasks as stoking and labouring. For these duties men are engaged by the Governors, with the approval of the Commissioners, as and when required : the night-patrols and stokers, and certain labourers whose jobs last for any considerable period, are employed as " quasi-permanent " officers on a weekly wage basis ; others are engaged as " temporary " officers by the day. Temporary officers are also engaged by Governors to fill vacancies in staff, pending the posting of established officers.

The subordinate ranks are organised as a uniformed body subject to a disciplinary code. The uniform is navy blue, with black buttons and a flat cap of military pattern, and distinctive marks for the higher ranks. No accoutrements are worn, and staves are carried in inside pockets. Firearms are carried only by sentries posted over parties working outside the walls of convict prisons.

Minor breaches of discipline by officers may be dealt with by the Governor by admonishment or reprimand : more serious offences are dealt with by the Commissioners, who may place an officer " on special probation," fine him, suspend his increments of salary, degrade him in rank, or with the Home Secretary's approval dismiss him from the service. Any officer in danger of dismissal is entitled to be heard in person by one of the Commissioners, and an appeal lies to the Home Secretary against any disciplinary decision of the Commissioners.

The subordinate staff of each establishment elects a Representative Officer, who is empowered to raise with the Governor or with a visiting Commissioner or Assistant Commissioner questions affecting the conditions of service of the staff. These representatives annually elect a Representative Board which meets the Commissioners twice a year to discuss conditions of service and matters of interest to the service, excluding questions of discipline, and acts as a negotiating body when questions of remuneration and conditions of service are at issue. There is also a Superior Officers' Representative Board, which meets the Commissioners annually for similar purposes, and the Commissioners hold periodical Conferences of each grade of the Superior Officers separately for discussion of questions affecting their work—first among themselves, and then with the Commissioners.

The numbers employed and the rates of pay for each grade of the service, as on 1st April, 1933, are set out in Appendix C.

3. Selection and Training of Staff

It is fully recognised by the Prison Commissioners that however high the ideals of an administration, however admirable its rules, it is on their application by the men in daily contact with the prisoners that the success of the system must depend. Something of that recognition was expressed, perhaps, when the name of " officer," with its connotation of a positive duty, of a " leader " rather than a " guard," was substituted for that of " warder." The cynic may here find occasion to smile, but the cynic will be wrong. It may be true that old traditions die hard ; that the opportunities which an officer will find of exercising, as man to man, an active influence for good on any individual prisoner, are necessarily restricted ; that, as was said by the late Home Secretary, prison life is apt to produce " callosities of mind " in officers as well as in prisoners—and let it not be forgotten how peculiarly difficult and exacting are the duties and the conditions of service of prison officers, who are not *ex officio* exempt from the common failings of humanity. But it is also true to say that the spirit which animates a prison staff to-day is definitely different from that of a generation ago, and that the ideals of the administration are loyally and sincerely interpreted by their governors and officers in a manner which has earned the well-deserved tributes of all who come into contact with the work of our prisons.

In order to maintain this high standard, it is necessary to devote the greatest care to the selection and training of officers, both superior and subordinate. The decisive factor is the Governor, on whom, as on the head of any disciplined unit or establishment, the tone of the staff must finally depend. The day is long past when a prison governorship was a suitable place of retirement for any half-pay officer of the Navy or Army with sufficient " pull " to get there. The control of one of our largest prisons, with its thousand or so prisoners and staff, extensive buildings and grounds, large manufactures, Prisoners' Aid Society, and Voluntary Workers of all kinds, calls for a combination of administrative, educational, and social qualifications of a high order : and in addition to these qualifications the successful Governor must possess those qualities of character and temperament, that vocation for a difficult social service, which are necessary to fit him for constructive work among prisoners.

Governors are appointed by the Secretary of State, on the recommendation of a Selection Board consisting of representatives of the Prison Commissioners and the Civil Service Commissioners. Candidates, who must be under the age of 41, are required to complete the prescribed form of application : on the occurrence of a vacancy a number of those who are *prima facie* most suitable are interviewed by the Commissioners, and a dozen or so are picked out to appear before the Selection Board, whose report is forwarded to the Secretary of State with the name of the candidate recommended for appointment. Following the decision of the Secretary of State, the Civil Service Commissioners are asked to issue a certificate of qualification, which involves a medical examination and inquiry into references. The aim of the whole procedure is to secure the best man available at the time, and it is perhaps worth while to emphasise that while due weight is given to testimonials from persons acquainted with a candidate's work and qualifications, any attempt to use " influence " is more likely to disqualify than to assist. A considerable proportion of Governors continue to be selected from retired or serving officers of the Navy, Army or Air Force, though candidates are also sought from a somewhat wider field. From time to time selected officers from the clerical or subordinate ranks are also brought before the Selection Boards, but appointments to Governorships from these grades are infrequent : the question whether a special avenue of promotion to the superior ranks can be opened for selected young officers is receiving consideration at the present time.

On the appointment of a candidate by the Secretary of State he is sent to a large prison for a three months' course of training, at the end of which, if he displays the necessary aptitude and personality, he is posted for duty as Deputy Governor on two years' probation. If his appointment is confirmed he will in due course become Governor of a prison of his own, and is eligible for promotion through Class III and Class II to Class I. The normal age of retirement on superannuation is 60, though in exceptional cases a Governor may be retained up to the age of 65.

The formalities of procedure for full-time Chaplains and Medical Officers are substantially the same, except that the Civil Service Commissioners are not represented on the Selection Board, their places being taken by clergymen or medical men as the case may be. Part-time Chaplains and Medical Officers are appointed by the Secretary of State, the former on the recommendation of the Bishop of the Diocese, the latter by selection from such local practitioners as apply.

The Housemasters and Assistant Housemasters of Borstal Institutions[1] are appointed by the Commissioners in substantially the same way as Governors, and Governors of Borstal Institutions are usually selected from senior Housemasters and not appointed from outside the service. Officers

[1] For the special qualifications required, see Chapter XVI.

of the Borstal Service are eligible for appointment as Assistant Housemasters, and a number of those so appointed have since become Housemasters.

Not less care is taken with the selection of subordinate officers. Written application on prescribed forms is made to the Prison Commissioners : these applications are examined by the Commissioners, and the candidates who appear to have the necessary education and qualifications are summoned to the prison nearest their homes to be medically examined, put through an "intelligence test," and finally interviewed by a Commissioner or Assistant Commissioner. What the Commissioners look for is not only a sound and reliable character with a good standard of education (ex-soldiers must have Class I or II Army Educational Certificate) but the right temperament and personality for the difficult work that a prison officer is required to undertake. A very large number of applications are received for these posts, and it is thus fortunately possible for the Commissioners to maintain a very high standard in their selections. In accordance with the policy of the Government preference is given to ex-regular Sailors, Soldiers, or Airmen, and a fine type of man is obtained from ex-N.C.O's of these services. But recruitment is not limited to ex-service men, and a considerable number of skilled tradesmen and men from various walks of life are selected.

Appointment does not however rest on paper qualifications, and the impression made at an interview. Those selected as *prima facie* suitable are in due course sent to a Training School, where they receive a general grounding in the bases of a prison officer's work. This School, with the consequent examination by a Commissioner, serves also to search out the weaker vessels, who are regretfully rejected : those who have survived the test are posted to prisons for two months' further training in the more detailed routine of their duties, and if still satisfactory they are then posted for duty on twelve months' probation. A subordinate officer, unless earlier discharged for misconduct or on medical grounds, will normally retire on pension at age 55, though in exceptional circumstances he may be retained till 60.

Promotions to the rank of Principal Officer are made from among officers who have qualified in a Promotion Examination, of which the first part is a written educational test, the second a *viva voce* examination by a Commissioner or Assistant Commissioner.

It is necessary to say a word in conclusion on the subject of " trafficking " between officers and prisoners ; that is, the illicit passing into or out of the prison by officers of letters or other communications to or from prisoners, or the purveying to prisoners of prohibited articles such as tobacco. It is well known that these practices are carried on by a small number of officers, who are prepared to risk certain dismissal for the not inconsiderable gain they may often secure by thus exploiting the needs of the prisoners and their friends. Perhaps no more need be said than that these practices are as vigorously condemned and repudiated by the staff as a whole as by the authorities, that Governors and their staffs are constantly on the alert to catch out these men who dishonour their service, that few escape detection for long, and that instant dismissal, and sometimes criminal prosecution, is the certain result.

4. *Visiting Committees and Boards of Visitors*

We have already noticed that Parliament, in transferring the local Prisons to the control of a Central Board, decided by one of our characteristic English compromises not to make the transference of powers complete, but to reserve to Visiting Committees, to be appointed annually by the Benches committing to the prisons, certain of the powers formerly exercised by the Visiting Justices appointed by Quarter Sessions. The composition, method of appointment, powers, and duties of these Committees are prescribed by the Secretary of State in the Statutory Rules.

The principal function of the Visiting Committee is in relation to discipline. They are the superior disciplinary authority of the prison, and to them are referred all reports against prisoners for breaches of discipline with which the Governor is not empowered to deal, or for which he considers the punishments he can award inadequate. To them also, subject to the confirmation of the Secretary of State, is reserved the power to award Corporal Punishment for the offences for which, under the Prison Act, 1898, this may still be awarded.[1]

They have a further and most valuable function as an impartial, judicial, and non-official body, having access to all parts of the prison and to every prisoner, to whom—or to any one of them—a prisoner may make a complaint or application. The Rules require them regularly to visit and inspect the prisons, to report any abuses to the Secretary of State, and to make an annual report to the Secretary of State : in these reports the Secretary of State receives their views on the state of discipline of the prison, the conduct of the staff, the health of the prisoners, the diet, the condition of the buildings, and any other matters which they wish to bring to his notice. It is usual for the Committee to meet as a Committee at the prison once in each month, and to draw up a rota to secure visitation by one member once in each week. The work is entirely voluntary and unpaid.

For Convict Prisons and Preventive Detention Prisons, which have no local connections, similar functions are exercised by Boards of Visitors, who differ from Visiting Committees only in that their members are appointed by the Secretary of State and not by the Sessions : a certain proportion of the members must be magistrates. The equivalent bodies for Borstal Institutions, also appointed by the Secretary of State, are called Visiting Committees.

This interesting experiment in dual control has worked decidedly to the advantage of the service. It must make for public confidence in the administration of discipline that it should be in the hands of a body which is not only extra-official but judicial, while the safeguard to the prisoners in being able to make any complaint to a magistrate unconnected with the administration is evident. Not less valuable is the maintenance of that connection with local interests on which, especially under the modern system with its reliance on voluntary co-operation in many directions, so much of value to the service must increasingly depend. Finally, the fund of experience and ideas accumulated by

[1] See Chapter VI, pages 84–5.

these men and women experienced in public work is placed
at the disposal of the administration through the medium
of an annual conference, at which representatives of all the
Visiting Committees and Boards of Visitors meet the Commissioners for the discussion of resolutions put forward by
the Committees for the Agenda. These conferences have
already had valuable results in many directions.

CHAPTER IV

BUILDINGS AND ACCOMMODATION

1. *Numbers and Distribution of Establishments*

THE process of economical concentration of prison populations begun in 1878 was resumed during the late war, and
since 1914 the fall in the number of prisoners and considerations of economy have brought about the closing of
no less than 29 local prisons. Of these 18 have been
formally discontinued and disposed of, one is in use by
another Department, five are earmarked as reserve prisons
for different areas, one has been reopened as a Convict
Prison, one as a Borstal Institution, one as a Preventive
Detention Prison, and two more recently closed are still in
the hands of the Commissioners.

The effect of this concentration has been to abolish, in
effect, the " county gaol," to which all prisoners from the
county Assizes and Quarter Sessions, and from the Petty
Sessional Divisions of the County, were automatically
committed. Instead we find the country divided into some
20 large " committal areas," each containing one or more
prisons, settled not by county boundaries but by convenience of communication.[1]

There are at present 25 prisons to which prisoners of all
classes are committed direct by the courts, and these are
known as " local prisons." There are also four prisons for

---

[1] By section 17 (2) of the Criminal Justice Administration Act, 1914,
a prisoner sentenced to imprisonment, or committed on remand or awaiting
trial, or otherwise, may be lawfully confined in any prison to which the
Prison Acts apply (this excludes " convict " prisons), and by subsection
(3) prisoners shall be committed to such prisons as the Secretary of State
may from time to time direct, and may by his direction be moved to any
other prison. A " convict," i.e. a person sentenced to Penal Servitude, may
be confined either in a prison declared to be a convict prison, or in any
other prison in the United Kingdom (Penal Servitude Act, 1853, section 6).

men and one for women[1] which are "convict prisons" under the Penal Servitude Acts ; one Training Centre (see p. 76) ; and one Preventive Detention Prison. There are six Borstal Institutions for boys and one for girls. A list of the 38 prisons and Borstal Institutions now in occupation, with particulars of each, is given in Appendix D.

The English administration does not like—nor, fortunately, does it require—the very large prison. In only six of our prisons does the nominal cell accommodation exceed 1,000, and it is only in the two largest London prisons, and during the exceptional pressure of 1932, that an actual population of 1,000 has been reached. In 1930 there were only four prisons with a daily average population in excess of 500, and even the high populations of 1932 have only increased that number to six.

2. *Planning and Accommodation*

The buildings at the disposal of the Commissioners present in an acute form the problem of pouring new wine into old bottles. The local prisons with few exceptions date from the middle of last century, those that are not of even earlier date following fairly closely the model set by Pentonville in 1842. It is evident that a prison built to serve a system based on punitive repression, strict separation by day and night, and mechanically repetitive "hard labour," will be ill designed for the modern conception of "training," with its productive work in association, careful classification, adult education schemes, and physical training. Public money has never been available for building a modern prison, so that there is none to which the administration can point as the expression of its own views as to what a prison should be : and as regards prison premises generally the most that can be said is that during the present century, by constant modification and reconstruction, the Commissioners have actively made the best of a not very good job.

There are two systems of planning for the cell-blocks which form the nucleus of the prison buildings—the

[1] Aylesbury : here there is also the Borstal Institution for girls.

" radial " system which, following the Pentonville model, was adopted for almost all the local prisons, and the " separate-block " system, which is more generally used for convict prisons and Borstal Institutions. The main advantages of the radial system, in which the cell-blocks radiate from a common centre in the form of a + or the spokes of a wheel, are economy of construction and facility of supervision. This form is also very elastic, being adaptable equally to the small prison of only two cell-blocks—or " halls " as they are usually called—and to the large prison with five or more, while additions and subtractions can be made without difficulty at the ends of the blocks. On the other hand the cells and rooms become increasingly dark and airless as the re-entrant angles are approached, while the ground in the angles is cramped and it is difficult to make it serve any useful purpose.

The halls are from two to five storeys high according to the size and general planning of the prison. On the ground floor the cell-doors give on to a central corridor, usually 16′ in width, which reaches to and is lighted from the roof. On the upper floors, or landings, the cells open on to railed galleries about 3′ wide, supported on wall-brackets. The well between the galleries is bridged at intervals, and the bridges serve also as landings for open stair-flights from floor to floor. At the gallery-level above the ground floor wire netting is stretched across the well, to check the fall of anyone who by accident or design drops over the gallery railings. Water-closets and slop-sinks with taps are provided at intervals on both sides of every landing, usually in annexes the width of a cell which project beyond the main wall from basement to roof. The interior walls are lime-washed to within four feet of ground level, where a line of green paint borders a cream-painted dado, giving a clean and light interior effect.

To this nucleus of cell-blocks the administrative and auxiliary buildings are attached in various ways. The offices and stores commonly form a " spoke " through which lies the entrance to the prison proper. For convenience of service and administration the kitchen and bakery and the chapel will be close to the centre : the laundry will usually be attached to the hall that is (or was) set aside for women. The hospital arrangements are described in Chapter IX. In a separate building towards the Gate is the " Reception," where prisoners on arrival are received, examined, bathed, fitted out with prison clothing, and detained till they have been passed medically fit for admission to the main prison. The stores for prison clothing and for prisoners' private clothing will usually be connected with this block. The general bath-house may be here or elsewhere.

The main task of the modern administration in connection with its buildings has been the provision of workshops for associated labour, and of rooms of a size suitable for lectures, educational classes, evening association of prisoners, gymnasia, and so forth. For long the ground floors of the halls were in many prisons the only spaces available for all or most of these purposes, and at some prisons they must still be used for some of them. A start was made with building workshops early in the century, and the pace has been so quickened since the war that at most prisons now all associated labour takes place in suitable workshops, while none[1] is without shop accommodation of some sort. The workshops are specially designed for their purpose, and are inspected by the Government's Factory Inspectors. Ingenuity has also been shown in knocking cells together and otherwise adapting existing accommodation for class-rooms and association rooms, while the Chapel or the Visiting Committee Room may serve for a lecture, and a shop or store or the floor of a hall for a gymnasium.

Most local prisons are built on restricted urban sites, and the limitations of space are often a severe handicap to proper development. In a few cases the Commissioners have been able to buy land adjacent to the prison, but generally speaking, the possibilities of additional construction are strictly limited by the area within the prison wall. In this area, in addition to the buildings, and the space required for light and air and necessary circulation, room must be found for exercising the prisoners. Nowadays this requires more space than when the prisons were built, for three reasons—classification breaks the prisoners up

---

[1] Except the prison for unconvicted prisoners at Brixton.

into separate parties, the policy of unbroken periods of work makes it necessary to have more prisoners out at the same time, and the partial substitution of physical training for walking round the paved concentric " exercise rings " calls for properly prepared drill-grounds of fair size. Where there is ample space within the walls vegetable gardens are often found, and in almost every prison brave and often surprisingly successful attempts are made to beautify the grounds with flowers.

Where additional land is available, vegetable gardens and recreation grounds may be found outside the walls, but normally the whole of the prison premises are enclosed within the sheer security wall, which may vary between 16 feet and 25 feet in height. Unless an additional gateway has been cut to give on to external land, there is only one way through the wall, and that is by the Main Gate, a massive entrance lodge with outer and inner gates (both must never be unlocked together), quarters for the gate-keeper, and often a room in which visitors wait before admission to the prison. Adjacent to the gate is the block of Visiting Boxes, in which prisoners receive their visits.

Outside the walls will be found the official quarters of the Governor and other full-time Superior Officers, and a certain number of official quarters for the subordinate staff. In the larger prisons there is usually a Recreational Club for the subordinate staff.

3. *The Cell and its Equipment*

Strict separation by night remains fundamental to the English system, and every prisoner has his separate cell in which he probably spends 14 to 16 hours out of every 24 : its construction and equipment are therefore of primary interest to him. There is no prescribed specification of a standard cell, but the Rules provide that every cell in which a prisoner sleeps must be certified by the Prison Commissioners as reaching a proper standard of size, construction, heating, lighting, ventilation, and equipment. The majority of cells in local prisons are $13' \times 7' \times 9'$

high, giving 819 cubit feet of air space : this was the size
adopted, after careful inquiry, at Pentonville, which as we
have seen was the model for most of the prisons built after
1842. It was intended to provide an adequate size for
strictly separate confinement with cellular labour. The
size of cell subsequently adopted by the Directors for
Convict Prisons was $10' \times 7' \times 9'$ high, giving only 630 cubic
feet of air space, since the convicts worked outside and not
in their cells.

The stone or brick wall surfaces and the ceiling are lime-
washed, with a dado painted like that in the halls : the
outer-wall surface only is plastered, and this is done for
security so that any attempt to tamper with the brickwork
would show up. The floors vary, cement, stone flags, tiles,
slate, and wood planks or blocks all being found.

Cell doors are of solid construction, both doors and frames
often being lined with sheet-iron to prevent tampering by
ingenious prisoners. A small glass peep-hole, covered by
a movable shutter, gives observation of the cell to the
patrolling officer. The lock is strong and heavy, and
inaccessible from the inside of the cell : it cannot therefore
be picked, but it has not infrequently happened that
prisoners have succeeded in cutting out or wedging the lock
to facilitate escape : each such incident, by disclosing
weaknesses, renders another less likely.

There are many patterns of cell-window : the majority
are of the old Pentonville type, with 14 small panes in two
rows : a later pattern was of 21 panes in three rows : during
the present century the pattern used has been of 35 panes
in five rows, each pane being $4\frac{7}{8}'' \times 6\frac{7}{8}''$. The panes are
glazed with clear glass, and two sliding panes give direct
access to the outer air. With older types of window the
sash was of cast iron, and this necessitated strong guard-
bars outside the window : the modern type has a manganese-
steel sash, which renders guard-bars unnecessary. With the
old 14 pane window the sill was approximately 6' 9'' above
floor-level, but with the modern type the height from floor
to sill is about 5 feet.

With few exceptions English prisons are still lighted by
coal-gas, though schemes have been prepared, and are being

F

carried out as funds permit, for the substitution of electricity as the old gas systems wear out. There are no gas lights actually in the cells : the burner (an incandescent mantle) is placed in a " gas-box " cut in the corridor wall : this has a glazed opening 9″×9″ on the cell side, through which the light shines immediately on to the prisoner's table. Where the cells are electrically lighted the light is within the cell.

The old system of heating and ventilation provided for fresh air, warmed in winter by low pressure hot-water pipes, to be passed into the cell by an intake flue near the ceiling and out by an extraction flue in the opposite corner near the floor. This system, originated at Pentonville, is with little modification still used with satisfactory results in many prisons. In systems of more modern installation heating is by direct radiation from low pressure hot-water pipes carried through the cells themselves, and ventilation is not by ventilating flues but by circulation from the outer air secured by the sliding panes in the windows and ventilators. A daily record is kept of the temperatures of different parts of the prison, which must be maintained in conformity with a prescribed standard.

Prisoners are required to open the ventilators on leaving their cells, and it is the landing officer's duty to see that at least once a day doors and sliding sashes are open for long enough to give the cells a thorough airing. The general intention is that all temperatures should be kept at about 60° F. in winter, and that both in summer and winter there should be a regular current of fresh air through the cells. Equal care is devoted to the heating and ventilation of halls, workshops, and other parts of the building.

The Rules require that every cell shall be fitted with bell communication, by which the officer on duty may be summoned in case of need.

The above relates to ordinary cells, but there are many special types of cell : the hospital cell is larger and lighter, and its plastered walls are painted ivory white : the observation cell, for certain medical and mental cases, has an iron gate as well as a door, the latter being left open to

allow full observation into the cell at all times : cells for
tubercular cases are similar to hospital cells, with a larger
portion of the window made to open, rounded angles, and
impervious floors : there are matted cells for epileptics, with
observation gates, coir floor mats, and coir matting round
the walls to a height of 5 feet, and padded cells for insane
prisoners who may endanger their lives without this protection : the " special " cells are fitted with a minimum
amount of immovable equipment that cannot be " smashed
up," and windows and gas-boxes high out of reach for the
same reason—a certain number of such cells are specially
isolated and fitted with double doors, for the discourage-
ment of those who disturb the prison by outbursts of shouting
and offensive noise.

Now we come to the ordinary equipment of a cell. The
plank bed takes up one side of the cell, and is stood against
the wall during the day : it is furnished with a coir-filled
mattress, blankets (two in summer, three in winter), two
sheets, pillow and pillow slip, and a bed rug. On one side
of the door under the gas-box is a fixed wooden table, and
across the other corner by the window a fixed corner shelf
for books, etc. : on table or shelf the prisoner may display
a few cards or photographs. There is a stool to sit on, but
chairs are now supplied instead of stools to all women, and
are being supplied for men as funds permit. Each year also
a further number of cells is equipped with washstands (to
take the enamelled iron washing-bowl, water-jug, and
covered chamber-pot), and with small looking-glasses.
Unless the cell has a wooden floor there is a two-yard strip
of matting. A wooden batten on the wall, with hooks ; a
plate ; salt cellar ; set of brushes, cloths, and other cleaning
materials ; and the prisoner's toilet articles, complete the
furniture.

Every prisoner also has in his cell a slate and pencil which
serve two purposes : first for the prisoner and his landing
officer or instructor to leave messages for each other—e.g. the
prisoner may write down the library books he wants, or the
officer may record some observations about the cleanliness
or otherwise of the cell, or the nature of the evening cell-
task ; second, for the prisoner's amusement or education.

The use of library books and note-books is discussed in Chapter VIII.

From another batten on the wall hangs a series of printed cards, which vary according to a prisoner's classification, but in all cases include "Notes for the Guidance of Prisoners" (a summary of the principal regulations which a prisoner should know), a Dietary card, and a card showing the library books, note-books, etc., which he has been authorised to keep in his cell. Others are added in special cases, e.g. the unconvicted prisoner has printed directions as to how he should seek bail and legal aid, and the recently convicted an explanation of his rights of appeal.

Outside the door a small wooden frame of cards contains information for the staff about the occupant. On one appears the name and register number, sentence, and classification : this card varies in colour according to religious denomination, so that Chaplains and Ministers may pick out members of their flock at a glance. Here, too, is kept the Stage Register (see page 79) and notes of the party the prisoner is allotted to for work, the tools he should have in his cell, any special diet he is allowed, and other such matters.

CHAPTER V

CLASSIFICATION OF PRISONERS[1]

CLASSIFICATION as understood to-day is essentially a problem arising out of the conditions of to-day, although, as we have seen, it has been discussed and to some extent practised at least from the time of Peel's Gaol Act. The idea that prisoners should be " classified " arose as one of the solutions of the problem of breaking down the contamination of the early gaols, and " prevention of contamination " is still at the root of the modern system—though we may find grounds for thinking that other tendencies are now working to modify this traditional conception.

The attempt of 1823 to classify convicted prisoners was never seriously pursued and was soon abandoned, but the desirability of separating and treating specially both debtors and unconvicted criminal prisoners was constantly reaffirmed, and remains by statutory requisition fundamental to the system of to-day. Both these classes are kept separate from all convicted prisoners and from each other, and are treated under special Rules. One may, nevertheless, question whether this clear-cut division is either so necessary or so desirable as may appear at first sight : it is true that in legal theory all the unconvicted are " held to be innocent till they have been found guilty," but in practice a given number of unconvicted prisoners may contain every degree of criminality, from the really innocent person who has never been in prison before to the cynical " old lag " awaiting trial for the twentieth time. And if the aim is prevention of contamination it might well seem more reasonable to associate the old lag with his convicted brethren than with the ingenuous novices of crime. As regards debtors, apart

---

[1] This chapter refers primarily to Local Prisons : the arrangements in Convict Prisons are slightly different—see Chapter XIV.

from the rather fine ethical distinction between some forms of " crime " and some forms of " debt," there is no obvious reason why a man who is imprisoned for not maintaining his wife or illegitimate child should be differently treated from one who has failed to pay a fine for some more or less technical motoring or street-trading offence, or for supposing that the former will be " contaminated " by association with the latter.

Our main concern, however, is with the problems connected with the classification of convicted prisoners—problems that were not raised in the gaols of the eighteenth century, which aimed at no more than safe custody, nor in those of the nineteenth century, which attacked contamination with Separate Confinement and the Rule of Silence, but which do arise in an acute form when it becomes necessary to reconcile both safe custody and the prevention of contamination with that constant association of the prisoners in workshop and class-room, and even at meals and recreation, that the modern system of training requires. And these problems further complicate themselves at the points where it begins to appear that this traditional, and somewhat negative, conception of " contamination " cuts across and conflicts with the more positive modern conceptions of " individualisation " and " training." But it will be best to begin by describing the system as it is, and to allow the difficulties to appear in the process.

The first attempt to distinguish between one convicted prisoner and another—apart from their arbitrary division by certain early statutes into " felons " and " misdemeanants," a division of no significance in practice or in common sense—was the institution, by the Prison Acts 1865 and 1877, of a provision under which " any person convicted of misdemeanour and sentenced to imprisonment without hard labour, might be ordered to be treated as a misdemeanant of the First Division, and as such was not to be deemed a criminal prisoner. Persons convicted of sedition or seditious libel, or imprisoned under any rule, order, or attachment, or for contempt of any Court[1] were to be placed in the First

[1] Under the Prison Act, 1898, the " contempt " cases are now treated as " debtors " : this applies even when no question of failure to pay monies is involved—a somewhat curious change.

Division."[1] This process was taken a step further when the Act of 1898 set up the Triple Division of Offenders, under which the Court passing sentence is enabled to give a direction, *in the cases of prisoners not sentenced to Hard Labour*, that the prisoner be placed in the First Division or the Second Division : if no such direction be given, the prisoner without Hard Labour passes into the Third Division.

Although it is necessary to describe the working of the Triple Division as an existing part of the Statutory system of classification, it may be said at the outset that it has long been to all intents and purposes a dead letter. This result would seem to have been due in part to uncertainty as to the real intention of the statutory provisions, in regard both to the kind of offenders to be placed in each Division, and to the kind of treatment there to be applied to them.

As to what offenders are to be placed in each Division, the Courts have no more guidance from the statute than that they are to " have regard to the nature of the offence and the antecedents of the offender," though the First Division must include the former " misdemeanants of the First Division." In practice, although the wording of the statute is not so limited, it has come about that the First Division is reserved " for strictly limited classes of prisoners, and mainly for those for whom First Division treatment is prescribed by statute, e.g. persons convicted of seditious libel."[2] It may be inferred that this Division is now used only for what are sometimes called " political " offenders, but neither the legislature nor the judicature of this country has shown any disposition to distinguish " political " offences as such, and in the result there are few years which see the reception of more than one of these prisoners. There should be, on the other hand, no doubt as to what class of offenders should go into the Second Division : the intention is clearly " to separate persons who are not depraved and not usually of criminal habits from those who are depraved or are usually of criminal habits. The former, therefore, should go into the Second Division, the latter into the Third Division."[3]

As regards the treatment intended for the different

---

[1] Ruggles-Brise, page 71.
[2] " Notes on Imprisonment, etc.," page 5.   [3] *Ibid*

Divisions, the position is reversed. The Rules for the First Division provide a régime which amounts to no more than deprivation of liberty, with such restraint only as is necessary for discipline and safe-custody. Those for the Second Division, however, provide for no different discipline or treatment than is received by prisoners of the Third Division, and it is clear that this fact is not generally realised either by the Courts or by the public. It may be that Parliament had in mind something more than a mere " classification," and indeed Sir E. Ruggles-Brise says that " in this way it was hoped to secure that ' *individualisation de la peine* ' which modern penitentiary science declares to be the ideal at which a good penal system should aim " :[1] but however that may be, in practice the Second Division has been treated simply as a medium of classification and not as setting up a different system of treatment.

It may be due in part to a failure to appreciate this position that Courts as a whole have not made full use of the Triple Division, though the true explanation seems rather to lie in the provision of the statute which limits its operation to prisoners sentenced without " Hard Labour " ; for although this phrase has had little or no practical significance for over 30 years, its traditions and implications are such that few Courts can resist it, and in the very great majority of sentences to imprisonment, the direction is still " with hard labour." In the result, the number committed to the Second Division in 1921 was only about 3% of those eligible for that Division,[2] and the position is not substantially different to-day. On the other hand it would seem that many prisoners wrongly placed in the Second Division are so placed because the Court, regarding Hard Labour as the only alternative, hesitates to pass this " sharp sentence " on an aged or infirm prisoner, however depraved : the course of passing sentence of imprisonment simply, leaving the offender to pass into the Third Division, is very rarely taken.

In practice, fortunately, this break-down of the statutory system is of little or no significance ; and indeed, if the Second Division was intended simply as an instrument of

---

[1] Ruggles-Brise, page 79.   [2] *Ibid.*

classification, it was unnecessary from the outset, for since 1898 the Commissioners have been required by the Rules to place in a separate class, known as the Star Class, every prisoner who has not previously been convicted of serious crime, and is not of habitually criminal or depraved habits —that is to say every prisoner who might properly have been sentenced to imprisonment in the Second Division. Prisoners of the Second Division and of the Star Class are, under the Rules, located together, and are kept so far as practicable separate from other classes of prisoners. The decision as to a prisoner's classification is made by a Reception Board, which sees him shortly after admission, and has before it all the information which can be obtained by inquiry into his character and antecedents. A prisoner found to be unsuitable for the Star Class can be removed to the Ordinary Class, though a depraved offender placed by the Court in the Second Division must unfortunately remain with the Second Division, however bad his influence.

The administration has taken a further step in the classification of adult male prisoners that is not required by the Rules. Experience would seem to point to the age-group 21–26 as being the main nursery of the " habitual criminal," and with the intention both of separating these young men from more hardened offenders while they are still of an age susceptible to better influences, and of providing a more active and strenuous training, there is formed in each Local Prison a " Special Class " in which are placed all male prisoners of the Third Division or sentenced to Hard Labour, under the age of 26, who by reason of their character are ineligible for the Star Class : the Governor may include prisoners of this type up to 30 years of age if he thinks they are likely to benefit and will not harm the rest of the class.

There remains only the Young Prisoners Class, in which, by requirement of the Rules, are placed all prisoners under 21, whether convicted or unconvicted. So long as these young people continue to be sent to prison, it is no doubt right to keep them separate from adults, but it is impossible to subdivide this class into " Stars " and " Ordinaries," and even among a batch of prisoners under 21, many degrees of

" criminality " are to be found, from the lad who cannot pay a 5s. fine for kicking a football about the streets, to the hardened member of a " motor bandit " gang with more than one previous conviction. Governors are, however, given a discretion to classify as " adults " and remove from the class those whose habits and character make them unsuitable for inclusion.

Thus in every Local Prison the prisoners, whether serving sentences of Penal Servitude or of Imprisonment with or without Hard Labour, fall, in addition to " Debtors " and " Unconvicted," into one of four classes : Stars[1] (including Second Division), Specials (men only), Young Prisoners, and Ordinaries. The extent to which the separation of the classes can be rendered effective depends in the first instance upon the numbers of each class in relation to the prison accommodation available in the area from which they are drawn. Thus in the area served by the London prisons, where a large prison population can be concentrated in several closely related prisons, it is possible to provide a separate prison for each main class—all women go to Hollo- way, unconvicted and debtors to Brixton, Stars and Second Division to Wormwood Scrubs, short term Specials to Wandsworth, and Ordinaries to Wandsworth and Penton- ville. Two separate blocks at Wormwood Scrubs are also set aside for Young Prisoners, one block for the convicted, the other for the unconvicted. The " Specials " from this area who have long enough sentences are concentrated at Lewes. At one time Nottingham Prison was set apart as a prison for Specials from the North and Midlands, but this scheme had to be discontinued in 1931 on grounds of economy. In the ordinary local prison, however, no more can be done than to set aside a hall, or in smaller prisons a landing, for each class, and so far as possible to keep one workshop or party for prisoners of a particular class ; though where, as in the smaller prisons is often the case, there is only one workshop for the whole establishment, the main- tenance of complete separation of six different classes is hardly within the limits of the practicable.

[1] All *convicts* of the Star Class go to either Maidstone or Wakefield Prisons.

A further step is taken with the Young Prisoners[1] with a view to their more effective separation from adults, not only physically but in the mode of treatment. A certain number of local prisons, which have better facilities for separation and for a more active and positive training, have been designated " Y. P. Collecting Centres," and to these are transferred all members of the Young Prisoners Class whose sentences are long enough[2] to enable them to benefit by the training. A similar, but less comprehensive, scheme is in force for the " Specials," those with sentences of an appropriate length[3] being sent to Wakefield from the Northern area and to Lewes from the London area.

But while something positive can thus be done for the younger prisoners with long enough sentences, it is evident that the classification above described is not the most suitable basis, within the four walls of a moderate sized mixed prison, for a system based on any conception of " training." It is true that where Stars can be adequately separated, and especially where they can be allotted a separate establishment—as in London at Wormwood Scrubs and for convicts at Maidstone—it is possible to permit a much greater measure of trust and responsibility and of unsupervised association than where their treatment must be regulated by what can be accorded to Ordinaries : but if one is to consider training first and foremost, there may be many who are technically disqualified for the Star Class who would derive much greater benefit from the treatment which can be accorded to that Class than some of those who are in the Class—indeed any " recidivist " who is not too hardened in crime is *prima facie* more in need of training than a " first offender." Again, in striving to avoid the contamination of the " good " prisoner by the " bad," it is possible to lose sight of the potentially beneficial effects on the not-too-bad of association with the " good "; and it is hardly likely that the general tone of a body of men of selected bad character will be improving—it may, for

---

[1] Again it is unfortunately necessary, owing to the very small numbers to exclude girls from these arrangements.

[2] At present three months or over.

[3] This varies according to numbers and accommodation, but would not normally be under six months.

example, be doubted whether such an outbreak as occurred at Dartmoor in 1932 would have happened in a prison with the steadying influence of an admixture of Stars. The problem of preventing contamination must also be viewed from the angle not only of Rules but of practice, which in effect means efficiency of staff, and there can be no doubt that with the staffs of to-day it is possible to obtain a close and intelligent supervision which can be relied on to a large extent to replace the rigid separation necessary under less favourable conditions.

This change in the traditional view of classification is reflected in the phraseology of the new Rules of 1933, which provide that classification is to be carried out with a view not only to " minimising the danger of contamination " but —and this is placed first—to " facilitating the training," and further give the Commissioners discretion to " authorise in particular cases or at particular prisons such departures from the provisions of this rule as are not in conflict with the intention thereof." The indications are therefore that in the future experiments on somewhat different lines may be expected, and it is interesting in this connection to consider the now well-established scheme in force at Wake-field Prison.

This prison, selected on account of its exceptional facilities for training, both industrial, educational, and physical, has for some time been set apart as a Training Centre, to which are transferred suitable prisoners from all the prisons in the North. The prime condition of eligibility for this Centre is length of sentence, and here we at once see the effect of " facilitation of training " on theories of classification. We have already noticed that of every 100 prisoners received only some 15 have sentences that imply any likelihood of reformative training (i.e. over three months), the bulk of the remainder (excluding debtors and the unconvicted) consisting of a " stage-army " of short-sentence prisoners drifting for ever hopelessly through the prisons. Not only can these prisoners receive no training themselves, but their presence is a real and constant handicap to the training of those who might profit. The Training Centre is therefore reserved for those with sentences long enough to make it

worth while to expend effort on them—normally six months
or over—whose character and physique are such that they
are likely to benefit : the aged, the infirm of mind or body,
and the hardened " recidivist " are alike excluded. The
system in force is substantially that of an ordinary prison,
but without those features inseparable from an establishment where the major part of the effort is diverted from
its main purpose to troublesome side-lines : all the best
features of the modern system can be intensified, greater
attention can be paid to the needs of the individual, and a
wider measure of trust and responsibility can be allowed.
And while the statutory classifications are maintained in the
broad, the interesting experiment is being tried of associ-
ating young men of the Special Class with the Stars—it is
understood that in many cases the effect on these " young
toughs " of a more responsible and respectable " public
opinion " has been surprisingly beneficial.

So far it has been possible to open only one such Centre,
and satisfactory statistical evidence as to the success of this
method in preventing reversion to crime is not yet available.
In any case any comprehensive scheme, outside the London
area, of " classification of prisons " presents difficulties
which in existing circumstances are evidently insuperable :
it would therefore be premature to suggest that future
development lies along these lines. But it is clear that
classification on present lines within the walls of a mixed
prison can be taken no further, and that the present system
is already entering on a stage of transition : as to what
may result, no clear conclusion can yet be drawn, save that,
as already indicated, classification must be a matter for the
prison administration and cannot, in present circumstances,
be effectively undertaken by the Courts.

CHAPTER VI

DISCIPLINE

1. *Earning of Remission and Stage Privileges*

" THE gain or loss of marks, either for remission or stages, constitutes the reward or punishment lying at the root of convict discipline."[1] We have earlier seen (page 27) how the "marks system," already in operation in the convict prisons, was introduced into the local prisons following the provision of the Prison Act 1898 that a local prisoner should be enabled " to earn by special industry and good conduct a remission of a portion of his imprisonment," and Sir E. Ruggles-Brise's dictum remains true of both convict and local prisons to-day. The underlying principle is that discipline should be maintained by constructive rather than merely repressive measures, by encouraging the prisoner to maintain a standard rather than by holding out physical punishments *in terrorem*. Although therefore other methods of maintaining discipline must be and are available, the forfeiture of marks remains the principal weapon which the Rules place in the hands of the disciplinary authorities, and except for the graver offences Governors are instructed to rely on the forfeiture of marks and privileges rather than on physical punishments such as cellular confinement and restriction of diet.

The Rules prescribe that a local prisoner serving more than one calendar month may earn a remission of his sentence not exceeding one-sixth. For this purpose, as soon as a prisoner is received, the total number of marks he must earn is calculated by multiplying the number of days in his sentence by five, which is the minimum daily allotment of marks. The number thus ascertained, together

[1] Ruggles-Brise, page 35.

with the earliest possible date of discharge on remission and the date of final expiration of the sentence, is then entered in the prisoner's "Record," in the "Discharge Diary," and on the " Stage Register " which hangs outside his cell door. A prisoner whose conduct and industry are satisfactory is allotted six marks per diem, and thus he may earn the required number of marks when he has served five-sixths of his sentence. The " earliest date of release " is the day after the number of marks has been earned. The marks earned are entered weekly on the Stage Register by the officer in charge of the hall, with any forfeitures awarded by the Visiting Committee or the Governor for offences against discipline. Thus a prisoner can always see at once how he stands and work out his date for discharge.

But although this system has many practical advantages as a simple and accurate method of calculating the date of a prisoner's discharge in whatever variety of circumstances, and although the fear of losing remission marks remains the prisoner's most powerful incentive to *good conduct*, it has admittedly ceased to operate as a direct incentive to *industry*. When the system was introduced the larger part of prison labour was cellular, and of such a nature that it could easily be " tasked " and the output measured : it was then a simple matter to relate marks to output, and a prisoner who did not complete his task would be allotted only five instead of six marks. To-day, when the prisoner's working day is spent in associated labour in workshop or outdoor party, " tasking " has come to be restricted to the relatively unimportant evening cell task, and in practice the daily award of six marks has become automatic, idleness being met by reporting the prisoner to the Governor for a disciplinary offence rather than by entering the minimum remission mark. This aspect of the question is further discussed in Chapter VII in connection with " earnings schemes " and the general problem of getting his best work out of a prisoner, and the operation of the marks system generally is at present under review by the Commissioners.

The " stage system," though it appears to have been regarded in its inception as a contribution to " reformative measures," has, fundamentally, always been a method of preserving discipline, the theory being that the well-behaved prisoner should have increasing "privileges" to look forward to as he passed from one "stage" to the next, and that fear of losing his privileges once they were earned would preserve him in well doing. No doubt the effect of such a system on the prisoner is better than that of purely physical punishments and deprivations, and to that extent the system may be regarded as having reformative value, but it is to be noted that in normal practice the deprivation of stage marks does not replace punishments of other types, it merely supplements them ; and the same effect might be gained by giving full privileges to start with and taking them away for misconduct. This latter method, however, would lack the psychological advantage of giving the long-sentence prisoner "something to look forward to."

To this extent the stage system, on the lines on which it was started, may be regarded as on the whole well conceived in relation to the circumstances then prevailing. But as we have already seen (page 21), "increasing privileges" were then made possible only by reducing conditions in the First Stage below what would now be regarded as tolerable, and the main privileges were the advance from "hard" to "useful" labour and the comfort of a mattress on a gradually increasing number of nights : the only other privileges were a very sparse allowance of letters and library books in the later stages.

With the employment of all prisoners on useful labour from the start of their sentences, and the growth of a more enlightened view as to the desirability of allowing prisoners to keep in touch with their families, and to read in their cells instead of meditating on their sins (both past and future), the foundations of the old stage system fell away. It was however continued on the traditional lines, a survival of little or no practical significance, until the present year, when a radical change was made.

Hitherto there had (in a local Prison) been four Stages, the first three each lasting a month : it was not till the prisoner reached the Fourth and last stage that the privileges really counted for anything, and as the long-sentence prisoner earned all he could earn in three months it was thereafter of no value as giving him hopes of better times to come. The new system recognises that for short-sentence prisoners it is neither necessary nor practicable to provide a system of increasing privileges : the First Stage therefore lasts for three months, and the Second Stage for six months, after which the prisoner passes into the Third and last Stage. The privileges are as follows :

Eligibility for concerts and lectures is a privilege of the Second and Third Stages.

Library Books.—The general idea is that good reading should be encouraged rather than restricted. Educational books, which include standard works of good fiction, are therefore supplied from the beginning of the sentence. The Second and Third Stages bring the privilege of choosing increasing numbers of fiction books from the catalogue.

Letters and Visits.—By statutory rule a Star prisoner is entitled to a letter and visit once a month, others once in two months : these are not " privileges " and cannot be forfeited for misconduct, except that the Star can be reduced to the two-month level. All prisoners in the Second and Third Stages have a letter and visit once a month. The period of the visit is 20 minutes in the first two stages and 30 minutes in the Third.

Recreations in cell approved by the Commissioners are a privilege of the Third Stage. These include cross-word puzzles, acrostics, chess and draught problems and boards, and jig-saw puzzles. Prisoners may have these things sent in to them by their friends.

Stage-marks, up to six per diem, are awarded, entered, and forfeited in the same way as remission marks.

2. *Offences and Punishments*

The acts which constitute offences against prison discipline, and the permissible methods of punishment, are set out in detail in the Rules, and no prisoner may be punished in any other way than is there prescribed. It would be *ex hypothesi* vain for any " authority " to state that unauthorised punishments are non-existent, but in view of the publicity accorded to " exposures " from various quarters, the rarity

G

of this particular allegation may perhaps be accepted as in itself sufficient.

Disciplinary measures may only be ordered by the Governor or by his Deputy or other officer appointed to act for him, following a formal written report which must be made forthwith by the officer witnessing the offence. The Governor adjudicates on reports every morning, except on Sundays and public holidays : he has before him both the prisoner and the officer making the report, and the prisoner is entitled to know the precise offence for which he is reported, to hear what the officer has to say, and to speak in his own defence, before the Governor comes to a decision.

If the Governor regards the offence as too serious for him to deal with, he may put the case back for the Visiting Committee, and it is in his discretion to order a prisoner " on report " to be confined to his cell—or, if necessary, in a special cell set apart for the purpose—pending adjudication by the Committee. Such confinement means only that the prisoner does not associate with others—he is not deprived of exercise, attendance at chapel, or library books.

The investigation by the Visiting Committee may be on oath or not, as the Committee decides, and if it is held on oath, the prisoner may also be sworn if he so wishes. It is also within the discretion of the Committee—as of the Governor when he is adjudicating—to decide what additional evidence should be called. The question whether other prisoners should be heard is, in the peculiar circumstances of a prison, always one of difficulty : the prisoner witness whose evidence conflicts with that of an officer is apt to fear, rightly or wrongly, that he will be " marked " by the staff, while he who " gives away " a fellow prisoner may find himself suffering from the *esprit de corps* of the prisoners. Not unnaturally, therefore, a prisoner may come to think that if he is reported it is his word against the officer's, and that the odds are on the officer : but one may well feel that there is in this a certain inevitability—there must also be occasions when the private soldier in the Orderly Room, and even the accused in the Police Court, feels that his word is carrying less weight than that of the police-constable or the company sergeant-major.

Apart from admonishments and the forfeiture of remission and stage marks, it is open to the Governor or the Visiting Committee to deal with a prisoner in one or more of the following ways :

(1) *Restriction of diet.*—No. 1 restricted diet consists of 1 lb. of bread per day, with water : after three days' bread and water the prisoner must be placed on ordinary diet for three days, so that the maximum period of 15 days No. 1 comprises nine days on bread and water and six days on ordinary diet. No. 2 diet consists of 8 oz. of bread, 1 pint of porridge, and 8 ozs. of potatoes per day, with water ; if this diet is given for more than 21 days, the prisoner after the first 21 days is placed on ordinary diet for 7 days, so that the maximum period of 42 days No. 2 comprises 35 days on the restricted diet and seven days on ordinary diet. A prisoner on No. 1 diet is not compelled to work if he does not wish.

The Governor may award up to three days No. 1 diet and 15 days No. 2 ; the Visiting Committee up to 15 days No. 1 and 42 days No. 2. A prisoner may not be placed on restricted diet unless he has been certified fit by the Medical Officer.

(2) *Forfeiture of associated work*—up to 14 days by the Governor, or 28 days by the Visiting Committee. This simply means that the prisoner works in his cell.

(3) *Deprivation of mattress* for a period not exceeding 15 days (men only).

(4) *Cellular confinement*—up to three days by the Governor or 14 days by the Visiting Committee (or up to 28 days for the more serious offences dealt with below) provided the prisoner has been certified fit by the Medical Officer. A prisoner in cellular confinement works in his cell, and is not entitled to go to chapel or exercise, though the Governor has discretion to allow him to do so : he forfeits his library books, letters, and other privileges. He may be confined either in his own cell or in a " separate cell," but the latter do not differ in size, lighting, or equipment from the ordinary cells : they are merely set apart for administrative convenience, and to prevent a prisoner from disturbing the prison by noise. A really violent or refractory prisoner, however, whether under punishment or not, who persists in

offensive noise or in "smashing up" his cell, may be temporarily removed to a "special" or "silent" cell—these are provided with double doors, and are made sound-proof so far as possible, with a minimum of fixed unbreakable furniture and a window well out of reach. A prisoner may only be kept here till he has calmed down—it is a precaution, not a punishment.

The offences of mutiny or incitement to mutiny, and of gross personal violence to an officer or servant of the prison, are dealt with under special statutory provisions, both these offences being punishable under Section 5 of the Prison Act 1898 by corporal punishment—provided the prisoner has been convicted of felony or sentenced to penal servitude or hard labour. For a prisoner over 18 years of age the maximum sentence is 36 strokes with the cat or the birch, for a prisoner under 18 it is 18 strokes with the birch. Reports for these offences can only be dealt with by the Visiting Committee, of whom not less than three, two being Justices of the Peace, must adjudicate, their inquiry being held on oath. If corporal punishment is ordered, the order must be submitted to the Secretary of State for confirmation, with the evidence. The Committee may order other punishments within their powers in addition to or in lieu of the corporal punishment.

Corporal punishment may not be awarded unless the Medical Officer certifies that the prisoner is physically and mentally fit for such punishment, and he must again examine the prisoner immediately before it is inflicted and satisfy himself as to his fitness to undergo it. As a further safeguard the Medical Officer must be present at the flogging and if he advises that it should stop, the Governor—who must also be present—must remit (not postpone) the remainder of the punishment and report to the Commissioners accordingly. This procedure equally governs floggings ordered by the Courts for criminal offences.

During 1931 there were ten cases of corporal punishment for prison offences : the average over the preceding five years was 12·6, as compared with 28 for the five years ended 1911–12. Full particulars of these cases are published each year in the Annual Report.

It is not proposed here to discuss the controversial question of corporal punishment in prisons, but it is worth while to indicate briefly the grounds on which it has been defended. These have been clearly and fairly stated, by an active opponent of corporal punishment,[1] as follows : " The case for the retention of flogging for breaches of prison discipline rests upon the need of defending prison officers against violence in the particular circumstances in which they are placed. An outstanding feature of the English Prison Service is the absence of brutality, or of the man-handling of prisoners by warders. The rule against brutality is rigidly enforced even in cases of violent attack. It is held that as individual retaliation is forbidden to the officer he must be specially protected, not so much for his own safety as in the interests of good discipline in the service."

The point has also been made that alternative punishments of suitable severity, such as periods of cellular confinement or restricted diet in excess of those already allowed, would be open to equally serious objections.

The subject of discipline can hardly be left without some reference to the question whether the post-war system has in fact been accompanied by that " relaxation of discipline " of which a good deal is heard from time to time. It is a question not susceptible of dogmatic answer or of statistical proof : certainly the percentage of prisoners punished has for some years past been round about 4% as compared with about 13% for pre-war years—but this might be used to show either that prisoners nowadays are better-behaved, or that authority is more leniently disposed. The Commissioners undoubtedly have inclined to the former view, and have expressed the opinion, based on the reports of Governors, that the tone of the prisoner is much improved as compared with that under the " old régime " ; nor have they hesitated to assert that " necessary discipline is maintained as firmly as ever."[2]

In part, perhaps, the explanation lies in the tendency of each generation to evolve its own conception of " necessary

---

[1] *Corporal Punishment—An Indictment* : George Benson and Edward Glover (Howard League for Penal Reform. Price 6d.), page 12.
[2] Annual Report for 1925, page 27.

discipline " and how to maintain it, whether in the Navy or the nursery. It may be, too, that there has been some confusion of thought : it is necessary to distinguish between the general treatment of prisoners and the maintenance of discipline. The removal from a system of elements making merely for repression and degradation, and the introduction of elements tending to constructive training, need imply no weakening of control by the staff. In such circumstances, as has been pointed out by the Commissioners[1], " the prisoner sees that the authorities instead of being merely repressive are working with his ultimate welfare in view " : it may be that all of the prisoners do not see this all the time—but however that may be, an objective view suggests that a system of constructive rather than repressive discipline would tend to produce a healthier tone and more willing response to authority among those to whom it is applied ; that these are the true objects of " discipline " ; and that they are more nearly attained in the prisons of to-day than in those of yesterday.

[1] Annual Report for 1925, page 27.

CHAPTER VII

EMPLOYMENT

1. *Problems of Prison Labour*

THE employment of prisoners has at all times and in all countries presented problems of peculiar difficulty to the prison authorities. The nature of these problems, with some of the solutions that have been attempted, is indicated in an interesting manner by the description given by Sir E. Ruggles-Brise[1] of the conditions in English prisons prior to the Act of 1877. " In some prisons there was complete idleness : in some, unregulated association : in some an active industry conducted with a view to commercial profit: and in some a close and melancholy adherence to the rule of separate confinement with its concomitant hard labour. . . . At Devizes 62 out of 78 prisoners were engaged on the tread-mill or oakum picking. At other prisons the question of providing remunerative employment received the keenest attention. One prison competed with another in finding a market for its produce. Governors and officers were encouraged to take an active interest in trade by bonuses and other payments, and the amount of trade profits was taken largely into account by Magistrates in dealing with applications for increase of pay. At Wakefield an extensive mat trade was carried on in which the sales averaged £40,000 a year. Steam power was employed. A commercial traveller was appointed to sell the goods . . . (at Preston Prison) the Governor was empowered to grant a sum of 2s. to every prisoner who had performed his fixed task diligently and well . . . and a further sum not exceeding £2 for all work done in addition to the fixed task."

This picture poses almost all the relevant questions, to

[1] *English Prison System*, pages 134-5.

many of which the satisfactory answer is still to be found. Grant the hypotheses that a prisoner should be required to work and that his work should be not punitive but productive—but how is a prisoner, in the peculiar circumstances of a prison, to be made or persuaded to work *his best*? Should he be paid wages, or any form of monetary incentive? Should the prisoners' labour be made to pay for the prison? Should it be let to outside contractors? Should prison-made goods be sold in free competition with outside industry? How is associated labour to be reconciled with proper classification and the prevention of contamination?

Different solutions of all these problems are to be found in the prison systems of Europe and America to-day. The picture presented by recent observers of labour in the prisons of the United States includes nearly every aspect of pre-1877 conditions in England, from complete idleness to the spectacle of a whole prison highly organised as a profitable industrial concern; while in certain European countries it is common for the prisoners to be handed over for labour purposes to a contractor, who installs his own plant in the prison, provides material, and pays wages to the prisoners.

The English administration after 1877, as we have seen, made up its mind very definitely on all these problems : fertile diversity of experiment was replaced throughout the Local Prisons by " close and melancholy adherence to the rule of separate confinement and its concomitant hard labour " : a certain amount of productive work was still done by convicts and by local prisoners not employed on First Class hard labour, but the conceptions of the self-supporting prison and the remuneration of prison labour disappeared, and a prisoner's work became simply part of the deterrent discipline.

New problems were presented after the Act of 1898, when even the " hard labour " prisoner, after the initial month of separate confinement, had to be employed in association on some productive industry—problems that to-day are still among the most considerable difficulties of the administration.

The first and most serious was the provision of the necessary workshops, and it is only quite recently that the position in that respect has become more satisfactory. With few exceptions now all indoor associated labour is carried out in properly constructed workshops, but there is still much work to be done in this connection. This problem interlocks to some extent with that of classification, since Stars should if possible be employed in a separate shop from Ordinaries, while Young Prisoners and Debtors ought also to be in separate shops or parties.

Much more difficult is the problem of finding suitable work for the prisoners to do, in face of the many limiting conditions that have no parallel in outside industry. Consider first the fitness for industrial work of the prisoners themselves, whose capacities, in the words of the Gladstone Committee, " range from the very highest to the lowest to be found anywhere in an almost endless variety." The large majority of prisoners are unskilled in any industry, and do not come into prison for long enough to learn. Many indeed are in prison just because of their mental or physical unfitness to earn a living. " In short," to quote the Gladstone Committee again, " a prison population . . . presents no favourable feature whatever for the development of industrial work." The conclusion would seem to be inevitable that for the prisoners with short or even moderately long sentences, who form the mass of a local prison population, the most that can be hoped for by the prison authorities is to inculcate habits of industry and ordered work : there can be no question of teaching a useful trade. For all this large class therefore must be found forms of work which are useful and productive, but at the same time easily learned without too much damage to valuable material, and for the product of which there is a steady demand.

This leads at once to a fresh problem—that of getting orders for prison work. It is almost a *sine qua non* of a prison industry that there should be a constant and reliable demand for the product, since unemployed prisoners cannot be turned off, and the taxpayer's money cannot be spent in making for stock without regard to potential demand. There is the further difficulty that the sale of prison-made goods in competition with outside industry is liable to arouse so much opposition both by Trades Unions and by employers' organisations, that with trifling exceptions prison industries are limited to manufacturing for use by the prisons and by other Government Departments ; and even in these activities they are not exempt from interested criticism.

For those prisoners who may be classed as trainable both by personal fitness and length of sentence, it is desirable to find a better class of work and to train them industrially in such a way as will assist them to earn a living when they go out. But again a fresh problem is introduced—to train a prisoner in conditions comparable with those outside usually means introducing power machinery and expensive plant, which would probably increase the product beyond all possible demand unless at the same time the number of prisoners employed were materially reduced.

Even when a good-class industry is started, with a reasonably certain demand for its orders, the responsible officers are often placed in positions of great anxiety by the uncertain relation of the amount of work available to the number of prisoners allotted to them. For the prison authorities have no control over the ebb and flow of the prison population, and the allocation of prisoners to labour is based on many considerations, among which the industrial efficiency of the prison can only take second place. The first consideration is medical : each prisoner is examined on reception by the Medical Officer, who classifies him as either (1), i.e. fit for all kinds of labour, including heavy manual work ; or (2), i.e. unfit for (1) but fit for ordinary industrial work ; or (3), i.e. fit for light labour only. The occupations at each prison are classified accordingly. Then length of sentence must be considered, prisoners with short sentences being in general employed (unless they are known bad characters) in the domestic service of the prison. In prisons which are large enough to have separate shops and parties for " Stars " " Specials " and " Young Prisoners " classification will also be a decisive factor. In the result it requires very careful organisation to prevent at one time loss of orders through inability to complete quickly enough, and at another time such shortage of work of a particular class as to lead to a tendency in the shops concerned to " go slow " instead of stimulating output—a deplorable tendency from the point of view of training, but difficult to avoid entirely in the peculiar conditions.

There remains one problem which, granted the hypothesis of " training " as fundamental to the prison system, is perhaps more important than any of the others and presents greater difficulties—that is to secure that the prisoner while at work really does work hard and well. It is of course easy to reprimand or punish a prisoner for definite idleness, but there is a considerable gap between obvious idleness and doing one's best, and the problem is to bridge that gap— and to do it among conditions and traditions all tending to a contrary effect.

The problem is very clearly stated by the Prison Commissioners in their Annual Report for 1929, pages 21–24. " The mark system," they say, " was originally devised with the idea that it should operate not merely as a negative check on misconduct and idleness, but also as a positive stimulus to industry." They go on to explain how, for the reasons indicated on page 79, the system is now " effective as a negative check on idleness but is not equally effective as a positive stimulus to exertion. Between the quantum which is sufficient to escape a report for idleness and the quantum which a worker can achieve if doing his best the gap is great." In these circumstances thought is moving towards the less stereotyped conditions of the pre-1877 prisons, and the Commissioners have conducted limited experiments in the provision of a " positive stimulus " by the introduction of " earnings schemes " at one or two selected establishments.

But without entering into the wider problems of whether it is right that a prisoner should be paid out of public money for his work in prison, and if so on what basis, and whether he should then be required to pay for his keep in prison, and contribute a fixed proportion to the upkeep of his family, and so forth, it is already evident that the mere administrative difficulties of such schemes are considerable, and it has yet to be shown that they will achieve the desired results. Already the Commissioners have found that " to devise a system of payments whereby the sums paid shall be accurately adjusted to the work done by the prisoner is by no means easy. Much of the work done in prisons does not lend itself to measurement, and the proper measurement of other work requires a large expenditure of time and clerical labour," while " any system which resulted in the automatic award of a weekly payment to every prisoner who had done a passable week's work would be no improvement on the existing situation." They also demonstrate the gap between the negative and positive quanta of diligence by mentioning that in one shop where the normal output had been under 500 units a week, an output of 836 units was reached, under a group-payment system, within a few weeks.

These experiments are continuing, and are of interest not only in themselves but as representing a fresh contribution of principle by the post-war administration in the sphere of employment. For the rest, much valuable work has been done of recent years in improving the conditions already set up before the war—notably, as we have seen, by increasing the number of workshops, but also by a determination to find good class work for trainable and especially for young prisoners, and to increase the number of hours spent in associated labour. A few years ago the policy was laid down that every prison should aim at an eight hour day— interrupted only by the midday meal—of associated labour, and generally speaking conditions had begun to approximate to that ideal in the majority of prisons by 1931. Unfortunately in that year the " financial crisis " arose, and the Commissioners were obliged to make such large reductions in their staff that it was necessary to suspend this policy, and under present conditions it is not practicable for associated labour to exceed five or six hours.[1] The remaining working hours (up to 10 in all) are spent in cellular labour.

In 1932, following a suggestion made in the Report of the Persistent Offenders Committee, 1931, the Secretary of

[1] Towards the end of 1932 the increase of population, combined with a considerable decrease of orders for canvas work from the General Post Office, created still further difficulties in maintaining the full period of associated labour, though it is to be hoped that this position is only temporary.

State appointed a Departmental Committee to consider the problems involved in the employment of prisoners, and especially whether their industrial training in prison cannot be linked up with their resettlement after release. It is much to be hoped that the Report of this Committee[1] will in due course afford guidance towards a satisfactory settlement of what is, in effect, the basic problem of prison administration.

One other aspect of employment may be mentioned here. As part of the policy of fostering the prisoner's self-respect and sense of responsibility, Governors are encouraged to extend the policy, which dates back as far as 1852, of selecting trustworthy prisoners for employment without supervision. Such prisoners are required to give their word to obey the rules and work their best. They may be employed singly—e.g. as stokers, orderlies, librarians, gardeners—when they are distinguished by a red armlet and known as "red-band men," or in "honour parties," working on their own in a shop or in the grounds under the general direction of a "leader." These leaders, however, have no disciplinary powers : they set an example and answer for the party to any inspecting officer and perhaps march them to and from their work, but they have no authority to give orders—they must rely on their personal influence to keep things going properly. It is indeed still a cardinal principle that no prisoner should be set over another, and the employment of "red-band men" and "leaders" has little or nothing in common with the American "trusty" system. Nor may a prisoner be employed, without the special authority of the Commissioners, in the service of any officer of the prison, and that authority is only given in rare cases, generally in respect of girls in a Borstal Institution who are being trained for domestic service.

2. Present-day Employment

The employment available in local and convict prisons falls into four main classes.

[1] Part I of this Committee's Report has now been published.

(1) *Domestic Service* of the prison, which includes cleaners, labourers, kitchen workers, gardeners, hospital orderlies, stokers, and laundry workers. Work of this class, except for individual jobs allotted to red-band men, is usually assigned to short-sentence prisoners and debtors.

Gardening work varies in value according to the circumstances of the prison : flower-beds are laid out in all the grounds, and where space permits vegetables are grown as well—indeed, several prisons have quite large market gardens either inside or outside the walls. The numbers employed may therefore vary from an odd man to a large regular party, doing work of a valuable nature both productively and as training. The Commissioners in this work have the advantage of assistance from the Prison Gardening Association, a body formed under the auspices of the National Gardens Guild to provide lectures on gardening in the prisons, with a view to stimulating the interest of prisoners in a healthy and profitable form of recreation.

The laundry work is done by women where there is a women's wing with sufficient able-bodied women : otherwise a small party of men, usually an " honour party," may be used once or more a week according to requirements. In a few prisons there are power laundries which, in addition to the prison washing, take in work from neighbouring Government establishments. Each prison has a trained laundry officer who has passed through a course at Wandsworth Prison, where there is an up-to-date power laundry with a trained Instructor.

The kitchens and kitchen-workers are under the supervision of the prison Cook and Baker, an officer who has passed through a special course of training arranged for the Commissioners by the Universal Food and Cookery Association, whose officials are good enough to hold an examination at the end of the course and report to the Commissioners on the results attained by the candidates.

(2) *Works.* During 1931 some $12\frac{1}{2}\%$ on average of the prison population was employed by the Works Department, in maintenance of buildings and new construction. This work, which is of great value both to the prisoner and to the State, includes not only bricklaying and labouring, but

plumbing, painting and whitewashing, glazing, slating, electrical work, and so forth. The bulk of the prison labour employed is utilised on labouring, painting, and white-washing, which account for some three-quarters of the " Works " employees : the remainder are employed on the more skilled occupations, reinforced by " free workmen " engaged from outside, and by " Trade Assistants " who are prison officers in receipt of a special allowance for work at skilled trades. The Trade Assistants also supervise the parties they are working with, but the general responsi-bility, under the Surveyor and his staff, rests with the Foreman of Works and Engineers in charge of the Works Department of the prison.

Since the War the Works Department, in addition to its ordinary maintenance work and a large programme of con-version, demolition, and reconstruction, has built 24 work-shops, 13 quarters for Superior Officers, and 665 quarters for Subordinate Officers. Meanwhile the convict prison at Portland has been reconstructed for the purposes of a Borstal Institution, and an entirely new Borstal Institution is under construction at Lowdham Grange, near Notting-ham. For all this work door and window frames, metal castings, concrete blocks, and other parts and materials are made in the manufacturing shops of the prisons and Borstal Institutions.

(3) *Manufactures*. The great variety of these will be seen by reference to Appendix E, which sets out in detail the daily average number employed on every kind of work and the computed value of that work, as shown in Appendix 6 to the Commissioners' Annual Report for 1931. The pro-ducts of the workshops are either sold to other Government Departments, e.g. mailbags and pouches for the General Post Office, ships' fenders, matting, brushes, overalls, for the Admiralty, furniture, baskets, etc., for the Office of Works ; or used in prisons and Borstal Institutions—e.g. materials for the Works Department, prisoners' clothing, boots, and underclothing, mats, and brushes : sales to the public of prison manufactures are of negligible proportions. There is also at Maidstone Prison a large printing and binding shop, which furnishes practically all the books and forms in use

in the Prison Department, and carries out work for the Stationery Office.

It will be seen that by far the largest number of prisoners is engaged in making mailbags and similar articles. This is the staple industry of most local prisons—unfortunately, for it is tedious, " soft," and of no " training " value : but it provides just such simple work as the majority of short-sentence prisoners are able to learn and carry out, it is suitable for men who are physically or mentally unfit for harder or better class work, it is the only work available in any quantity suitable for cellular labour, and it normally carries a steady and reliable demand for the product.

Next in size come the industries connected with the manufacture and repair of prisoners' boots and clothing—tailors, weavers, shoe-makers, needle-workers, etc.—all useful occupations not without value as training.

In the more skilled industries there is a valuable output from the tinsmiths' and brushmaking shops, and in addition to the materials for the Prison Works Department the carpenters,' smiths' and fitters' shops do much good-class work in furniture and fittings for Government Departments.

(4) *Farming and Land Reclamation.* This class of work is confined to the Borstal Institutions, certain Convict Prisons, and the Training Centre at Wakefield. There are farms of considerable acreage at Borstal and Lowdham Borstal Institutions and at Dartmoor, and smaller farms at some of the other Borstal Institutions and at Park-hurst. Stock-raising is undertaken in addition to crops and market gardening, and several establishments have their own dairies. Large areas of moor and forest have been reclaimed on Dartmoor and in the Parkhurst Forest by convict labour ; and at Wakefield the Commissioners have leased a considerable tract of woodland at some distance from the prison with a view to its reclamation and cultivation, the prisoners being taken to and fro each day by motor lorry.

The average annual value of a prisoner's labour has increased from a sum estimated at £5 18s. in 1878 to £14 9s. 4d. in 1911 and £36 11s. in 1931.

CHAPTER VIII

MORAL AND MENTAL WELFARE

1. *Religion in the Prison*

" IT is a commonplace, dating from the middle of the eighteenth century, that we must educate our prisoners, as it was also the common injunction that we must inspire them with the teachings of religion."[1] The modern conception of prison training seeks to make these " commonplaces " play a part both vital and effective. Much has been done since the war to make the influences of religion on the prisoner who can be touched by them real and stimulating. Perhaps the most important step in this direction was taken when compulsory attendance at chapel services was abolished: the present arrangement is that, while the Sunday morning service is a " parade " service in so far as a prisoner who does not wish to attend must ask to be excused, attendance at the Sunday afternoon and mid-week services is entirely voluntary. The general experience of Chaplains has been that following this change the services were approached in a much better spirit, and the Commissioners were able to report[1] " the numbers attending are practically unchanged . . . and the attitude of the congregation is more reverent and sincere."

At the same time every effort has been made to keep the spirit of the services fresh and interesting, and to remove so far as possible any prison flavour. The removal of the officers from high seats facing the prisoners to ordinary seats at the back and sides, where they take part in the service as ordinary members of the congregation, was a necessary and successful first step. Arrangements are often made for outside clergymen to take the services, or for special

---

[1] Ruggles-Brise, page 124.   [2] Annual Report, 1923–4, page 20.

H   97

Missions to be held, and the limitation of the period of service of a full-time Chaplain[1] was intended to help further towards this end.

Divine Service for Church of England prisoners is held in the chapel every Sunday morning, and in the afternoon there may be either a second service, or a concert of good music, or a suitable lecture. A short mid-week service is also held, and the Chaplain holds regular Celebrations of Holy Communion, frequently prepares suitable prisoners for confirmation by the Bishop of the Diocese, and forms classes for religious instruction. Cellular visitation also forms an important part of the Chaplain's duties, but the modern tendency is rather to get into touch with prisoners who will derive real benefit than to pay regulation visits to every prisoner irrespective of his disposition.

Every prisoner is required on reception to state his religion and is seen either by the Chaplain, or by the Priest or Minister[2] of his denomination if that is not Church of England. He has in his cell the books of devotion and worship approved by the authorities of his Church, and also certain books of " moral or religious instruction " ; these last are selected by the Chaplain, Priest, or Minister, according to the needs of the individual prisoner, from a list drawn up by the Commissioners in consultation with the authorities of the various Churches, and are changed by him at his discretion.

It is to be understood that the spiritual charge of the Chaplain is confined to prisoners of the Established Church, and that for others these duties are performed by the Roman Catholic Priest, or the Minister of their denomination, or the Jewish Rabbi, as the case may be. In some prisons there is a separate Roman Catholic chapel, and when the congregation of any faith is large enough arrangements are made for separate services if the Minister so desires. The Rules permit any prisoner who so desires to be visited by a Minister of his own religion, and if there is not one appointed for the prison the Governor must, if he can find one, specially call one in.

In the largest prisons the Chaplains are assisted by Church

---

[1] See page 50.   [2] *Ibid.*

Army Evangelists, who are employed by the Commissioners on a full-time basis : payment is made direct to the Church Army, who are responsible for their selection and with the Commissioners' approval change them from time to time. Devoted and valuable service on both the lay and spiritual sides of the Chaplain's work is given by these officers.

2. *Education, Recreation, and the Library*

The development of the attitude of the administration towards education in the prison is clearly brought out by comparison of a passage from *The English Prison System*, written in 1921, with an extract from the Annual Report of the Prison Commissioners for 1925–26. Sir E. Ruggles-Brise writes : ". . . the Prison Authority still remains in a sense an educational authority ; but the role it plays is not ambitious, and does not aim higher than to teach the illiterate to read and write, and in the small space and opportunity given, to raise to a higher standard those who are just a little better than illiterates." Five years later we read : " The adult education classes have shown some further development during the year under review. The number of classes held has increased and they have been attended by some 9000 individual prisoners. . . . The third annual meeting of Educational Advisers and teachers at the local prisons was held at the Home Office in January 1926 . . ."

This " Adult Education Scheme " was set up in 1923 with the advice and co-operation of the Adult Education Committee of the Board of Education. Its aim is not, primarily, to improve the " standard " of imperfectly educated prisoners, but to counteract the mental deterioration inevitably attendant on prison life, and to increase the prisoner's fitness for citizenship, by stimulating his mind and furnishing it with material for healthy activity in confinement, and of continuing value in after life. Evening classes are held in the prison after the hours of associated labour, and the subjects are chosen on the broadest basis to include not only "school " subjects such as history, mathematics, or modern languages, but " vocational " subjects, such as shorthand, gardening, technical trade courses, or handicrafts, and subjects of general interest like first-aid, literature, or drama—in fact, any subject, educational in the widest sense, on which qualified persons can be persuaded to give their help.

For this scheme depends entirely on the willing help of voluntary teachers from outside the prison—though many prison and Borstal officers also give up their evenings in this way—and the Commissioners in their Annual Report for 1929 reported that " the number of (teachers) giving their services week by week in a very exacting and difficult task has in 1929 reached the total of 400." To assist Governors in framing their educational schemes, and in enlisting the services of suitable teachers, Educational Advisers are appointed at each prison from among local gentlemen with suitable qualifications, and a list of these is published each year in the Annual Report. The Educational Advisers and Teachers are from time to time invited to meet the Commissioners in conference, so that full discussion may take place of the principles of their work, its day to day problems, and its relation to that of other Voluntary Workers and of the prison staff.

In local prisons any prisoner is eligible to attend evening classes, but in practice attendance must usually be restricted to those who have both the mental capacity to profit by education and sentences long enough[1] to cover a definite course. Attendance at lectures is commonly restricted to men in the higher stages, while Governors of course exclude any men whose influence in association may be undesirable.

The wider educational scheme has not entirely supplanted the elementary education of illiterates, but the continuing reduction (from over 18,000 in 1913 to 1027 in 1931, or from about 13% to about 2% of total receptions) in the number of illiterates received into prison, fortunately tends to reduce almost to vanishing point the amount of time spent by members of the prison staff who undertake this work. Elementary education for Young Prisoners, on the other hand, has been placed on a better basis by the employment

[1] Normally three months.

of certificated teachers from local schools, who take evening classes and are paid at the usual local rates. These teachers are employed at all Collecting Centres for Young Prisoners : the short-sentence boys in the local prisons are taught by voluntary teachers or members of the prison staff.

The objects of the educational scheme are promoted by other activities of a more recreational nature, which have been found by experience to make a useful contribution to the mental well-being of the prisoners. Periodical lectures, covering a wide range of subjects, are given in all the prisons by kindly well-wishers from outside, and in some prisons occasional evening debates have proved valuable. From time to time also concerts of good music are given. But it must be understood that the idea of " amusing " the prisoners plays no part in these activities—healthy mental stimulus is the sole object.

Another interesting innovation made after the war was the weekly reading of a " news-bulletin."[1] The Commissioners reported as to this (Annual Report for 1923, page 19) : " There is no question as to its value. A knowledge of current events helps the men to think during their imprisonment, while ignorance of them is a real handicap on discharge." More recently this has been supplemented by the provision of daily newspapers in the association rooms, for the use of the Star and other prisoners entitled to the privilege of association. It may well be that the use of newspapers and suitable periodicals could with advantage be extended, for apart from their mental value to the more thoughtful prisoner, it is evident that once prisoners are allowed to talk together it becomes necessary to provide some healthy topics of conversation, if only the football news—for prison topics are apt to be dark, dirty, and unprofitable. It follows that all newspapers are not permitted.

Finally, the prison library plays an important part in the mental welfare of the prisoner. This is maintained in part by a Government Grant based on the population of the

---

[1] At two prisons the experiment is now being tried of printing a weekly news-sheet, one copy for each prisoner : this may come to supplant the weekly reading.

prison, in part by gifts, which are always welcomed. Under the supervision of the Chaplain it is managed by one of the prison staff with the help of one or more prisoners. The books are divided into three classes—" Text books," " Non-fiction "—which covers the whole range of general literature other than fiction—and " Magazines and Fiction." Broadly speaking all prisoners may have books of educational value, either non-fiction or selected works of standard fiction, from the beginning of their sentences, and the use and frequent changing of these is encouraged : the number of books to be selected from the " fiction " catalogue depends, as we have seen, on the prisoner's progress in " stage." These arrangements are subject to modification for different classes of prisoners, and special facilities for frequent exchanges are provided for sick prisoners. Suitable picture books and magazines are available for the illiterate and weak-minded. The selection of books by or for prisoners, the arrangement and use of catalogues, etc., are matters for local arrangement, and much admittedly remains to be done to devise a system which will meet satisfactorily both the administrative difficulties of a prison and the varied and peculiar needs of its population. The guiding principle, however, is always, within the practical limitations, to encourage rather than restrict good reading.

The prisoners' reading facilities are not confined to the prison library. They may have books of an unobjectionable character sent in by their friends, or buy them out of their private money, and may have them in their cells in lieu of any library books to which they may be entitled.

The educational value of prison libraries has been enhanced by the formation of a special collection of books purchased from a fund originally made available by the generosity of the Carnegie Trustees, and administered by a small Committee known as the Prisoners' Education Committee. A central library and catalogue for this collection have been set up at Maidstone Prison, on which prisons draw according to their requirements, returning the volumes or passing them on in due course.

Note-books and pencils may be allowed to suitable prisoners to enable them to make the most of any approved course of study they may be following, and such note-books, if properly used, may on certain conditions be taken out on discharge.

3. *Prison Visitors*

Unless he is attending an educational class or lecture, a prisoner is normally locked up in his cell from sometime between 4 p.m. and 5 p.m. till next morning—a bleak and lonely period for many, since not all are capable of concentrated reading, and the cell task is monotonous and easily disposed of by the experienced prisoner. It is at this time that a visit from someone from the outside world, quite unconnected with the prison staff—someone to talk about ordinary matters of everyday interest, to take an interest in his family, perhaps to help him to understand how he has gone wrong and to discuss the future—may not only prevent the prisoner from solitary brooding over real or fancied grievances, but may actively direct his thoughts in profitable directions, give him fresh hopes and interests, and assist to restore his self-respect by letting him see that someone thinks it worth while to come and talk to him and take an interest in his affairs.

To this end the Commissioners in 1922 decided to extend to men the system of " unofficial visitors " which had for many years been so successful at certain women's prisons, and it would appear from their reports that their hopes have been realised with notable success. Notwithstanding the exacting nature of this voluntary service, and the difficulty of finding suitable persons who are both willing and able to spare the time for it, there were in 1931 557 men and 85 women acting as Prison Visitors. The work of the men has been consolidated by the formation of a National Association of Prison Visitors, an active and valuable body which not only serves to give the Visitors a corporate spirit, but by arranging annual conferences provides for the discussion of their common problems among themselves and with the Commissioners, and serves as the channel through which the views of Visitors about their work may reach the Commissioners.

Meanwhile, under the guidance of the National Association

of Visitors to Women Prisoners, the work among women has been extended to all women's prisons, and the experiment has been successfully inaugurated of inviting woman visitors to see young male prisoners under 21 years of age. The special work of the woman visitors at the Boys' Prison at Wormwood Scrubs is described later (see also Appendix H).

Visitors are invited to serve by the Commissioners on the recommendation of the Governor and Chaplain, who first satisfy themselves as to their suitability by local inquiries, by consultation with the Visiting Committee, and finally by a short trial on probation. The period for which the Visitor is invited to serve is 12 months ; all the invitations are reviewed annually, and are not renewed to those who have shown themselves unsuitable for the work or unreliable in their attendance.

Not every prisoner has a Visitor allotted to him : the Reception Board considers in each case whether a Visitor would be helpful, and the cases are so allotted that each is visited about once a week. The Visitor has a cell-key, and sees his man alone and in his own way, but he must not visit anyone not allotted to him by the Governor. The conditions governing the work are more fully set out in the memorandum issued by the Commissioners to all Voluntary Workers, which is printed as Appendix F. The views expressed about their work by both Visitors and Teachers may be studied in a series of extracts published by the Commissioners as Appendix 2 to their Annual Report for 1929.

CHAPTER IX

HEALTH AND CLEANLINESS

1. *The Medical Service*

SINCE 1898 one of the Prison Commissioners has been a medical man, to whom, though he is responsible with the other Commissioners for the general policy of the administration, falls the duty of directing the medical policy and administration of the prisons and Borstal Institutions. He is responsible not only for dealing with the detailed medical matters that are referred to him for decision and advice, but for co-ordinating the work of the different establishments, supervising the introduction of changes in medical and psychiatric practice made necessary by legislative changes or advances in medical science, and reorganising the diets from time to time on a scientific basis. He visits all establishments frequently, interviewing prisoners who wish to see him, carrying out a medical inspection of the establishment and considering all matters which concern the health of the prisoners and staff. He maintains personal contact with the Medical Officers and members of the prison staffs, and is available for consultation in any matters of peculiar difficulty.

The medical staff and equipment of a prison vary according to its size and population, but three elements are always present—the Medical Officer, the Hospital Officer or Nursing Sister, and the hospital.

The Medical Officer of a small prison will be a local practitioner who attends daily at the prison : in a larger prison he will be a full-time officer : in the largest the duties may be divided between two, three, or even four full-time doctors. A Medical Officer in the prison service must be a registered medical practitioner, preferably with experience

105

as resident on the staff of a general hospital, while other things being equal a candidate with experience of mental disease and defect would receive preference over others. A new full-time Medical Officer will usually be given experience as junior at a large prison before himself taking medical charge, and later in their service full-time Medical Officers are allowed periods of study-leave. A junior Medical Officer is also seconded to the Criminal Lunatic Asylum at Broadmoor from time to time. The responsibility of the Medical Officer includes not only attention on sick prisoners, but the general care of the physical and mental health of the prison population, including the staff and their families : this implies attention not only to the organisation of the hospital and the conduct of the nursing staff, but to the sanitation, heating, and ventilation of the prison, and to the diet, clothing, exercise, and cleanliness of the prisoners.

Every prisoner must be examined by the Medical Officer on the day of his reception, and he is kept in the separate reception block till this has been done. This examination serves to determine his classification for labour and physical training, as well as his medical condition and freedom from disease. He is seen from time to time by the Medical Officer during the sentence, and records of his weight are made periodically. He is again examined by the Medical Officer prior to discharge, both that his fitness for the journey may be assured, and that his medical condition may be on record in case of subsequent complaints. A prisoner may at any time apply to see the Medical Officer, whose regular duties also include the daily visitation of prisoners under punishment or mechanical restraint, and the special examination of prisoners who have been sentenced to corporal or dietary punishment, or ordered to be placed under mechanical restraint, before such orders are put into effect.

Not the least part of the doctor's duties lies in the preparation of written reports, either in respect of remand or trial prisoners on whom the courts require medical information, or in reply to inquiries by prisoners' friends, or at the request of the Secretary of State or the Commissioners in connection with prisoners' petitions or questions from M.P.s or members of the public about the health or medical treatment of individual prisoners. He is also on many occasions required to give evidence in court, and at the largest prisons the senior Medical Officers spend a considerable part of their time attending at Assizes and Sessions. Other miscellaneous duties include the medical examination of candidates for the prison service, the medical inspection of officers' quarters, attendance at executions and examination of the body (with a post-mortem should the Coroner require one), and reports on the medical condition of officers for superannuation and other purposes.

The dispensing of medicines in the largest prisons is done by a qualified Pharmacist; in the other prisons by a Hospital Officer, who has passed a departmental examination in the compounding of medicines, under the direction of the Medical Officer.

The nursing duties in men's prisons are done by a staff of male nurses called Hospital Officers, recruited from men with suitable nursing experience in the R.A.M.C. or R.A.F., or on the sick-bay staff of the Royal Navy, or as attendants in mental hospitals. A selected candidate is given the ordinary course of training of a Prison Officer and posted to a prison till a vacancy in the hospital staff is anticipated, when he is sent to a course of training in prison nursing at a large prison hospital, and if he satisfies the examiners is given a certificate and posted for duty as a Hospital Officer. For women's prisons there is a service of Nursing Sisters recruited from fully trained State Registered Nurses, who are required in addition to possess the C.M.B. certificate. There is a Sister at every women's prison, however small ; at a few larger prisons there are two or more Sisters ; and at Holloway Prison there is a large hospital, with a Hospital Lady Superintendent and a staff of some thirty Principal Sisters and Sisters, which serves also as a training-school for Sisters before they are sent out to provincial prisons.

The majority of prisons have separate hospital buildings within the walls. These vary in size : in a convict prison, a large local prison, or a Borstal Institution we may find a large, airy, and well-equipped building, with accommodation for 100 or more patients in association wards or ranges of large and well-lighted hospital rooms, with all necessary

offices. In the smaller prisons it is usually found that the
provision of a few special hospital-rooms in the main building
is sufficient for ordinary purposes, and avoids the opening
of the hospital—which is often an isolated building—save in
exceptional circumstances. Special cells are also provided
in the main building for tubercular prisoners, with large,
open windows, rounded corners, washable walls, and special
furniture : for prisoners subject to fits, with specially padded
furniture, floors, and walls : and for cases of itch, verminous
infection, and venereal disease.

In certain prisons major surgical operations are performed.
Generally speaking, however, it is unusual for any but minor
operations to be carried out in prison : where surgical
operation is needed, or where a disease cannot be properly
treated in prison, the Secretary of State has power under
Section 17 (6) of the Criminal Justice Administration Act
1914 to order the removal of the prisoner to a hospital or
other suitable place. A prisoner while absent under such
an order is deemed to be in legal custody, and the time spent
in hospital counts as part of his sentence. The hospital
authorities, however, are not responsible for his safe custody,
though it is quite exceptional for a prison escort to be
required, the prisoner being regarded as on parole : within
the last five years only five prisoners have abused this
privilege by escaping from the hospital. During 1931, 87
prisoners were removed under this procedure.

The number of deaths from natural causes in English
prisons (including prisoners dying in civil hospitals) was,
in 1931, 41 out of a daily average population of 11,676.
There were in addition four deaths by suicide.

The daily average percentage of sick in local prison
hospitals was 4·8 for men and 17·8 for women.

2. Mental Disease

Considerable advances have been made since the war in the
treatment of problems connected with mental disease among
prisoners ; indeed, it would seem that to-day the investigation and recognition of mental states, with the accompanying
administrative and forensic work in preparing certificates
and reports and giving evidence in courts, have come to

form the most important part of the Medical Officers' duties. Prior to the war all that was, broadly speaking, expected of the prison authorities was the recognition of cases certifiable under the Lunacy Acts ; though in practice a modified form of discipline was provided in the prisons for those who, though not certifiable as insane, were classified together as " weak-minded."

The Mental Deficiency Acts 1913–1927 (which only began to operate effectively after the war), together with the increasing recognition of the importance of the psychological factors associated with crime, have completely altered this position. It is of course self-evident that prison is not the place for an offender who is either insane or mentally defective, and both the Lunacy Acts and the Mental Deficiency Acts provide machinery enabling the courts to deal with such persons without sending them to prison. Nevertheless, a considerable number of convicted prisoners are found after reception to be insane or mentally defective, and it is important that these should at once be recognised, certified, and removed to Mental Hospitals or Institutions for Mental Defectives : in 1931 in local prisons 98 convicted prisoners were certified as insane, and 45 as mentally defective : in convict prisons seven men were certified as insane and two as mentally defective.

The procedure in cases of insanity is that in local prisons the certificate should be signed by two doctors and two magistrates, in convict prisons by two doctors and a Director of Convict Prisons : in cases of mental defect the signature of two doctors is sufficient. The prisoner is then removed by order of the Secretary of State to a Mental Hospital, or Criminal Lunatic Asylum, if a lunatic, and to an Institution for Mental Defectives if a mental defective. If a prisoner who has been certified insane recovers before the end of his sentence he may, by order of the Secretary of State, be returned to prison to complete his sentence.

There is a growing tendency for courts to remand to prison all cases where a doubt arises as to the mental state, in order that the prison medical staff may examine and report thereon. In 1931, 281 remand prisoners were found by the prison medical staff to be insane, and 182 to be

mentally defective : in addition 2,416 reports were furnished
to courts on the mental condition of remand prisoners.

But even when the clearly insane and defective have been
eliminated, there remains a considerable number of
" mental " or " psychopathic " cases, not certifiable under
any existing legislation, who are nevertheless unsuitable for
prison discipline and environment. As to these the Medical
Commissioner in the Annual Report for 1926 said : " These
people form a sub-normal group and include the simple
feeble-minded and those of border-line intelligence whose
offences are due to their low intelligence and high suggesti-
bility, and who are relatively incapable of social rehabilitation on account of their low mentality.

" This condition of feeblemindedness, though not sufficient
to warrant certification under either the Lunacy or Mental
Deficiency Acts, is a very marked condition, and includes
cases of mental deficiency of congenital origin with or without epilepsy ; imperfectly developed states of insanity ;
mental weakness after an attack of insanity ; senility ;
weakmindedness due to alcoholic excess ; and weakmindedness of undefined origin.

" These cases are reported to the Commissioners, and if
serving a sentence of a month or over they are transferred to
certain Prisons, parts of which have been specially set apart
for their location and employment, but they can naturally
be detained only for the duration of their sentences. Whilst
undergoing their sentences discipline is modified, and they
are given suitable work and some manual training by the
Brabazon Society. At the end of the sentence they are
brought to the notice of the local Agent for the Central
Association of Mental Welfare.

" I venture to think that something more is needed, and
that the time has come for consideration whether such
people should not be segregated permanently, or at any rate
until such time as there is a reasonable prospect of their being
able to work at a simple, suitable occupation.

" Most of them would probably work well at some simple
manual employment under supervision, but in the ordinary
conditions of life outside an institution they are unemployable.

" I give some particulars of 106 such cases reported to the
Commissioners during 1926."

In his Report for 1928 the Medical Commissioner further discusses the place in this group of prisoners with a history of encephalitis lethargica, though he points out that over a period of two years (1.4.25–31.3.27) the number of such cases detected numbered only 72, and since that date it has been continually less.

The Committee appointed by the Secretary of State in 1931 to enquire into the existing methods of dealing with Persistent Offenders considered the psychological approach to criminal problems in the light of evidence given by medical psychologists and prison medical officers, many of whom have paid special attention to the subject in recent years. The Committee recommended that " a medical psychologist should be attached to one or more penal establishments to carry out psychological treatment in selected cases," and considered that " action along these lines would determine whether the psychological treatment of delinquency is of sufficient value to justify statutory recognition as a means for the prevention and treatment of certain crimes." These suggestions, however, have not so far been implemented.[1]

In his report for 1931 the Medical Commissioner considers the psychological treatment of convicted prisoners under four headings : those who become relieved of the abnormal conditions without any special treatment ; those who become re-adjusted whilst serving their sentence as a result of an ordinary psychological investigation ; those for whom a complete psychological investigation seems worth a trial ; and those who do not respond to this form of treatment. The Medical Commissioner points out that no statistics are available at the present time to show the value of psychological methods in dealing with crime, and suggests that the proportion of successes in criminal cases is likely to be less than in civil cases. He calls attention also to the fact that many practical difficulties must be surmounted before progress is made along these lines. Meanwhile, he suggests, there is reason to hope that a certain amount of delinquency will be avoided by the psychological methods in use at Child Guidance and Mental Clinics.

[1] An additional part-time Medical Officer, with experience in medical psychology, will shortly be appointed at Wormwood Scrubs Prison to examine and treat selected cases sent by the Commissioners.

3. *Cleanliness and Sanitation*

In view of the filthy condition in which some prisoners are received, great care is required on the part of the reception staff to secure the elimination of vermin, and the isolation of cases of contagious skin disease, and the precautions taken are usually sufficient to ensure that there are no vermin about the prison. Every effort is made to enforce a decent standard of personal cleanliness : each prisoner is required to take a bath on reception, and thereafter once a week, and in every cell there is a wash-basin and water-jug, with soap and towel. Facilities are provided for regular shaving and haircutting : where proper arrangements can be made for looking after the blades, convicted prisoners may keep their own safety-razors and shaving brushes, with the consent of the Medical Officer—otherwise they are shaved by the prisoner who acts as " prison barber." The " convict crop " has been abolished, and both men and women may have their hair trimmed as nearly to their own taste as the " barber's " skill will run. Any prisoner's hair may, of course, be close-clipped by order of the Medical Officer on grounds of health or cleanliness. Toothbrushes and powder, hairbrushes, and combs are issued to all prisoners, and nail scissors are available on each landing.

Every prisoner receives on admission a clean set of outer and under-clothing, and thereafter the under-clothing is washed weekly : each set of outer clothing is washed and, if necessary, disinfected before re-issue. Mattresses and bedding must be aired for an hour daily before being folded, and sheets, pillow-slips, etc., are washed at prescribed intervals.

On each landing is a recess with sinks, running water, and water-closets : closets are also provided in the shops and exercise yards. Facilities are allowed at various times during the day, and particularly at morning unlocking and before " lights out," for prisoners to visit the recess to empty their chamber-pots and slops, get clean water, and use the water-closets.

The cells are swept and cleaned daily, and the plank beds are periodically scrubbed with disinfectant : they are also inspected weekly so that any trace of vermin may be dealt with. Detailed provision is made by the Standing Orders for the cleanliness of the halls, kitchens, and premises generally, and for a quarterly inspection by the Governor, Medical Officer, and Works Officer of all the buildings and the drainage.

4. *Exercise and Physical Training*

The Rules require that every prisoner should have not less than one hour's exercise a day, to take place in the open air when weather conditions permit. Until recent years the only form of exercise was walking round the concentric flagged rings of the exercise yard—the younger and more active on the outside rings, the older and infirm on the small inner rings. This somewhat depressing perambulation, conducted in single file at intervals designed to prevent conversation, is now in respect of at least half the daily exercise period confined to women, and to such men as by reason of age, ill-health, or infirmity are unfit for active physical training.

A male prisoner on his reception examination by the Medical Officer is classed " A," " B," or " Unfit " for physical training : the unfit are still confined to walking exercise, but the rest devote at least half the daily exercise period to physical training based on the tables in use in the Army, the " A " class being reserved for the young and fit, so that their training is not hampered by the presence of the less active.

At every prison, in the ordinary course, are one or more officers who have obtained the Instructors' certificate of the Army School of Physical Training at Aldershot, or some equivalent qualification approved by the Commissioners, while every new officer is required at his Training School to obtain a certain standard of proficiency in physical training. Arrangements have also been made for woman officers at the larger prisons to obtain instruction in the physical training of women, though the small numbers and poor physical condition of woman prisoners make it difficult to extend the physical training scheme to women's prisons generally.

I

In addition to this regular outdoor exercise almost every prison now has its gymnasium with apparatus, in which qualified instructors hold evening classes in gymnastics for younger men passed fit by the Medical Officer.

Except in connection with the Physical Training classes organised games form no part of the system at the ordinary local or convict prison, though week-end games of football have been found possible and valuable at the " Training Centres " and Y.P. Collecting Centres.

5. *Diet*

While the idea that the dietary of a prison should be specifically penal in conception has long been repudiated, the food provided is not designed to do more than maintain a prisoner in health and strength, and no doubt remains one of the least agreeable features of prison life to all but the poorest class of prisoner. The dietaries for each class of prisoner must under the statutory rules be approved by the Secretary of State : those at present in force are based on the recommendations of an expert Committee which reported in 1925. They are carefully arranged to provide a proper balance of the necessary dietetic elements without undue monotony, and the Commissioners report that their success is shown not only in the increased fitness of the prisoners, but in the reduction of waste food, " which has now fallen almost to vanishing point."[1]

The dietary for local prisons is printed as Appendix G. It will be observed that while breakfast and supper do not vary, there are 16 different dinners, and these are so arranged that the same dinner does not always occur on the same day of the week. The diet in convict prisons is substantially the same, with small additions and variations framed with regard to the longer sentences.

Convicted prisoners (other than those of the First Division) and debtors are allowed no food except that prescribed by the prison dietaries unless the Medical Officer so recommends for reasons of health. First Division and trial prisoners, however, are allowed to buy food from outside or to have it sent

[1] Annual Report, 1928, page 35.

in by friends : they are also allowed small quantities of
" light wine or malt liquor," but otherwise no alcoholic
drinks are permitted inside a prison.

Every prisoner has in his cell a Dietary Card, which shows
the weight of each item, and the prisoner is entitled to have
his meal weighed if he suspects " short rations."

Special diets are provided for sick prisoners, for vege-
tarians, and for Jews on their Holy Days, and on Christmas
Day a special dinner of meat and vegetables and plum
pudding is served.

There are also two restricted diets, No. 1 and No. 2, on
which prisoners may be placed as a punishment for periods
prescribed by the Rules (see page 83).

The contracts require provisions to be of unexceptionable
quality, and Governor, Medical Officer, and Steward all
have prescribed duties of inspection to ensure that the
supplies are of the required standard, and that the food is
properly prepared.

CHAPTER X

GENERAL TREATMENT

1. *Reception and Clothing*

THE various examinations, inquiries, and other formalities attending the admission of a new prisoner begin—though they by no means end—in the separate Reception Block to which he is taken on arrival. It will be convenient to describe these in related groups rather than chronologically.

First let us take the many inquiries that may be classed under the headings of Identification, Verification, and Documentation. These are initiated by the Reception Officer, whose duty it is before taking over the prisoner from the police or other officer of justice to satisfy himself both that the prisoner before him is the person named in the accompanying warrant of committal, and that the warrant itself is *prima facie* in order : a Governor would properly refuse to receive a prisoner on a warrant which on the face of it was illegal. This warrant is subsequently examined and checked in the office so as to establish the precise length of the sentence, the date from which it is held to run, and the earliest date of discharge on remission : all these calculations must finally be checked with the warrant by the Governor himself or his Deputy.

These particulars, with the information elicited by the Reception Officer as to the prisoner's age, address, occupation, religion, etc., are entered on the prisoner's " record," which eventually contains a complete dossier of his prison life during that sentence : should he be sentenced again another " record " will be made out, and with this his old ones (collected if necessary from his last prison) will be linked up to form a complete history of his prison life.

For this and other purposes it is necessary at once to

establish whether a prisoner has been in prison before. When a prisoner is received from a court of summary jurisdiction, it is usual for a list of his previous convictions to be sent by the police force responsible, but often a minor offender is convicted without his previous history becoming known to the police : in such cases an experienced Reception Officer usually has no difficulty in picking out a man who has " done time " before, even if the face is a new one, and discreet enquiry enables his previous " records " to be obtained from his last prison. There is also power to photograph, measure, and finger-print criminal prisoners in prison, and for all prisoners received on conviction (save of minor offences such as drunkenness, common assault, sleeping out, etc.) a descriptive form with photographs and finger-prints is automatically sent to the Criminal Record Office at New Scotland Yard, where the latest conviction is linked up with the previous record, if any. Unconvicted prisoners are only photographed and finger-printed at the request of the court or the police—if they object, the order must be confirmed by a Magistrate or by the Secretary of State, and if the objection continues force may then be used. Where prisoners are committed for trial at Sessions or Assizes the duty falls on the prison (whether the offender is in custody or on bail) of collecting, establishing, and entering in the Judge's copy of the Calendar an authentic list of the previous convictions. Thus from one source or another information is eventually received which enables the prisoner's various *aliases* to be sorted out, and his previous convictions and prison history to be placed on record.

Finally the prisoner is made the subject of a statistical card, and from these cards are compiled the statistics as to prison populations published in the Commissioners' Annual Reports.

The next set of reception formalities may be classed as " medical." The prisoner is required to strip, and is weighed and measured, notes being taken of his build and appearance, with any distinguishing marks and characteristics. He has a hot bath and is examined for traces of vermin or contagious skin disease. Finally, before he can be passed into the main prison he must be examined by the Medical Officer, who notes for insertion in the " record " the prisoner's physical condition and his classification for labour and Physical Training.

Now let us attend the conversion of the individual offender into the numbered prisoner. He is carefully searched—experience teaches Reception Officers that there are strange hiding places about the human frame—and all his personal property is taken from him, checked and listed in his presence, and signed for by him : there is an elaborate system of book-keeping to ensure that he gets everything back again. His private clothing is packed up, disinfected if necessary, and put away in a special store, though a prisoner with a long sentence may arrange to have it sent out to his friends.

Thus naked and purified, he is now reconstituted as a prisoner. Only prison clothing may be worn by a convicted prisoner : this, for a man, consists of vest and drawers (of cotton or flannel according to the season and the man's habits) ; shirt with an attached collar with which a plain narrow necktie is worn ; woollen socks ; shoes ; and a cloth suit of jacket, waistcoat and trousers. The colour of the suit varies according to the statutory classification—blue for debtors and unconvicted prisoners who do not wear their own clothes, grey for the rest. This clothing, which in recent years has replaced the familiar drab uniform with its " broad arrow " of historic memory (now quite obsolete), was designed on the lines of an ordinary civilian suit : the model has, however, been somewhat oustripped by fashion, and though warm and serviceable does not often contrive an air above its station. Caps are only worn on medical recommendation, and resemble the old cloth " forage cap " of the Army : capes are issued for out-door wear as required. Women wear jean dresses of blue or green according to their classification, with aprons and white washable caps ; woollen stockings ; strong leather shoes ; and underclothing that has recently been assimilated in pattern to the normal wear of women to-day, though the choice of materials points to a greater regard for service and economy. Young prisoners wear brown, with shorts and stockings insteads of trousers.

Thus clothed, our prisoner is allotted a registration number and a location number, e.g. B. 3–64, which means B. Hall, landing 3, cell 64 : by this latter number he is officially known and addressed in public by officers, though the old view that a prisoner should not be addressed by name before other prisoners is gradually dying out : it is perhaps worth mentioning that this use of the number is not a mere " soulless officialism " or " wanton degradation "—many prisoners do resent being called by name in front of others, while officers with fresh parties or new to the prison cannot always know all the names of a rapidly changing population—and many familiar faces have a different name on each reappearance : it is therefore a matter of general convenience to use the number, which is always prominently displayed for that purpose on a tag hung on the left breast pocket. With his number and his bag of cell equipment—slippers, toothbrush, books, and so forth, the prisoner is now ready to face the entry to the main prison and his cell.

On the following day he will come into touch with the superior officers of the prison. The Governor will see him, check over with him his sentence, date of discharge, and property, and will see that he has received and understands the card of Notes for Guidance of Prisoners—a brief explanation of the more important rules and regulations that every prisoner has in his cell. Later the Chaplain or Priest, or the Minister of his religion, will see him, form an impression of him, see to his books, and give him a helping word. Then his future in the prison will be determined by the Reception Board, which consists of the Governor or his Deputy, the Chaplain, and the Agent of the Prisoners' Aid Society. The Board has the prisoner before it, with his record, and decides in what class he should be placed, how he should be employed, whether one of the Prison Visitors should be allotted to him, what educational classes he might profitably attend, and what are likely to be his prospects on discharge.

2. *Communications with Friends*

A convicted[1] prisoner (other than First Division) may by rule write a letter on reception, so that his friends may

[1] For letters and visits of unconvicted prisoners and First Division, see Chapter XIII.

know what has happened to him, and thereafter he may write and receive a letter and receive a visit every two months (unless he is undergoing punishment by cellular confinement). Additional letters and visits may be earned as stage privileges, so that in the Second Stage (i.e. after three months in a local prison, or 18 months in a convict prison) a prisoner may write and receive a letter and receive a visit once every 28 days. If he is Star or Second Division he has a monthly letter and visit from the beginning. A prisoner whose friends cannot visit him may write and receive a letter in lieu of the visit.

At most local prisons visits take place in the Visiting Boxes, in which the prisoner and his visitor occupy a cubicle divided down the middle by glass and wire mesh, through which the conversation takes place without the possibility of contact, while an officer patrols the passage behind the line of cubicles. This arrangement is unfortunately necessary to ensure that proper precautions are observed without undue expenditure of the time of the staff in supervision, and that of visitors in waiting. It is admittedly unpleasant, particularly for prisoners of the better type and their friends, and at prisons where the use of boxes is necessary arrangements are made, whenever practicable, for at least the Young Prisoners, Stars, and Second Division to have their visits in an ordinary room : here prisoner and visitor sit on opposite sides of a table with an officer in the room. Visitors are limited to three at one time, and the length of the visit is 20 minutes, or 30 minutes in the Third Stage : Governors have discretion to extend the time in special cases.

Where there are business or domestic reasons of sufficient urgency, the prison authorities may grant letters and visits in advance of the normal date, or in addition to those to which the prisoner is normally entitled. This discretion is freely used, and though a prisoner cannot be allowed to carry on his outside business from his cell, it is fair to say that a deserving prisoner is allowed reasonable facilities to keep his affairs in order, while domestic crises are met with sympathetic latitude. When a prisoner is dangerously ill visits from his relatives are freely allowed.

All letters, inward and outward, are subject to censorship,

and anything objectionable may be stopped : " objection-able " matter includes undesirable discussion of criminals and crime, threats, indecency and the like, while com-munication with known ex-prisoners is also forbidden. A prisoner may not in his letters make complaints about his treatment in prison, since he has ample facilities for laying such complaints before the Visiting Committee or the Secretary of State, and he may not write to the Press, to M.P.s, or to any public authorities—the proper vehicle for any representations he wishes to make is a petition to the Secretary of State. A prisoner's letters are now posted in plain cream envelopes with no distinguishing mark or characteristic to suggest the prison.

Notwithstanding these restrictions, which are necessary on administrative and disciplinary grounds, the modern view regards the maintenance of close touch between a prisoner and his family and respectable friends as desirable and bene-ficial in itself, and so far as conditions permit progress is likely to be towards encouraging rather than restricting such humanising influences.

It should be added, and widely known, that to convey an illicit letter into or out of a prison is a criminal offence.

3. Petitions and Complaints

Not only is the prisoner fully informed as to his rights by means of the cards which must hang in every cell, but he has free and ample opportunity of making complaints and applications to the prison authorities, through no less than four channels. Any prisoner may apply to see the Governor, Chaplain, or Medical Officer, according to the nature of his complaint or application, and these officers must on every weekday hear the applications of prisoners who have put down to see them on that day. If the prisoner is not satisfied, or in the first instance if he prefers, he may apply to see a member of the Visiting Committee, and the Governor is required by Rule to see that all such prisoners are brought before the next member of the Visiting Committee to visit the prison. The third channel is afforded by the visiting Commissioners and Assistant Commissioners, who are also required to hear the applications and complaints of any prisoners who ask to be brought before them.

Finally, any prisoner may write a petition to the Secretary of State, whether about his conviction or sentence, or his treatment in prison, or his desire to leave prison, or indeed about any subject whatever, provided he expresses himself in proper and temperate language. If the petition raises a question with which the Visiting Committee is competent to deal, it is first laid before the Committee : the prisoner may then be satisfied and withdraw the petition, otherwise it is forwarded, with the Visiting Committee's observations and such reports as may be necessary, direct to the Home Office. Notwithstanding the common belief among prisoners that their petitions never go beyond the prison, or at most the Prison Commissioners, it is the case that all petitions are posted direct to the Home Office, that every one of them is read, and that whenever there seems to be a *prima facie* case for enquiry, or for other action, appropriate steps are taken.

A prisoner cannot be prevented from petitioning the Secretary of State : if he asks for a petition form he is given one without question, and whatever he writes is sent forward, though if he abuses the procedure of petition the Secretary of State may direct that the prisoner be not allowed to petition again for a specified period.

4. *Conversation*

The " Rule of Silence " associated with the nineteenth century prison régime was primarily intended to prevent contamination : there is no such rule to-day, but considerations of discipline, as well as the continuing necessity to prevent contamination, still require restrictions on talking among prisoners.

There are two important new factors in this problem of talking. In the first place modern classification has lessened, without of course removing, the risks of contamination ; and the provision of normal subjects of conversation through lectures, newspapers, and news bulletins has lessened, again without removing, the risk of undesirable conversation. In the second place, for decent and well-conducted prisoners many legitimate occasions for talking among themselves are provided at classes, debates, and associated meals ; and many prisoners have their Visitor to talk to one evening in the week.

The problem is therefore mainly one of restricting conversation when bodies of prisoners are associated under supervision, as at exercise or labour, or while passing to and fro along the landings, or waiting in parties to see the Governor or Medical Officer. As regards talking at labour " the view held by the Commissioners is that conversation . . . should not be more, and need not be less, than the conversation which takes place among workpeople . . . in properly managed workshops. That is to say, such remarks as the work requires may pass, but there is to be no idle talking on general subjects."[1]

In effect, at labour as at exercise and elsewhere, the question is primarily one of discipline : it is not an offence to talk, but it is an offence not to stop talking when ordered to do so. Evidently this leaves the position a little vague, and how it works must depend almost entirely on the discretion and experience of the officer in charge : but this is so when any body of men is brought together under discipline. It may be added that the Commissioners have authorised limited experiments at one or two prisons in talking at exercise, but the difficulties are many, and it is not possible to predict how this will develop.

As regards conversation between officer and prisoner beyond the bare requirements of the work, it rests again on the discretion of the officer to distinguish between that " familiarity " which the Rules properly forbid, and sensible conversation of the kind into which any officer, who means to take an effective part in helping the prisoner to re-establish himself, must from time to time find himself drawn. In fact here, as everywhere, the solution lies less in making regulations than in selecting and training the right men to administer them.

5. *Smoking*

No smoking is allowed by any class of prisoner in local prisons, though it has recently been announced that smoking

[1] Annual Report, 1921–22, page 72.

at exercise by remand and trial prisoners is being tried as an experiment at Brixton Prison, and that if the experiment is held to be successful its extension to remand and trial prisoners generally will be considered. In convict prisons certain long-sentence prisoners who have reached the appropriate stage are allowed to smoke in a prescribed place at specified times.

6. *Mechanical Restraints*

It is not much more than 100 years since Howard found prisoners chained to the floor on their backs, with spiked iron collars round their necks and iron bars across their legs, and a party of unconvicted women could be marched down the public road to take their trial at the Assizes, handcuffed, and chained by their necks. To-day no mechanical restraint of any sort is used inside a prison either for safe custody or for punishment. The only occasion on which a Governor may order a prisoner to be placed under restraint is " when it appears necessary, in order to prevent a prisoner from injuring himself or others, or damaging property, or creating a disturbance," and then only for so long as is necessary to achieve that purpose, and in no case for longer than 24 hours except with the authority of a Commissioner or Assistant Commissioner, or a member of the Visiting Committee. Every case of mechanical restraint must be notified at once to a member of the Visiting Committee, and particulars recorded by the Governor. The Governor is also required to secure the concurrence of the Medical Officer before restraint is applied.

No means of restraint are permitted except those authorised by the Secretary of State. Those at present in use are the body belt, a leather belt buckling behind the waist with a wrist cuff at each side—iron cuffs for men, leather for women ; and handcuffs, which may be used only if the prisoner succeeds in getting out of the body belt. An ankle strap is also authorised for use if a prisoner is violently resisting removal from one part of the prison to another, though it must be taken off as soon as the removal is complete : this is, however, rarely, if ever, used.

There is also a " loose canvas restraint jacket," to prevent prisoners suffering from a mental affection from injuring themselves or others, or destroying their clothing : this is only applied by direction of the Medical Officer.

When convicted adult prisoners (men) are being transferred from prison to prison, or taken to or from court, they are normally handcuffed, and if there is a party of three or more they may be secured by wrist cuffs to a light chain. Unconvicted prisoners, and prisoners under 21, are not handcuffed unless the Governor thinks it necessary and gives a direction to that effect. Handcuffs or chains are not used for women. Every effort is made to avoid the exposure to the public gaze of prisoners who are being removed. A cab is always taken from the prison to the station, a compartment is reserved on the train, and a cab ordered to meet the train. Where larger parties are to be moved, the whole journey is, whenever possible, made in a closed conveyance by road, and in the London district the Metropolitan Police keep a fleet of specially designed vans for use (on repayment) by the prisons. Special arrangements are made with the railway authorities to avoid exposure of parties of prisoners at busy stations.

To remove any misapprehension, it may be added that parties of convicts at work outside the prison walls do *not* work in chains !

7. *Discharge*

A local prisoner is discharged on the day after he has earned the requisite number of remission marks, unless that day falls on a Sunday, Good Friday, or Christmas Day, in which event he is discharged on the previous day : if he is a Jew, and the date of his release falls on a Saturday, he is discharged on the Friday. Discharges take place first thing in the morning, usually about 8.30, though the prisoner may legally be detained to the end of the day.

When the local prisoner is discharged his sentence is by law deemed to have expired, and he is under no sort of licence or supervision.[1]

[1] N.B. (1) Unless he has been ordered by the Court to be under Police supervision.

(2) Release on licence for other classes of prisoner is discussed in later chapters.

Every effort is made to send the prisoner out clean and neat and properly dressed, and to help him to reach his home—if he has a home—in good order. Private clothing is carefully stored, and when the prisoner gets his kit back he finds it washed and repaired, and the outer clothing pressed and brushed. Inadequate clothing is supplemented either by the Prisoners' Aid Society or from the prison funds. Every prisoner must be given an opportunity of shaving on the morning of discharge, and be provided with breakfast : if he is destitute and cannot reach his destination by midday he is also given a lunch of bread and cheese to take with him.

The prison authorities are required by statute to pay the fare of any prisoner " discharged from a prison situate beyond the limits of the county, borough, or place in which he was arrested . . . to the place in which he was at the time of his arrest or to the place where he was convicted, whichever is the nearer." But Governors have discretion to go further than this in assisting prisoners, and broadly speaking all who do not live within reasonable walking distance of the prison are sent home at public expense. In many cases where a prisoner wishes to make an expensive journey beyond the district from which he came the Prisoners' Aid Society will be prepared to pay the difference.

Before he leaves every prisoner must be medically examined, and is given an opportunity of making any complaints he may have about his private property or about his treatment generally.

A Hospital Officer takes home any prisoner whom the Medical Officer considers to be unfit to travel alone, and there are statutory provisions for the removal direct to a Public Assistance Institution of any prisoner who by reason of infirmity of mind or body is in need of immediate assistance. In special cases arrangements are made for the conveyance of sick prisoners direct to suitable hospitals on discharge.

CHAPTER XI[1]

AID ON DISCHARGE

It has been recognised since Howard's time that both prudence and pity should prevent a prisoner's being simply turned adrift outside the prison gate. The principle that a prisoner should be assisted to regain his own parish was recognised by Parliament in 1792. The Act of 1823 went further, and authorised Justices to provide, at the expense of the County Rate, for the provision of necessary clothing, and a sum not exceeding twenty shillings, to deserving prisoners whose sentences were shortened for good conduct : the Justices were further authorised to divert the various charitable bequests for providing poor prisoners with food and clothing to providing them with the means of returning home and with " implements of labour."

The next step is marked by the Discharged Prisoners' Aid Act of 1862, which sets out that : " Whereas divers Societies, hereinafter referred to as Discharged Prisoners' Aid Societies, have been formed in divers parts of England by persons subscribing voluntarily for the purpose of finding employment for discharged prisoners and enabling them by loans and grants of money to live by honest labour," these Societies might be recognised as the medium through which the Justices might assist prisoners, provided the Society had been certified by the Justices as an approved Society, and any sum which the Justices might have paid to the prisoner they were authorised to pay to the Society for the prisoner's benefit. Justices were also given power to pay to these Societies up to £2 for the benefit of each discharged prisoner, and this power was by the Prison Act 1877 passed on to the Prison Commissioners.

[1] This chapter relates to local prisoners only : aid on discharge for convicts and Borstal inmates is dealt with in Chapters XIV–XVI.

127

When the Prison Commissioners took over in 1878 they found 29 Aid Societies in operation, but they promoted their formation with such diligence that by 1885 there were " 63 Discharged Prisoners' Aid Societies working in connection with all prisons in England and Wales except one or two."[1] The sum expended by the Government on aid to Discharged Prisoners in 1884 amounted to £7,280, made up in part of gratuities earned by prisoners under the Progressive Stage System, which were paid to the Discharged Prisoners' Aid Societies for their benefit, and in part of a Government Grant of £4,000 distributed to the prisons in proportion to the number of prisoners discharged, but " with a proviso that an equal amount shall be provided by private subscription as a guarantee of that local and private interest in the work without which it cannot prosper."[2]

" Here are contained two important assertions of principle on which has been based the action of the Government since this date.

1. That it is the duty of the Government to make a charitable donation in aid of discharged prisoners in addition to the gratuities under the Stage System, which are an affair of prison discipline.

2. That the sum should be regulated by the amount of private subscriptions, provided that a maximum calculated on the total number of discharges is not exceeded.

In short, the State goes into partnership with bodies of charitable and benevolent persons, duly certified under the Act, in order to secure a double object : (a) the State object, that steps shall be taken at least to lessen the chances of a man's relapse into crime, (b) the private and charitable object of relieving misfortune and distress."[3]

The Gladstone Committee in 1894 found that " To each prison are attached one or more Societies. Some do admirable work—but it does not appear that there is either uniformity of action under definite principles, or that the various societies are so far organised as a whole that the effect of aid can be satisfactorily ascertained. There seems

[1] Du Cane, page 197.   [2] *Ibid.*   [3] Ruggles-Brise, page 170.

to be a great and unnecessary variation in the methods of working." While emphasising the importance of maintaining the voluntary and local side of Prisoners' Aid Society work, they thought there should be some central organisation and supervision, and " a representative conference in London for the purpose of securing common and uniform action providing for the most effectual distribution of the Government Grant, and for stimulating the considerable number of Societies which do little work or exist but in name." They also recommended that arrangements should be made for the agents of approved societies to see prisoners and make the necessary arrangements with them before discharge, instead of waiting for them at the gate.

In consequence of these recommendations the Commissioners made a special inquiry into the methods of Aid Societies, and a notable improvement in the work resulted. First, uniformity of procedure and organisation was secured. There is now one Society attached to each Local Prison,[1] managed by a Committee, with a Secretary and Treasurer, the actual work with the prisoners being placed in the hands of a paid Agent under the guidance of a Sub-Committee. In order to secure the Secretary of State's " certificate of efficiency " the Societies are required to comply with certain Regulations, and the Government Grant is paid only to certified Societies conforming with these Regulations.

This grant is divided into two parts—a Capitation Grant and a Variable Grant. In 1913 the earning of gratuities by convicted prisoners was abolished, and in addition to the existing grant of 1s. a head in respect of each convicted prisoner discharged to its care, each Society now received, as an equivalent of the gratuity, a further sum (averaging 1s. a head), which varied, as the gratuities had done, according to the length of the prisoner's sentence. In 1931 this complicated system was abolished, and a flat capitation rate of 2s. was substituted. For the first time now the grant was also paid in respect of debtor prisoners, in consequence of the abolition of the system of paying them allowances

---

[1] Though many of the prisons to which Societies are nominally attached are now closed. Some large towns also have their own Prisoners' Aid Society, which looks after prisoners from their area whatever prison they go to.

K

for their work in prison, and debtors and convicted are now assisted on the same basis. In addition to the capitation grants there is a supplementary grant of (at present) £1,500 a year, which after consultation at an annual conference is distributed by the Commissioners " in such a manner as they think best for the furtherance of the work." This procedure is valuable both in stimulating the less active societies, and in redressing to some extent the disparity between the richer and the poorer.

In 1918, in order to secure co-ordination of effort and ideas, there was instituted a Central Discharged Prisoners' Aid Society, with offices in London, and a Central Executive on which the various Societies are represented ; this Society also deals with special cases referred to it by the local Societies. Co-ordination with the Prison Commissioners was secured by the oversight of the Chaplain Inspector, who was especially charged with the care of education, aid-on-discharge, and other branches of welfare work,[1] and by the institution of an annual representative conference with the Commissioners for discussion both of general questions and of the distribution of the Annual Grant.

The problem of co-ordination, however, remains one of the most difficult aspects of Aid Society work. So long as the " partnership " between the State and voluntary local effort is maintained, the administration can exercise its guidance only by consent and good-will : the local traditions of Aid Societies are deep-rooted and spirited, and it is recognised that on the maintenance of that spirit must depend not only the funds but the energy and good-will necessary for the success of their invaluable work.

On the other hand many tendencies are at work to-day to break down the old local connections : there is no longer the simple unit of the County Gaol with the County Aid Society—so many prisons have been closed that one prison may now serve an area covered by several independent Aid Societies, and in these circumstances the Society on the spot necessarily tends to be more interested and active than distant Societies which can only operate, so to speak, at

---

[1] Since the abolition of his office in 1921 these duties have passed to one of the Assistant Commissioners.

second hand. Again, certain prisons receiving local prisoners, such as Wakefield, no longer have a specifically " local " character, while modern methods of classification result in many prisoners being transferred to distant prisons.

In consequence, increasing numbers of prisoners are discharged from prisons at a distance from the areas in which they live ; this situation causes difficulties both in the allocation of financial responsibility for such prisoners, and in the making of the best arrangements for their after-care, in addition to complicating the correspondence and organisation of the Societies. Various methods have been adopted by the Societies to meet these conditions, and in 1930 the Prison Commissioners addressed a letter of advice on this subject to Chairmen of Aid Societies. An important step was subsequently taken by the Societies connected with certain Northern and Midland prisons, which formed a " Federation of Northern and Midland Aid Societies " with a full-time Organising Secretary, whose salary and expenses are met in part from public funds. The practice now recommended and generally followed is that the Society for each area accepts financial responsibility for prisoners committed from that area, though the initiative in making arrangements for the assistance of a prisoner rests, in consultation with the responsible Aid Society, with the Society at the prison from which he is discharged. Where a Society has thus agreed to accept responsibility it receives the Government Grant in respect of all prisoners committed from its area.

In 1932 the Secretary of State appointed a Departmental Committee to consider the problems connected both with the employment of prisoners and with their aid on discharge. It may be that from the recommendations of this Committee will result not only better co-ordination of training in prisons with subsequent disposal, but a general re-casting of organisation designed to overcome the difficulties of the present position. It is in the circumstances premature to consider whether we may be heading towards a centrally organised system of positive " after-care," as distinct from the more limited conception of "aid-on-discharge," for suitable classes of prisoner, but it may well be that, in the future, development in this direction will be regarded as not less important towards a solution of the problems connected with crime than development of training within the prison walls.

The methods by which the assistance to be given to individual prisoners is settled are now fairly uniform. Each prisoner is informed on his cell-card that the Aid Society is there to assist him if he wishes, and is seen by the Agent of the Society soon after reception and some time before discharge. The Agent makes the necessary enquiries and arrangements, and eventually brings the prisoner before the Sub-Committee of the Society, which meets regularly at the prison, with his recommendation : the final decision as to what, if anything, should be done rests with that Committee.

It is very necessary that discriminating consideration should be given to each case, since the transitional period between leaving prison and settling down to work, during which the assistance of the Society is effective, is the most difficult part, perhaps, of an offender's punishment. The change from the passive and sheltered life of prison to the active competition of a hard and unsympathetic world, the cold shoulder of his former acquaintances to the man without previous criminal associations, the warm reception by his gang of the experienced " lag," all present to the ex-prisoner difficulties and temptations, past which the Prisoners' Aid Society must try tactfully to steer him—for they have no *power* of supervision : where a deserving man has no work to go to they try hard to find it for him, a difficult task indeed where millions of men with no prison history can find none, or they may provide tools for a tradesman who can use them : they may help where necessary with a few nights' lodging, food and clothing, or stock to set up a small shop or stall : in exceptional cases they may spend considerable sums and effort in establishing a really deserving man or woman, in others their long experience of the same old face and the same old story drives them to save their money for those that may turn it to some better use. But their power is limited to setting a man on the right road : they cannot, though with his co-operation they are usually willing to try, interfere to keep him to it.

It is the practice to see that a prisoner is not discharged

insufficiently clad, having regard to the weather and the time of year, and Aid Societies regularly supplement a prisoner's clothing, often to the extent of providing a good outfit to enable him to take a job.

They also in many cases assist prisoners with railway fares. There is a statutory requirement that " where a prisoner is discharged from a prison situate beyond the limits of the county, borough, or place in which he was arrested, the cost of his return to the place in which he was at the time of his arrest or in which he was convicted, whichever is the nearer, shall be paid out of moneys provided by Parliament " : in all such cases the Governor provides a railway warrant, and he is also authorised to provide the prisoner with a warrant to his home or any nearer place wherever he cannot reasonably reach his destination on foot by midday. But where the prisoner wishes to go further than the Governor has authority to pay for, the Aid Society is often willing to provide the supplementary fare.

With the consent of the Prisoners' Aid Society arrangements are also made for co-operation with such charitable agencies as the Church Army and the Salvation Army, and with the appropriate Voluntary Societies in the cases of blind and mentally defective prisoners.

The interests of Catholic prisoners are watched by the Catholic Prisoners' Aid Society, which supplements the efforts of the local Societies and looks after such cases as are referred to it.

CHAPTER XII

WOMEN AND YOUNG PRISONERS

1. *Women*

THE English penal system, and the English prison authorities, have never visualised the treatment of delinquent women as presenting problems to be solved separately from those of men : " in fact, the study of the English Penal System does not show that at any time the method of dealing with criminal women has engaged that close attention which might have been expected from the nature and importance and difficulty of the problem. . . . Generally speaking, the methods of punishment are the same."[1] Ten years later the position is substantially as Sir E. Ruggles-Brise described it in 1922 : the system of treatment for women to-day is the same as for men in principle, and—broadly speaking—in detail, and where practice differs this has generally been indicated in the course of the narrative.

There are, nevertheless, certain factors in the constitution of the female prison population that differentiate it in important respects from the male population, and it is worth while to consider these in some detail.

The outstanding feature is the very small number of women in custody, and the tendency of this number to fall at a rate proportionately greater than that for men. In 1913 women accounted for about 24% of the total receptions[2] on conviction, in 1931 for about 13%. The position is illustrated by the table on the next page.

This reduction in the female population is of course only one aspect of the general reduction in prison populations which is discussed in detail in Chapter XVII, and for the

---

[1] Ruggles-Brise, page 116.
[2] See page 195 for explanation of " receptions."

134

greater part may be ascribed to the factors of general application which are analysed in that chapter. There are, however,
certain special features. It is clear, for example, not only
that there has been a marked decrease in serious crime among
women, but that this decrease is proportionately much
greater than that among men : it is pointed out in the
Introduction to the Criminal Statistics for 1928 that whereas
in 1911 the incidence of convictions of indictable offences
per million of the sex was 261·3 for women and 1890·7 for
men, in 1928 it was 137·0 for women and 1387·5 for men,
with a percentage fall of 42 for women and 21 for men.

Year.	Receptions of Women on Conviction.	Daily Average Population of all Women Prisoners (including sentences to Borstal Detention).
1913	33,733	2,422
1923	9,076	1,031
1931	4,946	792

But it is among the non-indictable offences that the really
significant change is to be found : " the average annual
number of proceedings against women for non-indictable
offences in 1910–14 was 104,077, but in 1928 only 68,165 ;
a fall of no less than 34·5% in the short period of 17 years,
during which the number (i.e. the general population) of
women and girls of all ages had risen by 11%."[1] This change
is reflected in the fact that receptions into prison of women
convicted of non-indictable offences accounted in 1913 for
91·5% of all the convicted women received, and in 1931 for
only 56·7%.

Among the non-indictable offences the most significant
figures relate to offences connected with prostitution and
with drunkenness. The general decrease in offences of
drunkenness is discussed in Chapter XVII : so far as concerns women, it is sufficient for our present purpose to
emphasize that although the number of receptions of
" drunks " has fallen from 15,116 in 1913 to 2,366 in 1931,
this latter figure represents no less than 48% of the receptions

[1] Introduction to Criminal Statistics, 1928, page xxxiv,

of women on conviction (viz. : 2,366 out of 4,946), whereas only 16% (viz. : 5,118 out of 32,471) of the receptions of men are drunks. It is therefore evident that the problems of woman prisoners are much more bound up with the question of drunkenness than is the case with men.

It must not, however, be inferred that " half the women who come to prison are drunks," for the same woman may represent several " receptions " in the course of a year. Many of these drunken women spend a large part of their lives trailing in and out of the prison,[1] and indeed of the 2,366 receptions of female drunks in 1931 no less than 78% had been in prison before—610 of them over 20 times ! It is calculated that the 1,851 receptions covered by this 78% represent in fact not more than 400 to 500 women—a " stage army " of unhappy creatures, representing well over one-third of the receptions of convicted women into prison, on whom imprisonment has not the slightest effect either for deterrence or reform.

In their Annual Report for 1931 the Commissioners make the interesting point, which had not hitherto been brought out, that it is the figures of recidivism for drunkenness alone which make it appear that recidivism generally is much higher among women than among men—from which appearance " the inference has been drawn that the effect of imprisonment on women is even more demoralising than its effect on men."[2] It is true that among the " drunks " recidivism is worse among women than among men, but if these are excluded only 47% of the women received on conviction in 1931 were known to have been in prison before, as against 51% of men.

Drunkenness again affects the age-grouping of women. Whereas the largest proportion of men is found in the age-group 21–30, the largest proportion of women (29%) is in the group 40–50, and over half of these are drunks : and another 25% of the women, of whom nearly three-quarters are drunks, are over 50, as against some 10% of men.

Doubtless the decrease in other classes of minor offences

[1] Annual Report, 1931, page 17 : " The very high percentage of recidivism amongst this little group has long been recognised as an evil with which the prison authorities are powerless to cope."
[2] Annual Report, 1931, page 15.

is in general associated with the decrease in drunkenness, but it would seem that some other explanation, possibly changes in police practice, is to be sought for the fall in the number of receptions into prison for offences connected with prostitution from 8,063 in 1913 to 1,297 in 1923, and 205 in 1931. Of the other non-indictable offences, the majority are bound up with drunkenness and prostitution in one way or another.

To some extent also, changes in the practice of the courts in dealing with offenders may appear to have affected the female prison population more than the male. There is evidence that courts are in general more reluctant to send a woman to prison, and more ready to place her on probation, while it is a common practice to make it a condition of a probation order, in the case of a young woman, that she should reside in a Voluntary Home. There is also evidence that the closing of a large number of women's prisons, with the consequent additional expense of taking a woman to prison, has not been without effect on the committals of women for minor offences.

The more serious offences of women call for little comment : of the 1,290 receptions on conviction of indictable offences in 1931, 1,062 were for the various forms of larceny and false pretences, and 73 for offences of violence. Women convicted of these more serious offences also tend to be older than men, the age-group 30–40 containing the highest numbers. The group of offences classified as "akin to indictable," containing the more serious of the minor offences, includes assaults (116), cruelty to children (88), indecent exposure (78), malicious damage (66), and brothel-keeping (46).

The special characteristics of the female prison population are further reflected in the very high proportion of short-sentence prisoners among women. Sentences for periods of 14 days or less accounted in 1931 for 39% of the receptions of women sentenced to imprisonment, and 72·9% of receptions were for one month or less as compared with 53·1% of men. Of sentences implying any prospect of reformative training, viz. those of over three months, there were only 11·1% as against 22·9% for men.

The position as regards recidivism among women *convicted of offences other than drunkenness* is as follows :

There were 1,221 receptions of women known to have been in prison before, falling into the following groups :

1 to 5 previous sentences	.	.	. 714
6 to 10 ,, ,,	.	.	. 203
11 to 20 ,, ,,	.	.	. 151
Over 20 ,, ,,	.	.	. 153

In addition to this 1,221 (or 47%), there were 645 (or 25%) receptions of women known to have been proved guilty of previous offences but not sent to prison, and 714 (or 28%) not known to have previous proved offences.

We are now in a position to form a picture of our female prison population, as shown in the last available statistics, and to see how the conception of " training " as applied to women under present conditions must be modified to fit that picture. We must first remove, so far as training is concerned, more than half of the annual receptions into prison— that hopeless drift of minor offenders with short sentences —and concentrate on those convicted of crime. Of these there were only 1,290 receptions, of whom 476 were over 40 years of age, 302 had over five previous convictions, and only 711 had not been in prison before. There were only 536 with sentences exceeding three months.

The daily average population of all classes of women in 1931 was 792, of whom 113 were undergoing Borstal Training, leaving only 679 in the prisons. If we proceed to subtract from 679 those awaiting trial or in prison for debt (67) and those with sentences of under three months (205), we get a residue of about 400, of whom we may assume a considerable proportion to be untrainable either through age or prolonged recidivism : only about 40 would be under 26, and only about 50 eligible for the Star Class. Of this 679 approximately half would be found in Holloway, and another quarter in Manchester and Liverpool,[1] leaving only about 150 to be distributed among the remaining six[2]

---

[1] The women's prison at Liverpool is now closed, and the committals have been diverted to Manchester.

[2] Now reduced to five by the closing of Winchester Women's Prison.

women's prisons, the most important of which is Birmingham, with a daily average population of over 50.

In these circumstances the Commissioners have pushed to the utmost the policy of concentrating the female population in the fewest possible prisons : of the 100 female prisons taken over in 1878 there remained in 1921 only 26, and in 1933 there are only seven, plus one Borstal Institution. Beyond this, on present lines, the limitations of distance and transport would seem to make it impossible to go : Holloway already collects from the whole of the South-East, from Norfolk in the North to Hampshire in the South, and the remaining local prisons are as far apart as Durham, Manchester, Hull, Birmingham, Cardiff and Exeter. Convicts go to Holloway, and the Borstal Institution is at Aylesbury —here, too, are located, in separate parts of the establishment, Star Convicts and (when there are any) the Preventive Detention women.

At Holloway and Manchester, and to some extent at Birmingham, the numbers are such as to permit of the application of the principles of classification and training, though even here the numbers of " trainable " women, when the sick have been deducted, are very small, and the clogging of the machine by the non-trainable is accentuated, especially within the limited resources of a detached wing. But it is evident, if we remember the outcome of our analysis of the female populations, and apply it to numbers varying from—say—half a dozen to thirty, that the separation of " stars " and " young prisoners " might often amount to solitary confinement if too strictly conceived ; that the number of women capable of deriving benefit from continued education will hardly run to " classes " ; and that employment will be taxed even to provide for the necessary cleaning, washing, and clothing repairs of the prison.

In fact, the whole of the female criminal population of England and Wales with sentences of over three months could now be accommodated in two very modest establishments, nor is it obviously necessary that these should be castellated forts surrounded by 20 foot walls. How the remainder might be dealt with need not here exercise our imagination. It is perhaps worth while to make it clear that there is no

general practice of releasing women from prison in order that
their babies may be born outside, since the Secretary of
State's power under the Criminal Justice Administration
Act (page 108) does not apply to confinements, which can in
normal cases be quite well carried out in the prison. The
Nursing Sister always has the C.M.B. certificate, the prison
Medical Officer is in attendance, and the facilities generally
are perfectly adequate : there is usually a special room for
expectant mothers. The babies are well cared for in a
crèche which often contains several infants of various ages,
since nursing mothers may bring their babies with them
into prison and keep them there so long as necessary, though
they are required to make other arrangements when the
baby is a year old, or thereabouts.

It is hardly necessary to add that the separation of
women's wings is complete, that they are staffed only by
woman officers, and that no male officer has keys of the
women's wing or can enter without the attendance of a
woman officer.

The arrangements for women serving sentences of Penal
Servitude, Preventive Detention, and Borstal Detention are
mentioned in the appropriate chapters.

2. *Young Prisoners*[1]

Successive Home Secretaries have, in circulars and public
speeches, urged on the courts that where any other course
can properly be adopted the committal to prison of young
offenders under 21 ought not to be considered : and the
Prison Commissioners have on many occasions made it
clear that in their view prisons are not suitable for persons
of this age, and that whatever arrangements they may
make for them can only be regarded as a *pis aller*. These
views have been reinforced by the report of the Young
Offenders Committee, which stated (page 82) that " both
in the public interest and for the welfare of the young
offender concerned it appears to us to be the duty of the
legislature and of the courts to see that so far at any rate as

[1] i.e. Persons aged 17–21. The committal of young persons to prison
has now almost ceased (see page 39). Only one such person was received
in 1931 on conviction.

persons under 21 are concerned imprisonment is abandoned as far as practicable, and is only used when no other means can suitably be applied."

Nevertheless, in 1931 no less than 1,883[1] youths and 119[1] girls were received into prison on conviction, of whom 46% of the youths and 40% of the girls had not, so far as was known, been previously convicted.

And unfortunately these figures do not include by any means all the young people who are familiarised with prison conditions before they are 21 : in 1928[2] 2,549 youths and 348 girls were sent to prison on remand : of these only 562 youths and 43 girls were subsequently sentenced to imprisonment, the remainder being sent to institutions, placed on probation, fined, discharged, or otherwise dealt with. Making every allowance for the proper desire of many courts to have full information about a young prisoner before deciding how to deal with him, there can be no doubt that an increasing body of authoritative opinion views with concern a state of affairs under which this large number of young people, for most of whom the magistrates concerned eventually find prison to be unsuitable, are nevertheless subjected to the harmful conditions and social stigma of imprisonment. Special attention was devoted to this question by the Young Offenders Committee, which recommended that the requirements of remand in custody, and of the observation and examination of young offenders, should be met by the establishment, in at least three centres in different parts of the country, of Central Remand Homes, with expert staffs. Some indication of the sort of work that might be done in such centres is provided by the Collecting Centre for Borstal, now established at Wormwood Scrubs (page 178).

The Young Prisoners received in 1931 fell into the following age groups :

Ages	16	17	18	19	20
Boys	78	222	345	531	707
Girls	10	14	23	36	36

[1] These figures do not include persons sentenced to Borstal Detention.
[2] Comparable figures have not been published for subsequent years.

If we look at their offences, we find that whereas taking
convicted prisoners as a whole, whether men or women, a
clear majority of the receptions are in respect of non-
indictable offences—social nuisances rather than crimes—
the reverse is the case with these young prisoners. Of the
2,756 receptions of boys under 21 there were 1,912 receptions
of indictable offences, and of 166 receptions of girls the
number was 96. For further discussion of age-group
statistics see Chapter XVII, pages 203–5. It is of course
natural that young people should be less prone to those
minor offences which are due in the main to a low standard
of living and social behaviour, and are so closely bound up
with drunkenness : nevertheless, it is reassuring to find
only 28 receptions of boys and six of girls for drunkenness,
and that only eight girls under 21 were received for offences
connected with prostitution. Larcenies account for the
great majority of the offences of both sexes.

It is, on the other hand, far from reassuring to find a high
percentage of recidivism among these young people : the
figures shown in the following table suggest that, in spite of
the increasing number of committals to Borstal, the desirability of using this method of diminishing the chances that
young offenders will become persistent criminals is not yet
fully appreciated.

Previous Proved Offences.	One.	Two.	Three.	Four.	Five.	Six to ten.	Eleven to twenty.	Over twenty.
Boys (54%)	433	231	132	85	56	70	12	2
Girls (60%)	44	11	10	4	1	—	—	2

Yet another disturbing feature is the high proportion of
short sentences. It is unnecessary to emphasize the harm
done to a young offender by a sentence which serves no
purpose but to familiarise him with prison conditions ; to
remove the primary deterrence of imprisonment—that is,
the initial dread of it ; and to brand him with the stigma

of prison, without the slightest prospect of any beneficial influence. Yet we find that of the 1868 imprisonments of boys 946 were for a month or less, and of 117 imprisonments of girls 59 were for a month or less.

It should be clearly understood that when a person under 21 is sentenced to imprisonment he or she goes to an ordinary prison and serves his or her sentence under the same roof and substantially the same system as an adult offender. Mention has already been made of the misleading impression given by the use, some years ago, of the term " Modified Borstal System " : there is no such system. The differences between prison conditions and Borstal conditions are so great that it cannot be too strongly emphasised that nothing that can be done for young offenders in prison bears any relation to Borstal training.

Subject to these general considerations, every effort is made to provide a suitable régime for Young Prisoners. A distinction is drawn between those with short sentences[1] and those with longer sentences, the latter being transferred to one of a few selected local prisons, known as Y.P. Collecting Centres, where there are special facilities for the segregation from adults and the training of young prisoners.

The first step in the treatment of the " Y.P. Class " is to secure effective separation from the adult classes. In the Collecting Centres, where a separate wing or part of a wing can be allocated and cut off, the segregation is comparatively effective : in the ordinary prisons, particularly the smaller ones, it is hardly possible to make completely satisfactory arrangements, though the Y.P. Class is always confined to a separate landing and employed in a separate party.

Apart from segregation, the special treatment of this class consists in the intensification of the more formative elements of the system of training already described. The basis is a full day's associated work on the best class of work available in the prison—though for boys with short sentences in a small prison this may not amount to very much. Special attention is also paid to education, and they are kept out of their cells for as long as possible in the evenings by

[1] At present under three months.

" educational " and " hobby " classes. Above all, reliance is placed on careful individual attention by selected officers, and on the influence of Visitors, both men and women—for on some youths the influence of the right type of woman is of the greatest value.

To supervise and co-ordinate these efforts there is at every prison a Y.P. Committee, which consists of the Superior Officers of the prison, with representatives of the Visiting Committee, the Visitors, the Teachers, and the Prisoners' Aid Society, with any other persons the Committee may co-opt. This Committee is charged with two special functions. Young prisoners do not earn remission marks, but remission not exceeding one-sixth of the sentence may be granted by the Committee, which takes into account not only the prisoner's progress in the prison but his prospects on discharge. This last is the Committee's especial care, and in collaboration with the Prisoners' Aid Society and the voluntary workers they are responsible for both the disposal and the after-care of the young prisoner on his release.

In the Collecting Centres the principles are the same, but it is possible to do more to make them effective, and the longer sentences provide more scope for useful training and for making some impression on the boys' outlook and mentality. There is one important difference : in the Y.P. Class of an ordinary prison there is no Stage System, since the facilities for library books, letters, and visits which form the rewards of this system for short-sentence prisoners are made available for the young prisoners from the outset : but in the Collecting Centres there are two grades, Ordinary and Special. Promotion to the Special Grade may only be earned by steady and reliable progress, and not for at least three months : its privileges include a special dress, associated meals, indoor and outdoor games at week-ends, additional letters and visits, and eligibility to earn a small gratuity, to be used for the prisoner's benefit by the Y.P. Committee.

While the foregoing is applicable in principle to girls as well as to boys, it is clear that, with a daily average of only 28 girls spread over seven establishments, little that is effective can—except at Holloway—be applied in practice.

CHAPTER XIII

SPECIAL CLASSES OF PRISONERS

1. *Stars and Second Division*

IT has been made clear in Chapter V that the object of separating into a special class the prisoners classified as Stars and those ordered by the Courts to be placed in the Second Division, was not to provide any different or more lenient system of treatment, but simply to keep them away from the potential contamination of the " recidivist." There are in fact only two Statutory Rules differentiating this class from the general—the first provides for separation, the second for a monthly letter and visit, as compared with the two-monthly period of the Ordinary Class : this latter advantage, however, only lasts for the period that the Ordinary prisoner is in the First Stage, for thereafter he also is eligible for a monthly letter and visit. We may therefore say that separation is all that the administration is *required* to do for this class : the extent to which separation can be made effective has been discussed in Chapter V.

But in practice there is a good deal more in it than this. We have already considered the possibility that classification may in the future tend more and more to become an instrument primarily for the facilitation of training rather than for the prevention of contamination. And it is certainly true to say that, under the present system, the importance of the Star Class lies rather in the power it gives to concentrate the training resources of a prison on those who are regarded as *prima facie* most likely to profit, than in the purely negative prevention of possible contamination. Thus, while it must again be emphasised that there is no greater *leniency* in treatment, it comes about that the industry which provides the best training in the prison, after the Young

Prisoners, will be allotted to Stars ; that a Visitor will be allotted to a Star in preference to an Ordinary ; and that the greater freedom which can be allowed to Stars makes it possible to have them out much more frequently in the evenings for educational classes. Perhaps most important of all, it is possible to handle Star prisoners without the close and constant supervision that is required by Ordinaries : the ideas of " trust " and " responsibility " can be introduced. Thus we may find these prisoners doing their work in " Honour Parties," with no officer to supervise them, while dinner or supper, or both, may be taken in association : a copy of a daily newspaper is circulated during the times of associated meals. At Wormwood Scrubs, which is set aside for prisoners of this class, it is also possible to allow evening association for recreation, with approved games, for men in the higher stages.

2. *First Division*

The Rules for prisoners of the First Division are devised to provide a form of non-punitive detention as little irksome as is compatible with loss of liberty and with prison discipline. A First Division prisoner may not be compelled to associate with other prisoners (though he may do so if he prefers their company to solitude) : he may, for a small payment, occupy a specially furnished cell, in which he may at his own cost have private furniture and utensils approved by the Governor : he may also, on payment, be relieved of the cleaning of his cell and of other " unaccustomed tasks and offices " : he may wear his own clothing and provide himself with food and (within prescribed limits) drink, from outside : and he may if he so wishes go unshaven, unshorn and un-bathed for all his days in gaol—though should he wish to take a bath he may do so in private.

A First Division prisoner is not required to do prison work, but he can only earn remission of his sentence if he does so. If he does not choose to do prison work he may, so far as prison conditions permit, work at his own trade, employ-ment, or profession : and he may have such books, news-papers, writing materials, or other means of occupation as the Visiting Committee approve sent in to him, at his own expense. A letter and a visit are allowed weekly.

The general rules as to prison discipline apply to this Division, except that in lieu of the forfeiture of marks and of privileges under the stage system—which of course does not apply—they may be ordered to forfeit their special privileges relative to food, clothing, means of occupation, letters and visits.

3. *Prisoners on Remand and Awaiting Trial*

A difficult problem is presented by the necessity of detaining in prisons designed primarily for convicted prisoners a large number of persons charged with offences of all kinds who are still untried. Public opinion, properly emphasising the legal presumption of innocence until a prisoner is actually convicted, is reasonably disturbed by any suggestion of harshness in the conditions in which such persons are detained. The position is clearly defined by the Prison Act, 1877, which provides that " a clear difference shall be made between the treatment of persons unconvicted of crime and in law presumably innocent " and the treatment of convicted prisoners, and directs that special rules shall be made for the treatment of such persons " regulating their confinement in such manner as to make it as little as possible oppressive, due regard only being had to their safe custody, to the necessity of preserving order and good government in the place in which they are confined, and to the physical and moral well-being of the prisoners themselves."

There is, however, to-day the further presumption that in all proper cases the courts will release an untried offender on bail, so that when such a person is received into prison it must as a rule[1] be supposed that the court considers his detention necessary either to ensure his appearance for trial or further examination, or to prevent him from interfering with the course of justice. The conditions of detention of untried prisoners must, therefore, while complying with the provisions of the Act of 1877, be such as will secure not only safe custody but also adequate supervision, and will be

---

[1] There are, of course, many cases where bail is allowed but the prisoner is unable to obtain sureties.

compatible with the discipline and general régime of an establishment populated mainly by convicted prisoners.

It follows from our second presumption that the large majority of these untried prisoners are not, as may often be supposed, respectable and probably innocent people, but "old hands" with, in all probability, quite a string of previous convictions—whatever may be their fate on the charges pending. The prevention of contamination is therefore a matter of importance, introducing serious difficulties into the question whether trial prisoners should be allowed to associate together. Prisoners of this type may also endeavour to concoct false evidence or to arrange plans of escape, so that any relaxation of supervision may have serious results.

Prisoners awaiting trial are separated from all other classes of prisoner in a separate hall or landing, and they may on payment have specially furnished rooms like the First Division. In other respects, e.g. as regards food, drink, clothing, books, newspapers, and other means of occupation, the Rules are similar to those for the First Division. They are subject to the general discipline of the prison, but are not required to work : if they choose to work, they may after the first week's work receive payment in accordance with scales fixed by the Prison Commissioners (at present 6d. a day, or 3s. a week).

The Rules make generous provision to ensure that detention shall not hamper the prisoner in preparing his defence. He is allowed to see his legal advisers in private on any week-day at any reasonable time, and may hand to them personally any documents he has prepared as instructions for his defence without examination by a prison officer. The prison authorities are also required to provide him with all reasonable facilities, including writing materials, for preparing notes and instructions and writing to his legal advisers and friends.

The prisoner may be visited on any week-day by not more than three friends at a time, in addition to visits from his legal advisers, and there is no restriction on the number of letters he may write and receive. These letters are subject to censorship at the prison in order to detect matter tending to interfere with the course of justice—as by the concoction of evidence, intimidation of witnesses or prosecutors, and the like—or to the commission of further offences, or to the subversion of prison discipline. Where medical evidence is required, a trial prisoner may be examined by a doctor of his own choosing.

Special facilities are granted to those who are trying to obtain sureties for bail, and to foreigners who wish to communicate with their consulate or other representative ; and every prisoner is made aware by printed notices in his cell not only of the regulations relative to his class, but of the steps he should take if he wishes to seek bail, or to secure legal assistance under the Poor Prisoners' Defence Acts.

In short, though the conditions must be uncomfortable, and may seem to the respectable novice both degrading and depressing, they do aim to be humane, helpful, and fair.

At Brixton Prison, London, where the large population enables a separate prison to be set aside for trial prisoners and debtors, attempts have recently been made[1] to effect further improvements in the treatment of untried prisoners. A separate hall has been set aside for men not known to have been in prison before, and in this hall a superior type of cell furniture has been introduced. Experiments are also being conducted in permitting association among the prisoners, and smoking during the exercise periods. Similar arrangements (except for smoking) are being tried for women at Holloway, but it is too early yet to suggest that these improvements will become possible in the ordinary prisons with their limited facilities and small mixed populations.

4. Appellants

Under the Criminal Appeal Act 1907 a prisoner convicted at Assizes or Quarter Sessions may, under prescribed conditions, appeal against either conviction or sentence to the Court of Criminal Appeal ; and from the day on which he signs his notice of appeal to the day on which it is either

---

[1] A detailed account is given in the Annual Report of the Prison Commissioners for 1930.

abandoned or determined by the Court, his sentence is held to be suspended and he is treated under the special Rules for Appellants. It should be noted that these Rules do not apply to persons appealing to Quarter Sessions against convictions by Courts of Summary Jurisdiction : a person so appealing may be, and normally is, released on bail, but if he is not so released he continues to serve his sentence until his appeal is heard.

The object of suspending an appellant's sentence is primarily to discourage frivolous appeals, and where the Court thinks fit, even if the appeal is unsuccessful, it may order the time spent as an appellant to count as part of the sentence. The special Rules do not therefore provide any specially favourable treatment for the appellant, but only regulate certain technical details, and ensure for the prisoner the same freedom of access to his legal advisers, and facilities for preparing his appeal, as the trial prisoner has for the preparation of his defence. If the Court discharges him, he may be paid for his work in prison while an appellant at rates fixed by the Commissioners.

5. *Debtors*

It may first be convenient to explain what is meant, in prison, by a " debtor "—that is, what classes of prisoner are treated under the special Rules for Debtors. They include persons committed to prison[1] by Courts of Summary Jurisdiction, for non-payment of sums due under bastardy or wife maintenance orders, or non-payment of rates or taxes, persons committed by County Courts for non-payment of civil debts, and various other minor categories, including contempt of court cases, committed under other than criminal processes. Taken together they form a large and increasing proportion of the prison population, accounting in 1931 for 24·2% of the reception of male prisoners. Table I (page 217) shows in detail the composition of this group from

---

[1] The maximum period is three months if committed by a Court of Summary Jurisdiction ; six weeks if by a County Court ; 12 months if by the High Court in respect of a sum of money under section 4 of the Debtors Act, 1869.

1910 to 1931, while in Graph C (page 225) the figures are shown in diagrammatic form in relation to the movement of unemployment.

From these figures it is apparent that, whereas the numbers of criminal prisoners have fallen heavily since 1913, there has been no such fall in the numbers of non-criminal prisoners. On the contrary, there has during the last few years been a marked rise in the numbers of committals both by County Courts and by Courts of Summary Jurisdiction, and the recent figures are very little below the level of 1913. It further appears that this position is due in the main to the much higher numbers of commitments under Wife Maintenance or Affiliation Orders, which have increased from 3,554 in 1913 to 6,563 in 1931, though committals by County Courts, if still fewer than in the years before the War, have also increased very noticeably in the years following the War.

In view of the fact that County Court debtors are committed under an Act entitled " An Act for the Abolition of Imprisonment for Debt," it may be useful first to explain how they come to be in prison at all. The legal theory is that the debtor is not imprisoned for the debt but as a punishment for contempt of Court, the intention being, as stated by Halsbury in *The Laws of England*, that " a fraudulent debtor shall be punished, but that an honest debtor shall not." Thus the law[1] requires the Court, before making an order for committal to prison, to be satisfied that since the debtor was ordered to pay the sum found by the Court to be due, he has or has had the means to pay such sum but has refused or neglected to pay. In practice, however, the Court often makes in the first instance an Order for payment by instalments, and only commits to prison if and when the creditor applies for committal because the instalments are not being paid. There is therefore some ground for the view that whatever the legal theory the Act is used in fact as an instrument to enable creditors to enforce the payment of debts by the sanction of imprisonment, and from time to time doubt has been expressed whether under

---

[1] Debtors Act, 1869, section 5, and Summary Jurisdiction Act, 1879, section 35.

present practice committals are always confined to the " fraudulent " debtors.

This position was in 1908 the subject of an inquiry by a Select Committee, though no practical result was achieved ; half the members recommended the abolition of imprisonment for debt, and the other half reported in favour of very drastic limitations of the present system.

As regards the much larger question—so far as numbers are concerned—of whether, by any changes in the law or in the methods of its enforcement, some reduction can be made in the numbers committed by Courts of Summary Jurisdiction for non-payment under Maintenance or Affiliation Orders, the Secretary of State has recently set up a Departmental Committee.[1]

If the only persons sent to prison were in fact those who could have paid what they owed but would not, there would be no apparent necessity to separate such persons from convicted prisoners, of whom a substantial proportion are also committed for not paying sums of money, viz. fines, often in respect of social delinquencies of a much less unpleasant type than fraudulent debt. At present, however, the treatment of debtors is based on pre-Debtors Act assumptions, in so far as the Rules require them to be separated from criminal prisoners and to be allowed special privileges, e.g. to wear their own clothing, to associate together at exercise, and to have weekly visits and letters. They are, on the other hand, required to work at prison employments, and are no longer paid for such work, though since the abolition of payment they are entitled to facilities for getting home, and assistance from the Prisoners' Aid Society, on the same footing as other prisoners : and as regards accommodation, diet, and discipline the conditions do not differ from those of convicted prisoners. They do not, of course, earn remission of sentence, since they can always secure this by paying up or " purging their contempt," nor—in view of the three months limit of their sentences,[2] do they profit by the Stage System or enter into the scheme of " training."

---

[1] Committals for non-payment of fines are also within the terms of reference of this Committee.

[2] Save in the few *sine die* and other cases from the High Court

Figures specially taken out in 1929 show that a substantial proportion of the non-criminal prisoners committed by Courts of Summary Jurisdiction return to prison again and again, as appears from the following table :

Totals Received.	Numbers previously committed under Civil Process.								Totals previously committed.
	Once.	Twice.	Three times.	Four times.	Five times.	Six to ten times.	11 to 20 times.	Over 20 times.	
Affiliation .	2691	567	234	146	98	45	77	30	7	1204
Wife maintenance .	4188	913	403	201	127	74	140	28	1	1857
Non-payment of rates .	2001	393	205	127	60	48	73	9	1	916

6. *Prisoners under Sentence of Death*

Every care is taken to prevent a condemned prisoner from coming into contact with other prisoners, or from being exposed to their view at exercise or chapel. The " condemned cell " is usually set at the end of a landing, and is of double the ordinary size, with a bed for the prisoner, a table, and chairs for the prisoner and the two officers who remain in the cell day and night : washing facilities and water-closet are, if possible, placed in an adjoining cell, and under the most modern arrangement the execution chamber is reached through an intervening lobby, the whole set of rooms being self-contained.

The condemned prisoner wears prison dress, and except as to labour—which is not required of him—is subject to the general Rules so far as they are applicable. The prisoner may, at the discretion of the Medical Officer, receive additions to the usual diet, and be allowed to smoke, while books, games, and other means of mental occupation are freely permitted. He may see his friends and legal advisers at any reasonable time, in the presence of prison officers, but otherwise no person except an official of the prison or a member of the Visiting Committee may see him without the authority of the Prison Commissioners. Ample facilities are granted for correspondence and for the preparation, if desired, of an appeal.

Responsibility for carrying out the execution rests with the Sheriff of the county, whose Under-Sheriff fixes the date of execution, engages and pays the executioner, attends the execution, and decides whether representatives of the Press should be admitted. Immediately after the execution the Coroner for the district holds an inquest on the body at the prison. The burial takes place within the prison walls : a register of the graves is kept, but they are not distinguished by names or other marks.

CHAPTER XIV

PENAL SERVITUDE

1. *Development of Penal Servitude*

THE Penal Servitude Act of 1857 provided that " no person shall be sentenced to transportation," and that sentences of penal servitude should be passed for all offences punishable by transportation. The minimum sentence was three years, and though this was raised in 1864 to five years, it was in 1891 again reduced to three years : the maximum sentence is for life, and where the Royal Mercy has been extended to persons sentenced to death, the sentence is commuted to penal servitude for life. Every life sentence is reviewed periodically by the Secretary of State, and the length of time actually served depends on the facts and circumstances of the particular case. It is, however, rare for a prisoner serving a life sentence to be required to serve a longer term than if he had been sentenced to 20 years, i.e. about 15 years of actual detention.

The system as it stood after the Act of 1857 consisted of three distinct parts : (1) separate confinement for nine months in Pentonville or one of the local prisons ; (2) associated labour in a Public Works prison : this part of the sentence was divided into three equal " progressive stages," carrying increasing privileges and gratuities, so that the convict might have a definite stimulus to work hard and behave well ; (3) release on " licence " (the old " ticket-of-leave ") to be at large for the remainder of the sentence, the period of " licence " varying with the length of the sentence. It may be noted that under the Act of 1857 it was still legal for convicts to be " removed overseas " after their separate confinement, and for some years small numbers continued to be sent for their " public works " stage to Gibraltar or

Bermuda, or to the remaining penal settlement in Western Australia.

This system had not long been in force before an increase in crime led to some uneasiness as to the presence in the country of large numbers of convicts on licence—the fact being overlooked that for many years convicts had been at large under " pardons " with no licence at all—and a Royal Commission was appointed in 1863 to inquire into the working of the new Acts.   This Commission reaffirmed the desirability of the preliminary nine months separate confinement, and called generally for a " more deterrent character " in the system, and stricter supervision of licence-holders.[1]

This inquiry and the consequential Penal Servitude Act 1864 resulted in the introduction of the Marks System, under which the earning both of stage privileges and remission of sentence was standardised by requiring the convict to earn by labour and good conduct a number of marks proportioned to the length of his sentence : the marks were awarded daily and might be forfeited by misconduct.   At the same time the Stage System was elaborated and made more effective, the object being " to devise a useful system of progressive reformatory discipline, based upon a nice adjustment of the elements of hope and repression."[2]   These ideas of Progressive Stages and Marks, worked out in the convict prisons, were subsequently introduced into the local prisons when these came under the Government, and have remained the basis of prison discipline to the present time.

Another important step followed the Report of a further Royal Commission in 1878, when the first step towards the classification of convicted prisoners was taken by the formation in convict prisons of a " Star Class," in which were placed convicts with no previous convictions so that they might be separated from the more depraved.

Except as regards separate confinement, the legal position of the penal servitude system as it stands to-day was finally established by the Penal Servitude Act 1891, and the relevant sections of the Prison Act 1898.   By the latter

---

[1] For further details as to this see pages 162–165 following.
[2] Ruggles-Brise, page 29.

Act, as we have seen, the Directors of Convict Prisons and the Prison Commissioners became one body, and all Rules for both convict and local prisons were to be made by the Secretary of State. At the same time the Secretary of State was required to appoint at each convict prison a Board of Visitors of independent persons with judicial and other powers similar to those exercised in local prisons by the Visiting Committees. At this stage, then, penal servitude was a period of imprisonment, of any length from three years to life, of which by good conduct and industry a man might earn remission of a quarter, a woman of one-third : the first nine months were spent in separate confinement in a local prison—the remainder, until the necessary " remission marks " were earned, in a convict prison, with associated labour nominally on public works : finally came release on a licence, which might be forfeited by misconduct, to be at large under police supervision till the expiration of the sentence by efflux of time.

After 1898 the preliminary separate confinement slowly disappeared : the Gladstone Committee, while recognising that its *raison d'être* was now simple deterrence and expressing their dislike of it, did not do more than recommend that a reduction of the period should be considered. Shortly afterwards the period was reduced to six months for the " Intermediate " class and three months for the " Star " class ; in 1909 it was reduced to three months for Recidivists and one month for Intermediates and Stars ; and in 1922 it was finally abolished.

Except for this matter of separate confinement—and even this had its parallel on a smaller scale with " hard labour " prisoners—there has during the present century been no substantial difference in the conditions under which sentences of penal servitude and sentences of imprisonment are served. On the one hand local prisoners have been brought to work in association, and on the other the old " public works " tradition of the convict prisons has practically died out. At Dartmoor and Parkhurst a certain number of men are employed on land reclamation or on the prison farms, but these form a small proportion of the total population, and the majority are employed about the prison or in workshops in just the same way as a local prisoner.

There are no separate rules as to the accommodation, discipline, diet, or general treatment of prisoners serving sentences of penal servitude, and apart from the larger remission earned on such a sentence, and certain minor features incidental to its length, it may be said to differ from a sentence of imprisonment only in so far as the convict is released on a licence and not, like the local prisoner, absolutely.

As long ago as 1885 Sir E. du Cane said, " The distinction . . . no longer has any significance now that they (i.e. sentences of penal servitude and of imprisonment) are both carried out in the United Kingdom, and it is misleading. The only point to be kept in view is that the treatment should be adapted to the length of the sentence."[1] Again in 1932 the Persistent Offenders Committee said (paragraph 127), " The use of the two terms Imprisonment and Penal Servitude is liable to suggest that there is a material difference in the nature of the two sentences, and the abolition of the term Penal Servitude would have the advantage of making it clear that a sentence of five years differs from a sentence of one year in length only, or in such minor features as are incidental to length." We cannot therefore now regard the distinction between penal servitude and imprisonment as much more than an interesting historical survival.

It remains to describe shortly how " convicts "—as prisoners sentenced to penal servitude have long been described—are now classified, and the prisons to which the different classes are allocated.[2]

The Statutory Rules of 1898, as amended by the Rules of the 21st January, 1905, provided for the division of convicts into three classes, viz . : the " Star " class, which was formed for the purpose of keeping apart from others those who had not previously been convicted or were not habitually criminal ; the " Recidivist " class, which consisted of those who had been previously sentenced to penal servitude

[1] *Punishment and Prevention of Crime*, page 159.
[2] The following description is based on a circular letter sent by the Secretary of State to Judges, Recorders and Chairmen of Quarter Sessions 3.11.32.

or had been previously convicted of grave or persistent crime; and the "Intermediate" class, which consisted of those who by character or habits were unfit for the "Star" class, but could be distinguished from the "Recidivists" by their comparative youth, or by the fact that their previous offences had not been grave or often repeated.

This system of classification has now been revised, and men sentenced to penal servitude are, like local prisoners, divided into three classes, known as "Star," "Special," and "Ordinary," with a special class for Young Convicts under 26 who are eligible for the "Star Class."

1. The "Star" class consists of those who should be separated from others because they have not been previously convicted or not previously convicted of serious offences and are not of criminal or corrupt habits.

2. The "Special" class is for men under the age of 30 who are serving a first sentence of penal servitude, have previous convictions or records which show that they are not suitable for the "Star" class, and are not of poor physique or mentality. The object is to separate the younger men of criminal habits or tendencies who are vigorous in body and mind from those who are older or are of poor physique or mentality, with a view to subjecting the young and fit men to forms of employment and training appropriate to their age and character. Chelmsford Prison has been opened as a special establishment for offenders of this type.

3. The "Ordinary" class consists of persons who are unsuited for either the "Star" or the "Special" class.

In the past it has been the practice to set aside certain prisons or parts of prisons as " convict prisons," to use them exclusively for persons sentenced to penal servitude, and to keep offenders sentenced to penal servitude apart from those sentenced to imprisonment. There is, however, as we have seen, no such distinction of treatment that it is necessary to confine all persons sentenced to penal servitude in separate establishments from those in which persons sentenced to imprisonment are confined. Nor is such separation of establishments necessary for the purpose of classification by character and precautions against contamination. Some offenders of the " Star " class sentenced to penal servitude can properly be associated with persons of the " Star " class sentenced to imprisonment, and some Recidivists sentenced to penal servitude can properly be associated with offenders of the same type sentenced to imprisonment. Many of the persons serving sentences of imprisonment are old offenders who have previously served sentences of penal servitude. The Penal Servitude Act of 1853 (16 and 17 Vic. c. 99, Sec. 6) provides that persons sentenced to penal servitude may be confined in any prison in the United Kingdom, and arrangements by which offenders sentenced to penal servitude and offenders sentenced to imprisonment can in appropriate cases be placed in the same establishment conduce both to economy and convenience of administration. At the present time the arrangements with regard to males sentenced to penal servitude are as follows :

Those of the " Star " class are either at Maidstone Prison or Wakefield Prison : at Wakefield Prison they are associated with men who have been sentenced to substantial terms of imprisonment but are not of criminal habits. The Young Convicts are in a separate block at Maidstone.

Those of the " Special " class are sent to Chelmsford in the hope that by removing them from the corrupting influence of the more hardened criminals at Dartmoor and Parkhurst and subjecting them to a more positive and strenuous training a larger proportion may be diverted from the ranks of the habituals.

Convicts of the " Ordinary " class sentenced for terms not exceeding three years remain, as a general rule, in the local prison serving the Court at which the prisoner is sentenced. Convicts of this class sentenced for periods of over three years are mostly at Parkhurst and Dartmoor Prisons. Generally speaking, convicts of " Intermediate " type go to Parkhurst rather than to Dartmoor, and to Parkhurst also convicts of various classifications may be sent on medical grounds—there is a large hospital, and special arrangements for convicts of " weak-minded " type : here also is a special party of " Aged Convicts " over 67, for whom certain relaxations of the normal régime are permitted.

As regards women sentenced to penal servitude, those of the " Star " class are at Aylesbury Prison, and the others are at Holloway Prison.

No useful purpose would be served by detailed description of the régime of a convict prison since, as we have seen, it differs little from that of a local prison except for the somewhat greater possibilities—especially at Dartmoor and Parkhurst—of work outside the walls. At Maidstone, with its exclusively " Star " population, important printing industry, and extensive educational and recreational facilities, there is a more scholastic atmosphere than is found among the bucolic " bog " and " dairy " parties at " the Moor," but in general the differences are not such as to call for detailed description. It is of course necessary for a convict with a long sentence to serve to be able to look forward to some improvement of his conditions, nor is it desirable to subject a man over a prolonged period of years to a régime that may be suitable for one of two or three years. The privileges which may be earned in the later stages of a sentence in a convict prison are therefore more substantial than those available for shorter-sentence prisoners, and a man when he has served four years, a woman three years, may be eligible for admission to the Special Stage : in this stage there is greater freedom of association, a certain amount of evening recreation, and the possibility of earning gratuities which may be spent on articles of comfort and relaxation —such as newspapers and materials for smoking, which is allowed at fixed times in a prescribed room : women, instead of smoking, may make tea. Further, a special remission of three days may be earned by a prisoner spending less than six months with good conduct in the Third and Special Stages, and of seven days for periods of six months and over.

In special cases of long-sentence convicts where the relatives cannot afford the expense of a visit, arrangements are sometimes made through the Central Association for meeting the expenses of a visit from a grant kindly made by the Trustees of the Hector Sassoon Fund.

M

2. *Licensing and After-care of Convicts*

By Sections 9 and 10 of the Penal Servitude Act 1853 the King, by an order in writing under the hand and seal of one of his Secretaries of State, may grant to convicts licences to be at large within the United Kingdom and the Channel Islands during a portion of their term of Penal Servitude ; and by various provisions of the Penal Servitude Act 1864 as amended by the Penal Servitude Act 1891 such licences may be issued " printed, written or lithographed " either in the form prescribed in the statute or " in any other form that His Majesty may consider expedient." In practice the licence is a small printed sheet stamped with the signature of the Secretary of State, of which a copy, signed by one of the Directors of Convict Prisons, is handed to the convict.

Under the Statutory Rules a convict becomes eligible for licence when one quarter of his sentence has yet to run. Under the system now in force the actual date is worked out by a marks system : the total number of days in the sentence is calculated, and the sentence is represented by a number of marks calculated at six per diem, e.g. for four years, or 1,461 days, a total of 8,766 marks must be earned, plus any additional marks ordered to be earned as punishment. To enable a convict to earn remission of one quarter of his sentence he is allotted (provided he works satisfactorily) eight marks per diem ; so to ascertain the number of days to be served the total number of marks to be earned is divided by eight. The day after the necessary marks have been earned the convict will normally be due for discharge : this date may, however, be altered by various considerations, e.g. if his sentence has been suspended by appeal it may be postponed, or if he has earned the " Special Stage remission " it may be advanced, and if he is due for discharge on Sunday or Saturday he is discharged the previous Friday, or if on Good Friday or Christmas Day, or on a Bank Holiday, the day previous.

It has been held that a convict who has earned the necessary marks is not entitled to a licence as of right, and in certain classes of case the licence has been withheld irrespective of marks earned, e.g. where the convict has been certified as mentally defective, or if, owing to his low mentality, he is clearly likely to be dangerous, or where he is an alien who is to be deported : licences have also on occasion been withheld at the convict's own request, and in certain special cases *in terrorem*. On the other hand, the Secretary of State on occasion authorises earlier licence in special cases, e.g. as a reward for bravery or special services in prison, or as a form of compensation for accident or loss.

The names of convicts due for licence in each month are submitted to the Commissioners at the end of the preceding month, the calculations are checked, and the forms sent to the Home Office, whence the actual licences are issued on the form appropriate to the sentence.

Licences are granted subject to conditions, and by the Penal Servitude Act 1864 the following conditions must be inserted in a licence :

(i) the holder shall preserve his licence and produce it when called upon to do so by a Magistrate or Police Officer.

(ii) he shall abstain from any violation of the law.

(iii) he shall not associate with any notoriously bad characters such as reputed thieves or prostitutes.

(iv) he shall not lead an idle or dissolute life without visible means of obtaining an honest livelihood.

If the Secretary of State decides to impose any other condition he must within 21 days of making such condition lay a copy before both Houses of Parliament. Such conditions are not often imposed ; perhaps the most frequent relates to exclusion from a specified area, while others have related to abstention from drink and certain forms of publicity, and to special measures of supervision.

A breach of any condition of a licence by an act not of itself punishable constitutes an offence punishable by up to three months imprisonment. The principal sanction behind the licence, however, is the fact that on any breach of the conditions it may be forfeited or revoked : if the licence-holder is convicted on indictment of any offence the licence is automatically forfeited by virtue of such conviction, and at the termination of any fresh sentence he becomes liable to serve a term of penal servitude equal to the portion of the original term that remained unexpired when the licence was granted : if he is convicted summarily the Court sends a certificate of conviction to the Secretary of State, who may thereupon revoke the licence, with the same effect as regards the serving of the unexpired portion of the original term, which is always known as the " remanet " : the licence may also be forfeited by a Court for certain breaches of conditions, or revoked " at His Majesty's Pleasure " by order of the Secretary of State—in either case the licence-holder may be arrested without warrant and committed to prison, and he is thereby remitted to his original sentence, though he then serves not the " remanet " but so much of the sentence as is still unexpired.

To secure more complete control over the movements of licence-holders, the conditions of the licence were supplemented by various statutory provisions, which require them to notify their addresses, and any changes of address, to the police, by personally presenting themselves at the police station : the licence-holder must similarly notify his arrival in or departure from any police district, and (if a man) must report himself once a month—personally or by letter as the police may direct—at the police station. Failure to comply with any of these requirements is an offence punishable either by forfeiture of the licence or by imprisonment. The Secretary of State, however, has power to remit all or any of these requirements, and this is commonly done where it is thought they would serve no useful purpose. The police are automatically warned of the approaching release of a convict by the issue from the prison to the Criminal Record Office at Scotland Yard of a descriptive form giving the date of discharge, and intended address. This information is circulated by the Criminal Record Office to all police forces.

This cumbrous procedure, which involves a vast amount of labour at the prisons, at the Home Office, and among the police, is condemned altogether by the Report of the Persistent Offenders Committee, which considered that in modern conditions it serves no useful purpose commensurate with the trouble it gives. The Committee recommends that persons sentenced to penal servitude " should be allowed to earn absolute remission of a portion of their sentences in the same way as persons sentenced to imprisonment " : it is pointed out that the value of reporting to the police is considerably diminished by the increased facilities for rapid locomotion, that " the number of criminals subject to the licensing system is very small compared with those whose release from prison involves absolute discharge," and that in any case a much more effective machinery for the control of criminals at large is provided by the powers of Courts to order " police supervision " under Section 8 of the Prevention of Crime Act 1871.[1]

The after-care of all prisoners sentenced to penal servitude is undertaken by the Central Association for the Aid of Discharged Convicts, a semi-official body, with its head office in London, the expenses of which are met by a Government Grant. The Association is managed by a Council, and is under the Presidency of the Home Secretary. The Director, Sir Wemyss Grant-Wilson, controls the whole of the work through a small headquarters staff, whose conditions of service are subject to the approval of the Prison Commissioners, and a large number of voluntary " Associates " (who are usually probation officers or social workers) throughout the country. The assistance on discharge and after-care of convicts in local prisons is arranged in co-operation with the local Prisoners' Aid Society.

On reception of a convict full particulars are sent from the prison to the Central Association, and if he is in a convict prison the representative of the Central Association visits him some time before his discharge and discusses with him his plans and prospects. Where the man has no home to go to, the Association arranges for him to be received by their Associate, who finds him lodgings, if required, and assists him with maintenance, clothing, and tools for so long as is necessary or possible. The main task is to find work for the men, and in spite of the exceptional difficulties of the present time it is remarkable to learn from the Association's Report for 1932 that in 1931, out of 567 of these most

---

[1] " Police Supervision " under this section involves limitations of liberty similar to those imposed on a convict on licence. In practice it has come to be rarely used.

unpromising protégés, of whom 462 required work to be
found for them, work was actually found for 213—although
231 were unfit for ordinary labouring work, and 63 were
mentally or physically unfit for any work. Many men have
several jobs in succession found for them, and they are
accustomed to turn to the Association for help in times of
ill-fortune. The Central Association has, however, no
positive control over Penal Servitude licence-holders, as it
has over Preventive Detention licence-holders, or as the
Borstal Association has over its protégés.

The after-care work for women is carried out by the Aylesbury After-Care Association (see page 194) on similar lines.

The Central Association estimates that of the convicts
discharged to its care the following percentages do not again
offend :

Stars	.	.	.	90%
Intermediates		.	.	50%
Recidivists	.	.	.	30%

CHAPTER XV

PREVENTIVE DETENTION

1. *The Meaning of Preventive Detention*

" Preventive Detention is the name given to a form of custody, provided by the Prevention of Crime Act, 1908, for the protection of the public from the Habitual Criminal."[1] This was the first attempt in England to deal specifically with the problem of the criminal who is repeatedly guilty of offences, and is neither deterred nor reformed by sentences of imprisonment or penal servitude. Under the general principles and practice governing the award of sentences by Courts, apart from the statutory maxima in particular classes of offence, a Court does not award in respect of a particular offence a heavier sentence than is, under the general standards, appropriate for that offence, however many times the offender has been convicted of it before. Thus, in the record of the typical " recidivist " it is common to find a long sentence of penal servitude followed by several short sentences of imprisonment of varying lengths, which quite evidently, to a man well hardened to prison life, can only appear as inconveniences inseparable from his profession.

The extent of the problem of " recidivism " is indicated by the following passage in the Report of the Persistent Offenders Committee, 1932 (pp. 2–3) : " Of the 39,000 sentences of imprisonment (in 1930) 28,000 were imposed on persons who had been previously found guilty of offences. In many cases these previous offences had been dealt with by methods other than imprisonment, such as the use of probation, binding over, and fines : but in 20,384 cases the offenders had been previously in prison. Many of them had

---

[1] Ruggles-Brise, page 49.

served repeated sentences of imprisonment, as is shown by the following table :

4,740 had served 1 previous sentence.
2,952 had served 2 previous sentences.
1,949 had served 3 previous sentences.
1,499 had served 4 previous sentences.
1,115 had served 5 previous sentences.
3,382 had served 6–10 previous sentences.
2,622 had served 11–20 previous sentences.
2,125 had served over 20 previous sentences."

20,384

The Gladstone Committee had gone to the root of the matter in 1895 when they referred (para. 85) to " a large class of habitual criminals . . . who run the risk of comparatively short sentences with comparative indifference. . . . To punish them for the particular offence in which they are detected is almost useless . . . the real offence is the wilful persistence in the deliberately acquired habit of crime . . . a new form of sentence should be placed at the disposal of the judges by which these offenders may be segregated for long periods of detention during which they would not be treated with the severity of first-class hard labour or of penal servitude, but would be forced to work under less onerous conditions."

Part II of the Prevention of Crime Act, 1908, was the somewhat tardy outcome of this valuable suggestion : unfortunately this Act was so strictly limited in its approach to the problem that it has had little practical effect. Lord Gladstone, in proposing the Act, made it clear that it was intended to deal not with the generality of " habituals " but only with that more limited body of " professional criminals " or " persistent dangerous criminals " " engaged in the more serious forms of crime." Shortly, it provides that if a person with three previous convictions is convicted on indictment of a crime and sentenced to penal servitude, and is then found by the jury to be an habitual criminal, the Court may order him, at the end of his penal servitude, to be kept in Preventive Detention for not less than five nor more than ten years.

But in order to make more clear the "safeguards" and difficulties with which this procedure is hedged about, it is necessary to set out the steps in greater detail :

(i) the consent of the Director of Public Prosecutions must be obtained by the Police before they can charge an offender with being an habitual criminal.

(ii) the Secretary of State advised Police Forces that normally, they should only submit to the Director cases where, in addition to the qualifications expressly required by the Act, the criminal (a) is over 30 years old; (b) has already undergone a term of penal servitude ; (c) is charged anew with a substantial and serious offence.

If the consent of the Director is obtained, and if the offender is convicted on the fresh charge, and if the Court decides to pass a sentence *of penal servitude* in respect of that charge, then

(iii) the jury must be asked to find, on evidence, that he is an habitual criminal, and to this end they must be satisfied not only that since the age of 16, in addition to the fresh conviction, he has been at least three times previously convicted, but that he is "leading persistently a dishonest or criminal life." Should the jury find this charge proved, then

(iv) the Court must determine that "for the protection of the public it is expedient that the offender should be kept in detention for a lengthened period of years." For varied reasons the Court does not invariably so determine, so that it is relatively rarely that a case reaches the final stage—

(v) the passing of sentence of Preventive Detention.

2. *The Conditions in which Preventive Detention is Served*

The Prevention of Crime Act, 1908, directed that persons undergoing Preventive Detention should be generally subject to the rules governing convict prisons, but required

the Secretary of State by new rules to modify the conditions
" in the direction of a less rigorous treatment " : the Act
further directed that these prisoners should be subjected to
" disciplinary and reformative influences calculated to fit
them for earning an honest living on discharge." Accordingly, a new prison specially designed for the reception of
habitual criminals was constructed at Camp Hill in the Isle
of Wight, and on its completion in 1911 the Secretary of
State laid before Parliament draft Rules prescribing the
conditions in the new establishment.

At Camp Hill Prison prisoners serving Preventive Detention were detained until the end of 1931, when the immediate necessity of providing additional accommodation for
persons sentenced to Borstal Detention moved the Secretary
of State to authorise the appropriation of Camp Hill as a
Borstal Institution, and the preventive detention prisoners
were moved to a wing of the local prison at Lewes. In 1933
they were again moved to the former local prison at Ports-
mouth, which was reopened for the purpose.

In 1932, following the change of location, fresh Rules
were made for men sentenced to Preventive Detention :
these were similar in general effect to the earlier Rules of
1911 and 1925, but included certain changes which experience had shown to be desirable, and others rendered necessary
by the change of location. Their intention, as stated by the
Secretary of State in presenting the original rules to Parliament, is " to carry out the intention of the statute and to
make the conditions of Preventive Detention as easy as
circumstances will allow " : but it was also pointed out that
this intention could only be carried out in so far as it was
compatible with discipline, hard work, and safe custody,
and that all mitigation notwithstanding " the essential fact
remains that . . . the convict is completely deprived of his
liberty and remains under constant supervision, control,
and compulsion, in all he does." The Rules of 1932 now
form part of the general code of 1933.

Separation in cells by night and association by day is the
basis of Preventive Detention as of ordinary imprisonment.
The same kind of work is done, but the prisoner may by his
work earn money, starting at 2d. a day, and—providing he

earns the requisite good conduct stripes—rising after one year to 3d., and after two years to 4d. A stripe may be earned every six months, and each stripe carries a gratuity of 5s. The money thus earned is credited to an account kept for him by the Governor, and he may save it, send it to his family, or spend it on approved commodities at the Prison Store. These include articles of food, toilet requisites, smoking materials, etc. : smoking is allowed during the dinner hour and at prescribed times in the evening.

Meals are taken in association, and the prisoners also associate in the evenings and may play approved indoor games. Newspapers are provided in the association rooms, and prisoners may also purchase their own newspapers and periodicals. Visits and letters are on a somewhat more liberal scale than in the later stages of a sentence of Penal Servitude, and the diet is more varied and liberal than that of local and convict prisons. In short, " in the arrangements made to ameliorate the lot of these prisoners all that is reasonably practicable seems to have been done."[1]

Discipline presents little trouble. " It is common to find that the men who persistently revert to crime when at liberty are well behaved in prison. Discipline among the Preventive Detention men is usually maintained without difficulty and misconduct is rare."[2] The punishments available in a convict prison are available also in a Preventive Detention Prison, and are reinforced by power to forfeit work-money or gratuity, or to forfeit or restrict or postpone any privileges, or to reduce the prisoner to the Penal Grade : this involves forfeiture of all privileges and location in a separate part of the prison, with loss of association except at work.

For each Preventive Detention Prison the Secretary of State appoints a Board of Visitors in the same way, and with the same powers and duties, as for a Convict Prison.

Preventive Detention applies also to women, but the number sentenced under the Act is very small : such as there are are located in a separate wing at Aylesbury, but their numbers rarely reach half a dozen and usually average

[1] Report of Persistent Offenders Committee, page 56.
[2] Ibid.

two or three. So far as is practicable in these conditions they are treated under the same Rules as the men.

3. *Licensing and After-care*

The Act provides that the Secretary of State may " at any time discharge on licence a person undergoing Preventive Detention if satisfied that there is a reasonable probability that he will abstain from crime and lead a useful and industrious life, or that he is no longer capable of engaging in crime, or that for any other reason it is desirable to release him from confinement in prison." In order that the reasonableness of this probability may in each case be assessed from time to time he is further required to appoint at each Preventive Detention Prison an Advisory Committee, selected like the Boards of Visitors from unofficial persons in the neighbourhood, which is required by Rule to meet at least once a quarter at the prison, " and as occasion arises shall make such individual reports on prisoners as will assist the Commissioners in advising the Secretary of State in regard to the discharge of such prisoners on licence."

" The members of these Committees interview the inmates, make themselves acquainted with their careers and characters, and after consultation with the Governor and Chaplain do their best to estimate the probability of an offender's abstaining from crime if released on licence. . . . The practice is in comparatively hopeful cases where the sentence is five years to grant a licence usually after $3\frac{1}{2}$ years, in less hopeful cases after $4\frac{1}{2}$ years, and in some apparently hopeless cases to grant no licence. When the sentence is six years a licence is usually granted in comparatively hopeful cases after four years, and when the sentence is 10 years after seven years."[1]

The licence granted differs materially from that granted to a convict : the latter may be described as " negative," in so far as it simply permits the licence-holder to be at large, provided he abstains from crime and complies with the regulations as to reporting to the police, whereas the former

[1] Persistent Offenders Committee, page 58.

is " positive " in that the licence-holder is placed under the definite authority of some society or person, whose directions as to where he shall work and live must be obeyed, the sanction being revocation of the licence by the Secretary of State. The licence may also be revoked by the Secretary of State following a reconviction. In such case the prisoner becomes liable to serve, in addition to any fresh sentence, a period of Preventive Detention equal to the period from the date of revocation to the date of expiration of the original Preventive Detention sentence, and on return to the Preventive Detention prison he is placed in the Penal Grade for such length of time as the Advisory Committee consider necessary.

The after-care of prisoners released from Preventive Detention is undertaken by the Central Association, and it is to their care and supervision that the licence-holder is committed by the terms of his licence. The arrangements which the Association makes are similar to those already described for convicts, but in these cases it has the added responsibility of making reports to the Secretary of State where a man in not behaving satisfactorily. For women, this work is done by the Aylesbury After-Care Association (see page 194).

4. Results of Preventive Detention

In 1928, when the Act had been in operation for 20 years, the Commissioners in their Annual Report (pp. 12 to 18) published a detailed account of the operation of Preventive Detention, which showed conclusively that it had not had the effect which was intended. This view was confirmed by the Persistent Offenders Committee of 1932, which recommended that Part II of the Act should be repealed, and that further provision should be made for dealing with habitual criminals on lines which it is no part of our task here to consider. It is, however, interesting and pertinent to note briefly the grounds on which these conclusions have been based.

The first is that insufficient use has been made of the Act. " Between the date when the Act came into operation in August, 1909, and 31st December, 1928, 901 sentences of

Preventive Detention have been passed, of which 735 were for the minimum period of five years and 34 for the maximum period of 10 years . . . in recent years the average number of sentences has been for men 31, for women 0·6 each year. How insignificant are these figures compared with the number of recidivist criminals can be seen by taking any sample batch of convicts and noting how numerous are those who have three or more previous convictions of crime. For example, in 1928 there were discharged from the convict prisons 434 men, of whom 308 were ' recidivists.' Of these 308 there were 54 with one or two previous convictions of crimes, and 254 with three or more previous convictions of crimes. One hundred and fifty-nine of them had six or more such previous convictions and 134 of them had served previous sentences of penal servitude. . . . Seeing that this sample batch of 308 recidivists represents only a portion of the total number of recidivists who at any one time are at large . . . it is clear that 31 sentences a year of Preventive Detention can have no appreciable effect on the problem of recidivism."[1]

It would seem that there are three explanations of this position. The first lies in the cumbrousness of the procedure itself, which has been explained in Section (1) of this chapter. The second, in the opinion of the Persistent Offenders Committee, lies in " the scheme of treating the sentence of Preventive Detention as supplementary to the sentence for the substantive offence . . . . all the evidence we have received points to the conclusion that the sentence of detention should be alternative to, and not supplementary to, any other sentence " : not only are Courts often reluctant to add a sentence of Preventive Detention to a substantial sentence of Penal Servitude, but where the particular offence of which the criminal is convicted does not justify a sentence of Penal Servitude according to accepted judicial standards the Court is precluded from passing a sentence of Preventive Detention. And thirdly, as is shown by the Commissioners in their Annual Report for 1928, far fewer sentences of Penal Servitude are passed nowadays than in 1908, notwithstanding that the volume of indictable offenceshas increa sed (in

[1] Annual Report, 1928, pages. 13 and 15.

1908 there were 1,182 sentences of Penal Servitude ; in 1928 only 483), so that a much smaller proportion of " habituals " can now become eligible for Preventive Detention than in 1908.

The third ground of failure alleged against the system is that it has been unsuccessful in " the steps taken to comply with the provision that persons undergoing Preventive Detention shall be subjected to such disciplinary and reformative influences and shall be employed on such work as may be best fitted to make them able and willing to earn an honest livelihood on discharge."[1] The figures published by the Commissioners in their Annual Report for 1928 speak for themselves : taking the men released from Camp Hill in the seven years from 1st January, 1920, to 31st December, 1926, the total number licensed for the first time was 55, of whom four died and one became insane. Of the remaining 50, only three had not reverted to crime by the end of 1928. Of the 26 discharged on expiration of sentence, three died, and of the remainder only four had not reverted to crime by the end of 1928.

[1] Persistent Offenders Committee, page 56.

CHAPTER XVI

THE BORSTAL SYSTEM

1. *Introductory*

WHAT is essential in the law relating to Borstal training is so completely stated by Section 1 (1) of the Prevention of Crime Act, 1908, that it is unavoidable that it should be quoted in full. It provides (as amended by Section 11 of the Criminal Justice Administration Act, 1914) as follows :

1.—(1) Where a person is convicted on indictment of an offence for which he is liable to be sentenced to penal servitude or imprisonment, and it appears to the court—

(*a*) that the person is not less than sixteen nor more than twenty-one years of age ; and

(*b*) that, by reason of his criminal habits or tendencies, or association with persons of bad character, it is expedient that he should be subject to detention for such term and under such instruction and discipline as appears most conducive to his reformation and the repression of crime ;

it shall be lawful for the court, in lieu of passing a sentence of penal servitude or imprisonment, to pass a sentence of detention under penal discipline in a Borstal Institution for a term of not less than two years nor more than three years :

Provided that, before passing such a sentence, the court shall consider any report or representations which may be made to it by or on behalf of the Prison Commissioners as to the suitability of the case for treatment in a Borstal Institution, and shall be satisfied that the character, state of health, and mental condition of the offender, and the other circumstances of the case, are such that the offender is likely to profit by such instruction and discipline as aforesaid.

Sub-section (2) provides that the Secretary of State may by order raise the maximum age to 23, but the power has never been used, and if effect is given to the recommendations of the Persistent Offenders Committee as to detention of habitual offenders over 21 it is unlikely that it will be. The minimum age is at present 16, but the Young Offenders Committee 1927 has recommended that when the upper age limit for Home Office Schools is raised to 17,[1] the minimum age for Borstal should also be raised to 17, with an option to Courts to send to Borstal offenders of 16–17 who are certified to be too developed for Schools.

It may be added here that a Court of Summary Jurisdiction may commit direct to Borstal a young offender charged with escaping from or breaking the rules of a Reformatory School, and that the Secretary of State may transfer to Borstal suitable young offenders sentenced to penal servitude or imprisonment, and equally may transfer to prison unsuitable young offenders who are reported by the Visiting Committee to be " incorrigible " in a Borstal Institution.

Sentence of Borstal Detention can only be passed (save for Reformatory School offences) by a Court of Assize or Quarter Sessions. For Courts of Summary Jurisdiction a special procedure is provided by Section 10 of the Criminal Justice Administration Act, 1914 : if a young offender who has been previously convicted or has failed on probation is convicted summarily of an offence punishable by imprisonment for one month or more, and the Court thinks Borstal Detention appropriate, it may on conviction commit the offender to Sessions[2] for sentence to Borstal Detention. This procedure has some disadvantages—since the offender is convicted bail cannot be allowed, and he must therefore await sentence in a local prison for a period which may be as long as three months : and in practice the higher Court

---

[1] Provision has now been made for this by the Children and Young Persons Act, 1933.

[2] Or to the next convenient Assize under Section 46 (1) of the Criminal Justice Act, 1925.

N

rarely declines to commit to Borstal. The Young Offenders
Committee therefore recommended that power of direct
committal to Borstal should be given to Summary Courts.
A Summary Court before dealing with a case under
Section 10, or a higher Court before passing sentence of
Borstal Detention, is required to consider a report made to
it by or on behalf of the Prison Commissioners as to the
suitability of the case for Borstal training, and to satisfy
itself that " the character, state of health, and mental condition of the offender, and the other circumstances of the
case, are such that the offender is likely to profit by such
instruction and discipline as aforesaid." These reports are
made to the Courts by the local prison Governors on behalf
of the Commissioners, whom they consult in doubtful cases.
The correct procedure for a Summary Court which contemplates proceeding under Section 10 is to remand the
case to prison and to request the Governor to furnish a
Borstal report : where a young offender between 16 and 21
is for trial at Assizes or Sessions on any charge for which he
could be sentenced to Borstal Detention, the Governor
automatically inserts a report on his suitability for Borstal
in an Appendix to the Calendar : the Governor is also
present at Assizes or Sessions to give evidence if required.

For the preparation of a Borstal report inquiry forms are
sent out to the parents, employers, school-teachers, and any
others who can give useful information ; also to the Police
and (where indicated) the Probation Officer, or Headmaster
of a Home Office School. For the London district, from
which all lads under 21 on remand or for trial are collected
in the Boys' Prison at Wormwood Scrubs, these reports are
supplemented by those of the Woman Visitors, whose
special work is described in Appendix H. In a few provincial prisons similar work is also done by one or two
Woman Visitors. For the whole of this aspect of the work
reference should be made to *Boys in Trouble*, by Mrs. le
Mesurier, who first organised and until 1933 led the Visitors'
work at the Boys' Prison. The information which the
Governor obtains from these reports is of course supplemented by the opinions which he and the Chaplain form
from their personal observation of the case, and is com-

pleted by the report of the Medical Officer on the mental and physical fitness of the offender to profit by Borstal training. The question whether a Borstal sentence is permissible, having regard to the terms of the statute, is of course a legal question which it is for the Court to decide : the function of the Commissioners' Report is to furnish the Court with information as to the habits and character of the offender, and as to whether he is mentally and physically fit to profit by Borstal Detention if the Court finds that sentence to be permissible under the statute.

The view was formerly held that some offenders had such bad records that they were " too bad for Borstal," but with the increase in the number of Borstal Institutions classification has so far developed that the risk of contamination of younger and less experienced offenders by the more hardened is now very much reduced ; and incorrigible cases can always be transferred to prison. On the other hand, improved classification also makes it possible to take lads who might once have been thought " too good for Borstal." The Court of Criminal Appeal has held that it may be right to infer " criminal tendencies " from the nature of the offence or offences of which the accused stands convicted, even if there is no previous conviction, and although in such circumstances the Court may often prefer to make a Probation Order, in many cases the circumstances are such that a sentence of detention is thought necessary : in such cases, in view of the objections to short sentences of imprisonment for young offenders, a Borstal sentence will often be the most appropriate course.

The minimum Borstal sentence is two years, the maximum three years, and the Prison Commissioners have power to release on licence at any time after six months (three months for girls) " if satisfied that there is a reasonable probability that the offender will abstain from crime and lead a useful and industrious life." On the expiration of his original sentence the offender remains for a further year under supervision of the Prison Commissioners. The course of training in the Institutions is based on a normal two-year period, so that with a three-year sentence the total period of control is four years, of which two would normally be spent under training in the Institution and two under supervision outside. (The nature of the training, and the arrangements for licensing and supervision, are described in the subsequent sections.) It follows that a two-year sentence has no effect on the period the normal lad spends in the Institution, but it does curtail the period under supervision : it is therefore unhelpful, and the Young Offenders Committee has recommended that all sentences should be for three years.

As soon as possible after sentence, the offender is sent to the Boys' Prison at Wormwood Scrubs, or if a girl direct to the Borstal Institution at Aylesbury. The object of this " collecting centre " for lads is primarily to enable the authorities to complete their observation and decide to which of the Institutions he should be allocated.

There are at present six Institutions for lads, at Nottingham, Portland, Camp Hill (Isle of Wight), Borstal, Feltham, and Lowdham Grange (Notts) : to Nottingham and Portland are sent the more hardened lads, with the worst records, the older lads of this type going to Nottingham : to Camp Hill, those approximating to the Portland type : to Borstal the " intermediates " : to Feltham those who are more hopeful still, and those who are mentally sub-normal or unstable : to Lowdham Grange the most hopeful cases, for whom the full period of training will probably not prove necessary. The special characteristics of the various institutions will be described later on.

To determine the lad's allocation, and for the guidance of the authorities of the Institution to which he is sent, a careful record is made at Wormwood Scrubs of his history and characteristics : these are studied from the medical standpoint by a special staff of Medical Officers, who devote their whole time to mental, temperamental, and physical examinations, and from the social standpoint by the Women Visitors, who from conversations with the lads, visits to their homes,[1] and inquiries from any helpful source, endeavour to produce a complete picture of the social and temperamental circumstances that have formed their lives and contributed to their lapses into crime.

[1] In London cases : in provincial cases home visits can often be arranged through local helpers.

In the cases of young offenders between the ages of 16 and 17 who are remanded to Remand Homes under the Children and Young Persons Act, 1933, and for whom Borstal reports are required by the Courts, arrangements have been made with the London County Council for collaboration between their officers and the officers of Wormwood Scrubs and Holloway Prisons.

Finally, the allocation is determined by the Commissioner or Assistant Commissioner responsible for the Borstal Institutions, and as soon as a vacancy occurs the lad is sent off with the next party. Meanwhile he has been receiving valuable preliminary instruction in the meaning of his sentence, what it entails, what sort of life he is to expect at the Institution, and so forth. Lantern slides of Borstal life are shown, and generally every effort is made to put the lads into a frame of mind to benefit by the training they are now to undergo.

2. *Training*

"Borstal training is a combination of mental, moral, physical, and industrial training of a strenuous kind. It is not a fixed system, but like other progressive systems is in a state of flux."[1] Certainly the Secretary of State has power to make Regulations for Borstal Institutions, and indeed in 1919 made some, but they are for the most part buried in respectable obscurity : a system that is growing all the time, both in scope and in method, that lives by experiment and fresh thought, cannot be contained within a code of regulations. And subject to these Regulations, the Prison Acts and the Rules made thereunder apply to a Borstal Institution " as if it were a prison " :[2] but a Borstal Institution is in fact many steps removed from a prison—the gates stand open all day, and neither at work nor at play are the lads confined within the walls.

The objects of Borstal training were described in a recent memorandum issued by the Home Office in these words : " The object of Borstal Detention is training rather than punishment. The aim is to give young offenders, whose

[1] Young Offenders Committee, page 95.
[2] Section 4 of the Prevention of Crime Act, 1908

minds are still plastic, a new outlook and a new bent, and, by the personal influence and example of the staff to create a corporate spirit and a standard of social behaviour which may persist after release " : and to this should be added, " The task is not to break or knead him into shape, but to stimulate some power within to regulate conduct aright . . . it requires that each lad shall be dealt with as an individual and shall not be regarded as being the same as any other lad, requiring the same universal prescription."[1]

To sum up these pronouncements, the Borstal system aims to provide a positive training, mental, moral, physical, and industrial, based on sympathetic study of the needs of each individual, and aiming at the development, through trust, increasing with the individual's progress, of personal responsibility and self-control. Work of this sort is, above all, personal work : " The Borstal system has no merit apart from the Borstal staff. It is men and not buildings who will change the hearts and ways of misguided lads. . . . The foundations of the Borstal system are first the recruitment of the right men."[2] The greatest care is therefore taken to select men of the right type with a definite vocation for work of this sort.

To enable the staff to develop the corporate spirit of the lads, and to facilitate individualisation, the House system has been introduced into the Institutions, and is now fundamental to their organisation. Each Institution is divided into from four to six Houses : the numbers in each House vary with the pressure on accommodation, but ideally a House should not contain more than about 70 lads, who again are divided into " groups " or " sections." Each House has its separate block of buildings, with its own sleeping, dining, and recreational accommodation, and its own staff of Housemaster, Assistant Housemaster, Principal Officer, House Officers (usually two) and Matron. The Housemaster stands for each of his lads *in loco parentis.* On him, with the advice and co-operation of his Assistant and the House staff, falls the responsibility of getting to know

---

[1] *The Borstal Book*, page 10. (This is a handbook drawn up by the Commissioners for the guidance of the Borstal staff.)
[2] *Ibid.*, page 17.

each member of his House so intimately that he makes no error in the policy of training which he outlines for him, in the work to which he assigns him, in the reading and recreation in which he encourages him, and in the recommendations which he makes to the Governor for his promotion and, eventually, as to his fitness for discharge. But however susceptible a lad may be to the influence of a good Housemaster, that influence may always be undone unless the " spirit of the House " is also good. The greatest care is therefore taken in the selection of prefects or group-leaders, on whom rest a general responsibility for the tone and good order of each group and of the House, and special responsibilities for looking after certain aspects of the House life, such as games, the library, the dinner tables, etc.

The second main instrument by which the staff can assess the responsiveness of each lad to the training, the growth of his sense of responsibility, and ultimately his fitness for release, is the Progressive Grade System, which aims to confer, in proportion to the lad's progress, increasing trust and freedom of choice and action, increasing responsibility, and increasing privileges. Great care is taken to secure that promotion represents real progress and is not merely mechanical—" Steps must repeatedly be taken to ensure the difficulty of ascent, so that the minimum of promotion may reward a maximum of effort. This can be done by emphasising the responsibilities rather than the privileges associated with each grade, and by a merciless reduction when these responsibilities are not fulfilled. . . . He must show that he justifies the trust and is indeed growing more fit for freedom. If he fails, he must return to the lower order where it is easy to be good."[1] To put it another way, for the first year it is not desirable that the conditions should be brought too close to those of outside life, because the lad has *ex hypothesi* shown himself unfit to live in those conditions. He must prove his fitness through training in a harder school before he can be admitted to the comparative freedom of the higher grades.

For his first year then, or longer if necessary, a lad wears the brown dress of the earlier grades, but at the beginning

[1] *The Borstal Book*, pages 32 and 33.

of his second year he ought to be eligible for the blue dress of the Special Grade. From the " blues " are chosen the leaders—jobs which carry no privileges, but a good deal of extra work and responsibility : the " blues " move freely about the Institution, and take charge of small parties of " browns " : they are allowed outside the Institution, without an officer, for walks, or to attend service at a neighbouring church, or classes at the local technical school. There is nothing but their sense of honour to stop them from absconding at almost any time, but " out of a daily average of special grade lads of approximately 300 . . . during 1926 . . . only eleven abused the confidence placed in them."[1] The privileges to be earned by promotion consist, in the " brown " stages, of increased facilities and time for games and recreation, and in the " blue " stage, besides the trust and comparative liberty of movement, and a gently mounting scale of earnings (which may be spent on cigarettes and so forth at the canteen) in becoming eligible for the annual camp.

The camp has become not only a pleasant and healthful change from institutional routine, but a valuable element in the training. Every summer each Housemaster takes his " blues " to camp at the seaside or in the country for a week. Here " the freedom of life in common, where deception is so much more difficult, establishes a relation between officer and lad which on return to the Institution, so far from endangering discipline, does much to strengthen it. The mutual knowledge gained is invaluable. The officers win the added respect of the lads when seen at closer quarters, the lads show their true colours. Erstwhile paragons reveal a soft or cunning streak, and the lad who was always a nuisance under the necessary restraints of institutional life frequently emerges as a loyal stand-by at every crisis."[2]

In the Borstal Institutions, as in the prisons, the influences of religion can often play a determining part, and here the Chaplain has much greater scope for his work, owing to the freer life and the longer periods for which the lads come

---

[1] Young Offenders Committee, page 96.
[2] *The Borstal Book*, page 55.

under his care. There is also greater opportunity in a Borstal Institution for his work to be seconded by the lay staff, and particularly by the Housemasters and their Assistants.

It remains to fill in the details. " The routine of the Institutions is that of an active day of 15 hours, beginning with physical training, continuing with eight hours work in workshop or outdoor party, and ending with 1½ or 2 hours of school or study."[1] To place first things first, the work a lad does during his training falls into three stages. First with the " cleaners," doing the necessary domestic work : then, while awaiting a vacancy in the trade party to which he has been allotted, he may have a spell of heavy outdoor work with a labouring party, which is good both for his character and his physique. Finally, he passes into a trade party. In the workshops good class work in carpentry and metal work is carried out with power machinery, and employment is also found at tailoring, shoe-making, cooking (especially training for sea cooks), gardening, farming (some institutions have farms of considerable size, all have some land and stock), various adjuncts of the building trades, and other minor trades. At Lowdham Grange the whole of the lads are engaged on building the new Institution, and the conversion of old or the erection of new buildings is a regular source of valuable work. Clearly in two years a lad cannot learn a skilled trade, but they are trained to use tools and simple machinery, and get a grounding which fits them for jobs as improvers and mates on release. The lad's wishes are consulted as to the trade he is to be taught, and to assist in reaching the right decision the Housemaster may consult the parents, the results of the Vocational Tests[2] at the Collecting Centre, and the Borstal Association—who will have to find him work on release.

Education is by means of evening classes. " The whole purpose of continued education at a Borstal Institution is not to impart information or to make dullards into scholars, but to get rusty and ill-controlled brains to work, to enlarge the sphere of interest, and to discover a point of contact with

[1] Young Offenders Committee, page 96.
[2] Carried out under the supervision of the Institute of Industrial Psychology.

each lad."[1] The syllabus therefore is widely varied, and—
while it provides elementary education for the exceptionally
backward, and hobbies and handicrafts for those whose
brain is best approached through eye and hand—by classes,
study circles, societies, lectures, and any other appropriate
methods it seeks to discover and develop interest in nature,
art, literature, music, or any branch of useful knowledge.
Facilities are also given for advanced students to take
correspondence courses, or to attend sessions at the local
technical schools. Closely bound up with this work is the
Library, and not the least valuable influence of the Housemaster may be in guiding a lad along the paths of good
reading.

Physical training under skilled instructors is part of the
daily routine, and in addition each Institution has a well-
equipped gymnasium in which are held evening classes in
gymnastics. The intention is not only to improve physique
but to teach correlation of mind and body. Similarly,
outdoor and indoor sports and games of all kinds are
encouraged, not for amusement only, but as a definite
element of the training : the corporate spirit is encouraged
by the inter-House games, and much may be learned about
a lad on the football field that does not appear in the House.
Each Institution has its playing fields and several have
swimming baths—of course, outside the walls.

A full day's work and study and play for a growing youth
calls for a plentiful diet, and this, though plain, is necessarily on a fuller and more varied scale than that of the
prisons. Meals are taken in the House dining-rooms, the
general arrangement being that each " group " has its own
table. The clothing must also be adapted to the uses it has
to be put to, and it has been found that a grey flannel shirt
with an open neck, shorts,[2] and a jacket, with shoes and
stockings, are the best wear. The turn-down tops of the
stockings are of the House colour, as is the tie supplied for
wear when the lad is not at work. It may here be added
that the staff do not wear uniform, but ordinary " plain
clothes," and the " Borstal tie " (to which reference is

---

[1] *The Borstal Book*, page 50.
[2] Trousers are worn by the older lads at Nottingham.

sometimes heard on the music-halls) is worn by the officers, not by the inmates !

Although administrative necessity must place some limits on letters and visits, the wish of the authorities is to foster any link a lad may have with the outside world, provided the influence promises to be a good one. The letters and visits of parents and relatives are encouraged, and every effort is made to secure the co-operation of parents in encouraging their boys to take full advantage of the opportunities afforded them. Thanks to the generosity of Sir William Morris, a fund exists, under the control of trustees, for paying the expenses of a visit by parents who would otherwise be unable to afford the journey.

We come last to discipline, because most of what is to be said on that subject is already implied. A Borstal officer is expected quietly to control his lads by his personal influence ; there is no demonstration of the " weight of authority." The removal of his uniform and staff sufficiently explains what is intended. Minor offenders are dealt with by their Housemaster, by deprivation of privileges : if a lad comes before the Governor, he may be reprimanded, or deprived of privileges, or reduced in grade, or (in bad cases) placed in separate confinement on restricted diet for not more than 14 days, or placed in the Penal Grade, where he is taken out of his House and located in the punishment cells, employed on some unpleasant work like bone-crushing or stone-pounding, and deprived of all privileges. Longer periods of separate confinement may be ordered by the Visiting Committee,[1] who may also recommend to the Secretary of State the removal of an incorrigibly bad influence to a prison. This expedient, however, is rarely necessary, since the Commissioners have power to transfer such a lad to the Borstal Institution wing at Wandsworth Prison, which is set apart for such cases and for lads whose licences have been revoked.

The Staff of a Borstal Institution consists of Governor and Deputy Governor, Chaplain, Medical Officer, a Steward

---

[1] The Visiting Committee is appointed by the Secretary of State in the same way as the Board of Visitors of a Convict Prison, and exercises similar powers and functions.

and clerical staff, the House staffs already detailed, a Chief Officer at the head of the discipline staff, Works and Hospital Officers (including a Nursing Sister), skilled Instructors in the various trades, and sufficient officers to take charge of the various outside parties. The conditions of service are the same as for the prison service generally,[1] but subordinate officers are specially selected and trained at one of the Borstal Institutions. The Assistant Housemaster, usually a young man of good education (many are University men) with experience of and vocation for work among boys, is appointed by the Prison Commissioners, on the advice of a Selection Board, in an unestablished capacity in the first instance : should he prove fitted for the work, he may after a year or more become established. Housemasters are established officers who may either be appointed direct or—more usually—promoted from among the Assistants. Governors are usually promoted from among the Housemasters. The Matrons are selected either from suitable woman officers of the prison service or from outside applicants.

As one method of securing freshness of thought, fertility of experiment, and circulation of ideas, the Commissioners arrange conferences attended by all Governors, Housemasters, and Assistant Housemasters who can be spared, and a Matron and representatives of the discipline staff from each Institution. The Housemasters and Assistant Housemasters also have an annual camp at which they hold conferences and discussions.

A word may be said in conclusion about the buildings. The Young Offenders Committee said, " The development of Borstal training has undoubtedly been handicapped by being started in old prison buildings, though much ingenuity has been exercised in adapting them. None of the present buildings are wholly suitable for the purpose, and it is to be hoped that when the next Borstal Institution is provided it will be found possible to erect special buildings." Soon afterwards the Commissioners purchased a site at Lowdham Grange, near Nottingham, and they are here erecting a substantial set of buildings designed to express their idea of what a Borstal Institution should be. Of the other five

---

[1] See Appendix C.

Institutions for lads, Borstal and Portland are old convict prisons, but with great structural ingenuity they have been converted to fulfil very adequately the purposes of a Borstal Institution, for which they are now much better adapted than the buildings at Feltham, which was formerly a L.C.C. Industrial School. Camp Hill, formerly a Preventive Detention Prison, was taken over as a Borstal Institution in 1931, and with a very little conversion will do very well. Nottingham Borstal Institution is housed in the old local prison, which was reopened as an emergency measure in 1932 to meet the continued pressure on accommodation : there is land outside the walls, and though a prison can never make an ideal Borstal Institution it is not altogether unsuited for the older and more hardened type of lad and somewhat sterner conditions of training at this Institution.

At Borstal there is a considerable farm with 272 acres of land outside the walls, at Lowdham there is also an extensive farm, at Feltham and Portland there are smaller farms with some 70 acres of land, and at Camp Hill there is a considerable tract of forest land under reclamation.

There is some difference of opinion as to whether the dormitory system or the separate room system is better suited to the needs of a Borstal Institution. Until recently all the Institutions, save one House at Borstal, had separate rooms, and generally speaking this system seems to be suitable for and preferred by the majority of lads, besides having certain administrative advantages. On the other hand many lads can be handled more successfully in dormitories, and the whole of Feltham Borstal Institution is being converted to this system, while an additional dormitory House has been added at Borstal. Opinion being evenly divided as to the relative advantages, the more economical dormitory system is being adopted throughout the new buildings at Lowdham, and more experience will be gained when this Institution has been for some time in use.

The Institution for girls is at Aylesbury : here, within one wall, stand the Women's Convict Prison and the buildings of what was formerly a State Inebriate Reformatory. These latter, which are quite separate from the prison buildings, are light and pleasant, and have proved well adapted to the uses of a Borstal Institution. Girls who misbehave in the Institution, or whose licences are revoked, are confined in a separate wing of the prison building. Prison and Borstal Institution are under one Governor and a common staff, but there is no contact between the woman prisoners and the girls. Outside the walls are some 20 acres of farm land, on which a number of girls are employed, both with stock, dairying, and market gardening. The industrial employment is mainly in laundry work, cooking, and needlework, and girls are fitted for domestic service by special courses in cooking and other subjects. The intention and spirit of the system are the same as in the boys' Institutions, but the method is adapted both to the smaller numbers (see following table) and to the special problems presented by delinquent girls. The House system, for example, is not applied at Aylesbury.

The Governor is assisted by a Deputy Governor, and there is also a fully qualified teacher of physical training, to which special attention is given, while outdoor games are also encouraged. Education is largely in the hands of paid teachers from outside, who take evening classes in both handicrafts and general subjects.

The numbers committed by the Courts to Borstal Detention have noticeably increased of recent years, as is shown by the following table :

Year.	Numbers sentenced to Borstal Detention.			Daily Average Population in Borstal Institutions.		
	Male.	Female.	Total.	Male.	Female.	Total.
5 years ended 31st March, 1924 (average)	524	55	579	—	—	—
Year ended 31st December, 1927	568	34	602	1179	74	1253
1928	635	48	683	1203	85	1288
1929	679	51	730	1232	104	1336
1930	725	49	774	1285	116	1401
1931	873	47	920	1488	113	1601
1932	1011	47	1058	1781	114	1895

In consequence the pressure on the accommodation of the Institutions during the last two years has been such that, even with the addition of Camp Hill and Nottingham, it has been impossible to keep the Houses down to the optimum population, and lads have had to wait for vacancies at the Collecting Centre for longer than is desirable. The number of committals for 1932, moreover, showed so marked an increase over those for 1931, that the opening of a seventh Institution may become necessary in 1934.

3. *Licensing, After-care, and Results*

The period which a lad must serve before earning his release on licence is not arrived at by any automatic system. The promotion of an inmate from grade to grade is only made on the recommendation of the Institution Board, composed of certain of the senior members of the Staff, and it is not till that Board is satisfied that the lad has derived all the advantage he is likely to get from his training that his case is brought before the Visiting Committee with a view to licence : this stage is reached in a few cases in a comparatively short time ; in others it may be necessary to keep them for $2\frac{1}{2}$ years or more ; but in the majority of cases it is found that the maximum benefit is derived in about two years. If the Visiting Committee are satisfied, they send a recommendation for release to the Prison Commissioners, who then issue a licence.

This licence is subject to conditions, the principal condition being that the lad shall place himself under the care of the Borstal Association, and shall obey their instructions as to where he shall live, and as to his employment, and generally shall conduct himself to their satisfaction. If he is reconvicted, or if the Borstal Association report to the Commissioners that his behaviour is unsatisfactory, his licence may be revoked and he will then be arrested and returned to the special Borstal Institution wing at Wandsworth.

The work of the Borstal Association is not less important than the training in the Institution. This Association is a semi-official body, the expenses of which are met in part by voluntary subscriptions and in part from public funds. It acts under the Presidency of the Home Secretary and an Executive Committee, with central offices in London, and some thousand " associates " throughout the provinces. The Director is Sir Wemyss Grant-Wilson, who controls the whole of the work throughout the country : he has at his London office a full-time staff, whose pay and conditions of service are approved by the Prison Commissioners, and there is a branch office at Liverpool with a full-time paid staff. The provincial associates are usually probation officers or social workers : the latter act on a voluntary basis, charging their expenses to the Association.

The Association is in close touch with all the Institutions, and the Director is a member of each Visiting Committee. Its work begins as soon as a lad is received, when the local associate gets in touch with his home. In due course a representative from the Central Office visits the lad in the Institution, discusses his plans with him and with the authorities, and writes to the local associate : where the report from him shows that the home is a good one and work can be found, disposal is easy—but this is a rare combination. Of 783 lads who were discharged to the care of the Association in 1930 over 400 had no homes at all or homes from which one or both parents were missing : in many more cases the home influence was bad or unhelpful, and in such cases it is often necessary to find lodgings as well as jobs. It is a remarkable tribute to the Association and its associates that in only 30 out of these 783 cases—of whom 209 were discharged for a second time after revocation—was there a complete failure to find work, and this at a time when some 2½ millions of men were out of work.

When all plans have been made, and the licence has been received, the lad is given a good outfit of civilian clothing and taken to London to the offices of the Borstal Association. Here he is given some admonition designed to prepare him for a world somewhat less sympathetic than the one he has just left, and sent off to report to his local associate, on whose tactful and sympathetic handling in the first difficult days of freedom much may depend. During the two years or so that the Association has a lad under its supervision, it has to act in two capacities, the reconciliation of which requires a good deal of tact—first as friend and adviser, then as " policeman " : and even the first of these needs boundless sympathy and understanding, for firmness must be combined with persistent patience if the feet of a wayward youth, too apt to throw up an uncongenial job or resent the hard word of a foreman, are to be kept firmly along the narrow path of hard work and right living. But while the Association is ready to make allowances and to help again and yet again, its aim is to make the lads stand on their own feet, and as soon as it becomes evident that there is a decided preference for standing on other peoples', then friendly advice must change to stern warning : if this is ineffective a report must be made to the Prison Commissioners, and revocation of licence will probably follow.

When a licence has been revoked, whether on reconviction of the licensee or on a bad report from the Borstal Association, the failure is sent to the Borstal Institution wing at Wandsworth, where he may be kept for the unexpired portion of his period of licence or for 12 months, whichever is the longer. In practice a " revokee " is rarely kept more than six months—unless he has been given a fresh sentence of imprisonment by a Court, in which case he must serve that out. For at Wandsworth the conditions are substantially those of prison life, and the purpose is not to give further Borstal training, but to make it clear to the lad that he has been a fool and that the way of the transgressor is hard, and also to allow the authorities to find out why he has failed. For this purpose an Investigation Committee meets once a month and reviews all the cases, examining the lad's Borstal record with reports from the police and the Borstal Association, and hearing his own story : this Committee consists of the Commissioner or Assistant Commissioner responsible for the Borstal Institutions, representatives of the Visiting Committee, of the staff of the Borstal Institution wing, and of the Borstal Association. When they have made up their minds about a lad they fix the time he is to serve, and in due course he is licensed again. It is not often that a licence is revoked more than once—a lad who persists in going off the rails after revocation is, unless

o

he is young and not evidently hopeless, usually written off as a loss.

For girls the work of the Borstal Association is done by the Aylesbury After-care Association, a similarly constituted body with headquarters at the Institution, whose Director, Miss Lilian Barker, C.B.E., J.P., is also Governor of the Institution (and of the Convict Prison).

It is the opinion of the Commissioners, which has been endorsed by the Young Offenders Committee, that the Borstal system has justified itself by its success. In the Annual Report of the Commissioners for 1924–1925 it was stated that out of 6,140 lads discharged from Borstal Institutions since their first establishment in 1910, some 35% were known to have been reconvicted, and 65% were satisfactory : of those reconvicted, a substantial number settled down after their first lapse, so that roughly speaking seven out of ten of these persistent young offenders have been restored to a decent and honest standing in society. Comparable figures have not subsequently been published, but in 1929 the Borstal Association reported that :

Of lads whose period at Borstal was their first experience of Institutional treatment over 71% have become satisfactory.

Of those who had been to prison before Borstal only 55% have become satisfactory.

Of those who had been sent both to a reformatory and prison before Borstal less than 49% had made good.

The Association points out that these figures suggest that Borstal is most likely to be effective if it is tried at an early stage.

CHAPTER XVII

PRISON POPULATIONS : STATISTICS

A. Composition and Characteristics

IN this chapter we shall consider, so far as the published statistics[1] inform us, the composition, characteristics, and numbers of the present-day prison population ; and in the second section of the chapter we shall see what influences affect those numbers and how they are related to the general movement of crime. It must, however, be understood at the outset that inferences as to the state of crime cannot be drawn from statistics of prison populations. It is not paradox but sober fact to state that the majority of prisoners are not criminals and that the majority of criminals do not come to prison : only about one quarter of the persons received into prison are convicted of crime in the ordinary sense, i.e. of indictable offences, and some two-thirds of those convicted of indictable offences are not sent to prison.

It is also necessary to understand that in considering numbers reference will be made both to " receptions " and to " daily average population." But x receptions in a year does not mean that x separate individuals have been received : many persons are " received " more than once in a year, and a special record kept in 1927 showed that in that year 35,964 individuals accounted for 43,674 receptions. There is no fixed ratio between the number of receptions and the daily average population,[2] which reflects not only the volume of receptions but the average length of sentences : thus x receptions for an average of three months would give a d.a.p. only half as large as x receptions for an average of six months. The varying relation between

---

[1] The latest figures available are those for 1931.
[2] Hereafter referred to as " d.a.p.".

receptions and d.a.p. over a period of years shown in Graph A (page 221) represents, broadly, variations in the practice of the courts as to length of sentences, or in the relative numbers of major and minor offenders.

Size and Distribution of Population.—In 1931 there were 53,043 receptions of men and 6,442 of women, giving a d.a.p. in all the establishments under the control of the Commissioners of 10,884 men and 792 women, or 11,676 in all. This population was distributed over the different types of establishment as follows :

	Local Prisons.	Convict Prisons.	Borstal Institutions.	P.D. Prisons.	Totals.
Men	7,909	1,363	1,488	124	10,884
Women	628	48	113	3	792
Total	8,537	1,411	1,601	127	11,676

In 1932 the d.a.p. increased to 12,803, and for the first six months of 1933 it was 13,006. These figures must, however, for analysis and explanation, await the publication of the prison and criminal statistics for 1932. Their relation to the general movement of prison populations and of crime is discussed in Section B of this chapter.

Composition of Population.—The receptions for the year 1931 may be analysed as in table on opposite page.

It will be observed that of the receptions of men 41·3%, of women 41·7%, were for non-payment of sums of money —fines or debts ; that only 44% of the receptions of men, and 38% of women, were under sentence of detention in any form without the option of a fine ; and that only some 26% of men and 19% of women had been sentenced to such detention for indictable offences.

These figures will, however, take on a different aspect when translated into terms of d.a.p., since prisoners on remand or awaiting trial, or those committed for minor offences or non-payment of monies, are in prison usually for quite short periods. Thus, while the numbers of prisoners serving longish sentences received during a year may be comparatively small, the proportion of such prisoners in prison at any one time will always be comparatively large. Of a d.a.p. in local prisons of 8,537, " remands and trials " accounted for 632, or about 8%, and "debtors " for 897, or about 10·7% : the remaining 81·3% were convicted prisoners of whom only 456 (some 5·3% of the d.a.p.) were fine cases. These figures should be remembered when estimating the effect of alternative methods of dealing with

	Men.		Women.	
	Numbers.	%	Numbers.	%
Committals on remand or for trial, not followed by imprisonment . . .	7,588	14·3	1,299	20·2
Committals under civil process	12,818	24·2	197	3·0
Committals in default of paying fines	9,051	17·1	2,492	38·7
Imprisonment without the option of a fine				
(i) non-indictable offences	9,704	18·2	1,235	19·2
(ii) indictable offences .	12,498	23·6	1,144	17·8
Sentences of Penal Servitude	511[1]	1·0	28	} 1·1
Sentences of Borstal Detention	873	1·6	47	
Totals . .	53,043	100·0	6,442	100·0

fines and debtors : but it should also be remembered that it is just as much trouble to go through the reception of a prisoner for seven days as for seven years, and that both the cost and the efficiency of the prison service are affected by the pressure of merely routine work involved in receiving and discharging short sentence prisoners.

Length of Sentences.—The following tables show the position as regards length of sentences for 1930 and 1931 as compared with 1913 : the figures published for the intermediate years since the war are, unfortunately, not on a comparable basis :

[1] Nineteen men were sentenced to P.D. to follow the P.S. : no woman was sentenced to P.D.

(a) *Imprisonment.*

Length of Sentence.	Percentage of Total Receptions.					
	1913.		1930.		1931.	
	M.	F.	M.	F.	M.	F.
1 month and under	78·8	87·8	55·3	75·5	53·1	72·9
3 months and over 1 month . .	13·4	8·8	23·6	14·9	24·0	16·0
6 months and over 3 months . .	4·0	2·6	12·4	6·7	12·4	7·5
12 months and over 6 months . .	2·5	·7	6·1	2·4	6·0	2·2
18 months and over 12 months .	1·0	·1	2·0	·4	2·2	·6
Over 18 months .	·3	—	·6	·1	·7	·2

(b) *Penal Servitude.*

Length of Sentence.	1913.	1923.	1930.	1931.
3 years	522	319	344	335
Over 3 and under 5 years .	89	43	56	96
5 years and upwards .	222	116	136	102
Life	12	3	—	—
Totals . .	845	481	536	533

Of the receptions for one month and under in 1931,
sentences of not more than 14 days accounted for 9,012 men
and 1,900 women, or 29% and 39% of the total receptions of
persons sentenced to imprisonment.

Remembering our criterion of three months as the
minimum period of any value for training purposes, it is
interesting to note that in 1931 no less than 77·1% of the
receptions of men and 88·9% of the receptions of women
were for periods of three months and under—a little better
than in 1913, when the relative percentages were 92·2 and
96·6. The higher proportion of longish sentences of
imprisonment is no doubt to be explained by the very
considerable falling off since 1913 in the number of sentences
of penal servitude : it is, however, to be noted that there is

a marked tendency to pass more sentences of penal servitude now than was the fashion a few years ago, though the very long sentence tends increasingly to fall out of favour.

It is worth while again to note the different aspect assumed by these figures when translated into d.a.p. In 1931 the percentages of the d.a.p. in the different groups were as follows :

Under 1 month	7·7
1 month and under 3 months .	14·9
3 months ,, ,, 6 ,, .	18·2
6 months ,, ,, 12 ,, .	28·3
12 months ,, ,, 18 ,, .	18·7
18 months and upwards . . .	12·2

From these figures it appears that of the convicted prisoners actually in the local prisons at any one time over 77% are serving sentences of three months and upwards.

Committals in Default of Fines.—The recent appointment by the Secretary of State of a Departmental Committee to investigate, among other things, the question of committals to prison in default of payment of fines, makes it of especial interest to consider the present position in this respect and to compare it with that in previous years.

In 1931, of 32,471 receptions of men and 4,946 of women after conviction, 9,051 or 28% of men, and 2,492 or 50% of women, were imprisoned for non-payment of fines. The d.a.p. of " fines " in local prisons was, however, only 5·3% of the total.

The following table shows the position in 1913 and during the last five years :

Year.	Total Receptions on Conviction.		Receptions in Default of Payment of Fines.		Percentages.	
	M.	W.	M.	W.	M.	W.
1913	105,510	33,550	52,286	22,866	49·6	68·2
1927	36,038	7,636	10,743	4,178	29·8	54·7
1928	34,423	6,026	10,104	3,156	29·0	52·0
1929	31,734	5,208	8,937	2,642	28·0	50·0
1930	33,541	5,458	9,716	2,781	29·0	51·0
1931	32,471	4,946	9,051	2,492	28·0	50·0

Two facts emerge from this table—first that the position has completely changed since 1913, and second that the change is no longer progressive. It has already been suggested in earlier chapters that the major change is due to the operation of those sections of the Criminal Justice Administration Act 1914 which provided for the allowance of time for payment of fines.

To test this assumption let us look at the position from another angle. In 1913, of 502,659 persons fined on conviction, 75,152 or 14·9% were committed to prison in default : for 1930 the figures were 496,247—12,497—2·5%. It is true that conditions have materially changed since 1913, when nearly one-third of the fines were for drunkenness, and 1930, when less than one-tenth were for drunkenness and nearly one-third for motoring offences. But the elimination of motoring offences makes no significant change in the relative percentages, and the elimination of drunks gives for the remainder a percentage of committals of about 9% in 1913 and 1·3% in 1930. Again, of the persons fined for drunkenness the percentage of committals was 26·2 in 1913 and 13·6 in 1930. It is therefore clear that the improvement has been a real one, and the percentage of committals is now so small that the field for further improvement has been considerably narrowed—for it must be conceded that in the absence of an alternative sanction imprisonment in default remains essential, and evidently effective, to secure the payment of fines.

Nevertheless, out of the 11,543 cases of imprisonment in default in 1931, there were no less than 6,920 in which time to pay had not been allowed, and there were 501 committals in default of young people under 21 years old. And doubt has been expressed whether Section 5 of the C.J.A. Act 1914, which requires the means of the offender to be taken into consideration when the amount of a fine is fixed, is always present to the minds of magistrates. There is, therefore, still scope for improvements which would be both socially beneficial and administratively economical.

Nature of Offences.—The following table gives in respect of 1931, with comparable figures for 1913 and 1924, information as to the numbers of persons committed to prison

in respect of each of the main classes of offence into which
crime is generally divided for statistical purposes :

Offences.	Men.			Women.		
	1913.	1924.	1931.	1913.	1924.	1931.
Indictable offences.						
Crimes of violence against the person . . .	514	300	395	114	76	73
Sexual crimes (including bigamy) . . .	1,064	1,057	809	10	29	12
Crimes against property with violence. . .	1,956	1,690	2,304	—	—	—
Crimes against property without violence . .	16,806	10,474	10,626	2,593	1,277	1,106
Forgery and coining . .	115	106	148	—	—	—
Other offences . . .	543	434	270	154	92	99
Totals . . .	20,998	14,061	14,552	2,871	1,474	1,290
on-indictable (akin to indictable).						
Assaults	7,486	2,798	2,037	1,136	301	116
Frequenting, etc. . .	1,770	1,392	1,412	—	—	—
Malicious damage . .	1,650	712	746	392	113	66
Indecent exposure . .	866	525	484	242	159	78
Cruelty to children . .	1,028	379	156	731	139	88
Other offences . . .	1,558	354	305	553	122	87
Totals . . .	14,358	6,160	5,140	3,054	834	435
Other non-indictable offences.						
Drunkenness . . .	37,033	7,407	5,118	15,116	3,989	2,366
Begging and sleeping-out .	14,822	2,544	1,818	1,049	193	114
Breach of police regulations	5,982	1,070	1,037	2,730	644	298
Offences against the Poor Law	4,343	2,030	1,684	—	—	—
Prostitution offences . .	—	—	—	8,063	1,086	205
Offences in relation to railways	866	246	187	—	—	—
Other offences . . .	7,108	2,357	2,935	850	327	238
Totals . . .	70,154	15,654	12,779	27,808	6,239	3,221
Grand Total . .	105,510	35,875	32,471	33,733	8,547	4,946

202   THE MODERN ENGLISH PRISON

Classification.—An analysis of the d.a.p. in local prisons in 1931 gives the proportions of the different categories into which convicted prisoners are divided, in round figures, as follows :

Ordinary Class	56
Star Class (with II Division) . . .	23
Special Class	11
Young Prisoner Class	5
Convicts and B.Ds. awaiting removal . .	5
	100

Degree of Education.—The following table summarises the statistical information as to the degree of education of prisoners received on conviction in 1931 :

1. Illiterate.		2. Read and Write Imperfectly.		3. Moderate Proficiency.		4. Read and Write Well.		5. Superior Education.		6. TOTALS.	
M.	W.	M.	W.	M.	W.	M.	W.	M.	W.	M.	W.
839	138	2,631	340	26,884	4,137	1,953	263	164	18	32,471	4,946

Too much importance should not, perhaps, be attached to these figures, which are based on somewhat rough and ready tests relative to school " Standards."

It is of greater significance to note that, in an investigation carried out by two prison Medical Officers in 1926,[1] the conclusion was reached that the average mental age of the ordinary adult male remand prisoner of not more than 35 was " equal to that ascertained in the general population by the authors of the *Report on Mental Deficiency* of the Boards of Education and Control in 1929," i.e. 14 years.

Occupations.—The following table summarises the statistical information as to the occupations of prisoners received on conviction in 1931. This information, being based solely on the prisoners' own statements, is not always reliable.

[1] Drs. Grierson and Rixon, *Lancet*, August 7th, 1926, quoted by Dr. Young in " Character in Young Delinquents," the *British Medical Journal*, August 26th, 1933.

(1)	(2)	Offences.		
OCCUPATIONS.	Total Number of Convicted Prisoners.	(3) Indictable Offences.	(4) Non-Indictable Offences (akin to Indictable Offences)	(5) Other Non-Indictable Offences.
Vagrants and prostitutes and others of known bad character	2,474	425	318	1,731
Labourers, charwomen and other unskilled workpeople .	18,497	7,077	3,096	8,324
Domestic servants. . .	1,510	603	130	777
Miners, farm hands, factory operatives, merchant seamen and other skilled workpeople	10,860	5,420	1,680	3,760
Members of the Army, Navy or Air Force . . .	337	255	29	53
Shop assistants, clerks, waiters, etc.	1,702	1,220	123	359
Shopkeepers, tradesmen, farmers, etc. . . .	180	118	16	46
Professional employments, merchants and persons of independent means, etc. .	96	85	5	6
Unclassified	1,761	639	178	944
Total . .	37,417	15,842	5,575	16,000

Sex and Age.—The following table shows the grouping by sex and age of each main class of the convicted prisoners received in 1931, with a percentage comparison of the totals with 1913.

We have already (in Chapter XII) reviewed the questions peculiar to women.

As regards men, what is most noticeable is the definite preponderance of the age-group 21–30, and—as compared with 1913—the increased weightage of the groups 16–21 and 21–30 at the expense of the older groups. This aspect concerns rather the causes of crime than the state of the prison population, and is further discussed in the second part of this chapter. It is, however, worth suggesting here

Offences.	1. Total of Convicted Prisoners.			2. 16 and under 21.		3. 21 and under 30.		4. 30 and under 40.		5. 40 and under 50.		6. 50 and under 60.		7. 60 and above.	
	Totals.	M.	W.	M.	W.	M.	W.	M.	W.	M.	W.	M.	W.	M.	W.
Indictable	15,842	14,552	1,290	1,912	96	5,449	324	3,642	394	2,027	297	935	135	587	44
Non-indictable (akin to indictable)	5,575	5,140	435	313	9	1,801	98	1,392	147	894	129	446	41	294	11
Other non-indictable	16,000	12,779	3,221	531	61	2,703	375	3,423	793	2,912	1,008	1,750	603	1,459	381
Totals	37,417	32,471	4,946	2,756	166	9,953	787	8,457	1,334	5,833	1,434	3,131	779	2,340	436
Percentages 1931				8·5	3·3	30·6	15·9	26·0	27·0	18·0	28·9	9·6	15·8	7·2	8·8
Percentages 1913				6·1	2·6	24·8	18·4	29·0	34·1	21·3	29·0	9·9	11·3	8·7	4·4

that this change in disposition of age groups may be ascribed not only to an increase in the number of young people committing indictable offences, but to the much smaller proportion, in 1931, of receptions for non-indictable offences, with which young persons are not so much concerned as older ones.

But that there is nevertheless a noticeable increase in the number of young men of 21–30 committing serious crime is shown by reference to the age-groups of persons convicted of indictable offences : in 1903 the proportion of such persons falling into the age-group 21–30 was 26·6% ; in 1913 it was 28·7% ; in 1931 it was 33·6%.

Recidivism.—A recidivist is, for prison purposes, one who serves more than one sentence of imprisonment, and recidivism may be defined shortly as persistence in crime. The statistics of recidivism are therefore of primary interest in the study of any prison system, since they are commonly accepted as the criterion by which the effect of the system may be estimated.

It is nevertheless open to question whether conclusions of real value can be drawn from such figures in relation to any particular period of prison administration. In the first place, their true meaning cannot be accurately estimated in isolation : it is necessary to consider them in the light of the practice of the Courts over the same period, and also of the state of crime and of relevant social conditions. Further, it would in all probability be impossible to present them in such a relation to comparable figures relative to other prison systems, or to earlier periods of the same system, as would enable conclusions to be drawn as to the relative success of the period in question in preventing recidivism. No more, therefore, is attempted here than to present the latest available figures.

In their Annual Report for 1931 the Commissioners for the first time published statistics of recidivism distinguishing between persons convicted of drunkenness and others—a valuable departure, since the merging with figures relative to crime of the high proportion of receptions for drunkenness has evidently obscured to some extent the real meaning of the figures. This is one of the factors which adds to the difficulty of any comparison with pre-war years, when the receptions for drunkenness were enormously higher.

Of the receptions in 1931 of prisoners convicted of offences other than drunkenness, 51% of men and 47% of women were known to have been in prison before ; 18% of men and 25% of women had previous proved offences but had not previously been sentenced to imprisonment ; and only 31% of men and 28% of women were not known to have previous proved offences.

The extent of recidivism among those known to have been in prison before may be judged from the following table :

	M.	W.
1 to 5 previous sentences . .	9,252	714
6 to 10 ,, ,, . .	2,309	203
11 to 20 ,, ,, . .	1,454	151
Over 20 ,, ,, . .	824	153
Totals . .	13,839	1,221

Of the receptions for offences of drunkenness, which accounted for 15% of the imprisonments of men and 48% of women, 57% of men and 78% of women were known to have been in prison before ; 21% of men and 19% of women had previous offences but had not been in prison ; and 22% of men and 3% of women were not known to have previous proved offences.

The high rate of recidivism among these " drunks " may be judged from the following table :

	M.	W.
1 to 5 previous sentences . .	1,642	627
6 to 10 ,, ,, . .	419	306
11 to 20 ,, ,, . .	437	308
Over 20 ,, ,, . .	412	610
Totals . .	2,910	1,851

The Commissioners in their Annual Report for 1931 estimate that this considerable proportion of their annual reception is accounted for by 7–800 male and 4–500 female alcoholics.

The Departmental Committee on Persistent Offenders, on a survey of these figures, concluded that " a very large proportion of ' first-timers ' are not reconvicted. Of the comparatively small number of persons who return to prison on a second sentence a large proportion, however, come back repeatedly ; the probability of relapse increases with the number of previous sentences, and a substantial part of the prison population consists of a ' stage army ' of individuals who pass through the prisons again and again. The inference is that the present methods not only fail to check the criminal propensities of such people, but may actually cause progressive deterioration by habituating the offenders to prison conditions which weaken rather than strengthen their characters." It is perhaps fair both to the prison authorities and to the Courts to add that, in the light of the context, this grave conclusion appears as a condemnation primarily of the inadequacy of the weapons which the present system allows them to use.

But this problem cannot be estimated only by considering the careers of those " who are neither deterred nor reformed " by their first sentence of imprisonment, which is, in the words of this Committee, " a turning point in an offender's career, and his treatment in prison on this first occasion will often have a decisive influence on his future career." Fortunately it is now possible to give a definite answer to the question what effect a first sentence has on offenders in general : figures are now available, which were not available to the Committee—though they accurately anticipated their general effect—showing what proportion of persons sentenced to imprisonment for the first time during the year 1930 had not been recommitted by 31st December, 1932. The effect of these figures is, that of those who had no previous offences, 90·5 had not returned to prison, while of those who had previous offences (but had been dealt with otherwise than by imprisonment) 82·8 had not returned. Of all those who had not previously been sentenced to imprisonment taken together, 88% had not returned to prison. These figures refer to local prisons, but it has been noted at

the end of Chapter XIV that the Central Association
estimates that of the Star Class convicts 90% do not again
offend.

These figures will of course have greater value when they
have been tested over a longer period than 2–3 years, and it
is not possible to compare them with similar figures for other
periods : but taken by themselves they do seem to suggest
a conditions of affairs not altogether unsatisfactory.

B. Fluctuations in Prison Populations

Fluctuations from 1880–1932.—The fluctuations from 1880
to the present time of the total annual receptions into and
the daily average population in English prisons are shown
in diagrammatic form on Graph A.

This graph shows four distinct periods of movement—
first a slow fall, followed by a steady rise from 1890 to the
period of the Boer War ; second, a sharp rise during the
early years of the twentieth century to the highest recorded
level about 1904 ; third, a prolonged fall, checked about
1908, but sharply accelerated during the Great War, to the
lowest recorded figure in 1918 ; and finally a short rise,
followed by ten years of minor fluctuations with peaks in
1922 and 1932—the last year giving the highest population
since 1914.

The most striking feature of this graph is the totally
different levels of population that are divided, roughly, by
the decade 1908–1918. In the earlier part of this century
over 150,000 receptions were recorded annually, and for
much of the time the daily average population exceeded
20,000 : between 1920 and 1930 receptions never reached
50,000, and only once did the d.a.p. reach 12,000. In 1932
the d.a.p. was 12,803, and for the first half of 1933 it has
exceeded 13,000.

It is of more than historical interest to examine the
possible reasons for this major change, as compared with
pre-war years, in the general level of prison populations,
since such an inquiry may throw light both on the general
considerations which affect the numbers in prisons, and on
the important question whether the change is permanent or

whether the sharp rise of the last two years may be leading us up again to something like pre-war figures.

Reduction of Non-Indictable Offences.—Our first clue is found in the table of figures on page 201, which shows that while the receptions of persons convicted of serious (indictable) offences are to-day about two-thirds of what they were before the war, those of minor (non-indictable) offences are only about one quarter of the pre-war figure.

There can be no doubt that, although the allowance of time for payment of fines has considerably reduced the number of minor offenders sent to prison, the reduction in the number of such persons in prison is primarily due to an enormous and continuing reduction in the volume of minor offences. This is shown by the following table, which gives for certain years the numbers of persons actually dealt with by the Courts for the kinds of non-indictable offence most commonly leading to imprisonment. See also Graph C.

Offence.	Annual Averages.		1930.	1931.
	1910–14.	1925–29.		
Drunkenness . . .	193,354	68,491	58,609	46,846
Assaults . . .	43,032	29,000	26,001	22,317
Prostitution . . .	10,682	3,278	1,323	1,438
Begging. . . .	25,419	4,803	4,675	4,016
Sleeping-out . . .	8,594	2,163	1,995	1,612

What is the explanation of this most gratifying improvement—gratifying especially in that—at any rate up to 1931—it was continuing with increasing momentum ?   In general, since of all these offences it may be said that they connote a low standard of living and of social behaviour, it may be assumed that any marked reduction in their volume would suggest an improved standard of living and behaviour among the poorer classes.   Conditions during the war, when wages were high and employment plentiful, no doubt laid the foundations of such an improvement, and it was during the years 1915–1919 that the numbers of persons dealt with for non-indictable offences reached their lowest point : the consolidation of this position must be ascribed primarily to the effect of the restrictions on the sale of intoxicants

P

imposed in 1914 and 1915. The convictions for drunkenness have fallen from 183,828 in 1914 to 84,191 in 1916, and 46,846 in 1931 ; and it may confidently be assumed that this diminution of drunkenness has also tended to reduce the minor offences bound up with drunkenness, both directly, and, so far as it contributes to an improved standard of living, indirectly.

It is a noteworthy fact that the prolonged industrial depression of recent years, with its figures of unemployment far exceeding, year after year, anything hitherto recorded, so far from witnessing an increase in these offences, has seen them decreasing ever more rapidly (see Graph C). If motor car offences are excluded, the number of persons dealt with for non-indictable offences was in 1931 far less than in the prosperous years 1920–1924 or the war years 1915–1919. During a pre-war period of depression (1905–9) the numbers were nearly double those of 1931. It does, therefore, seem safe to assume that in modern social conditions unemployment is not accompanied by any increase in the volume of non-indictable offences.

Increase of Indictable Offences.—When we turn from social nuisances to crime proper, as represented by indictable offences, we find a different situation and a different set of considerations affecting the numbers received into prison. Whereas, as compared with pre-war years, non-indictable offences have decreased and are decreasing, indictable offences have increased and are increasing.

On the whole, the best available index of the volume of crime in any year is the ratio of the number of indictable offences reported to the police to the size of the population. It has been pointed out in the Introductions to the Criminal Statistics that deductions from this index must be made with the reservation that some part of the increase of recent years may be due to improved police methods of recording and other purely statistical factors, and this consideration should be borne in mind in looking at Graph B, on which this index number is shown in diagrammatic form from 1857 to 1931. It will be seen that since 1926 the index has been higher than at any time since about 1880.

Space does not permit, nor is this the place for, any close

analysis of the figures relative to serious crime or of the social and other conditions that affect them : the whole subject is very fully treated in the Introductions to the Criminal Statistics from 1928 onwards. It is, however, of some interest to our study of prison populations to summarise broadly the conclusions arrived at in those Introductions.

These offences fall roughly into three groups—offences against the person, including murder, manslaughter, felonious woundings, sexual offences, etc. ; offences against property, and miscellaneous (see table on page 201 for fuller details). The position as regards the first group is entirely satisfactory—offences of violence are not increasing, but decreasing. The position is the same as regards many of the offences in the third group. Nevertheless, whether we look at the numbers of indictable offences known to the police, or the numbers of persons tried for such offences, the total figures for 1931 are notably higher than for 1930, and considerably higher than for any previous period of the present century.

The explanation lies in the increase of offences against property, and particularly those classed as " with violence," i.e. robbery with violence, burglary, housebreaking, shop-breaking, etc. Special interest attaches to the first of these crimes owing to the exceptional publicity given by the Press to almost every instance of it that comes to light, but in fact its incidence is very small : in 1931 there were 208 such cases reported to the police, which is fewer than in 1930 though greater than in the three or four preceding years and in the years 1910–14 : there are not nearly so many of these crimes as there were in the early part of the century and the years after the war. Burglary is another " sensational " crime which is definitely decreasing. The major increase is connected with crimes of " breaking in," which have practically doubled as compared with 1910–14. Attention has also been drawn to the very high incidence of this class of offence among the young : of the 3,200 persons convicted of shop-breaking in 1931 some two-thirds were under 21, and nearly 44% were under 16 ! We may therefore with safety assume that most of these " breakings-in " are not due to a " wave " of professional crime but to unfavourable social influences among the young.

In this connection it is interesting to note that on consideration of the relation between industrial depression and crime, no evidence is found that unemployment has increased the incidence of crime among men over 30. So far as a connection is traced, the class principally affected is shown to be juveniles under 16 in the depressed areas, whose offences are mainly petty " picking and stealing " : the crimes of violence against property tell most heavily against young men in relatively prosperous areas.[1] Probably the majority of these men under 30, whose youth or adolescence was passed under the unfavourable influence of the war years, have been faced ever since they left school with the hopelessness of unemployment : they have not fallen out of work—they have never been able to get into work.

But to arrive at clear and well-authenticated conclusions on this complex subject would be an independent labour of no small dimensions, requiring a special technique and experience. Sufficient has perhaps been said to suggest that too facile dogmatisms as to the " causes of crime " should be accepted with reserve. The diagrams given in Graph C include the curve of unemployment, but this can hardly be taken as evidence of the actual state of unemployment on a basis of absolute comparison throughout the century, as it is based at different times on different methods of recording, and is materially affected by administrative factors, e.g. in 1911 and 1920 when new Acts came into force.

Reduction in Committals for Indictable Offences.—Why is it then, in face of a definite increase in the volume of indictable crime as compared with pre-war years, that fewer criminals are in fact coming to prison ? Before an offender gets to prison three things must happen—the police must catch him, he must be convicted, and the Court must decide that imprisonment is the proper punishment. It is said that certainty of punishment is a more efficient deterrent

---

[1] It is worth drawing attention to the fact that the high incidence of serious crime in the age-group 21–30 is not peculiar to this generation (cf. pp. 203–5).

than severity of punishment, and though this proposition
is not susceptible of statistical proof, it is interesting to
consider certain considerations which bear on it. It has,
for example, been suggested (Introduction to Crim. Stats.,
1928) that no statistical connexion can be shown between the
practice of the Courts in passing more or less severe sentences
and the increase or decrease in the general volume of crime :
it does not, however, follow that in the case of a particular
type of offence—especially an offence of a new type which
shows signs of becoming fashionable—a determination on
the part of the Courts to impose really long deterrent sentences in all such cases will not have the effect of nipping
the fashion in the bud.

But the fiercest determination on the part of the Courts
would lose in effect if the offenders could reckon on the odds
being against their being caught : it is therefore of some
interest to see how far we can gauge the relative " certainty
of detection " by reference to published statistics. There
is published annually a table showing what proportion of the
offences known to the police are cleared up to the point
where proceedings are justified, and this index, over a period
of years, is shown in diagrammatic form in Graph B. Conclusions from these figures can only be drawn with reservation (cf. p. 210), and it should in particular be noted that the
reduction in the percentage cleared up is not general, but is
due in the main to failure with the recent increase in
" breakings-in."[1]

The next stage in securing certainty of punishment is that
the guilty offender should be convicted. It may be that in
some countries this factor would be of greater statistical
weight than it is in fact in England, but it is not without
interest to set out the position here as shown by the figures
for—say—1930. In that year 147,031 indictable offences
were reported to the police, and 66,049 persons[2] were proceeded against in respect of them. In 49,846 cases the
summary court found the charge proved and dealt with the
case, in 8,710 cases they committed for trial, in 1,367 cases

---

[1] Introduction to Crim. Stats., 1928, p. xix.
[2] Proceedings against one person may of course cover several separate
offences.

they discharged the prisoner, and in 5,816 they acquitted him of the charge : 310 were "otherwise disposed of" (e.g. died, absconded, removed to asylums). During the same year there were 8,384 persons for trial at Assizes and Quarter Sessions, of whom 1,443 were either acquitted or not tried, 20 were found guilty but insane, and 6,921 were convicted.

The third—and decisive—factor is that Courts are no longer sending so many convicted offenders to prison. The real explanation of the reduction in the imprisonments for indictable offences is the increasing use of the Probation Act, 1907 : this factor of course also operates to a lesser extent in regard to non-indictable offences, while the effect of allowing time for fines is also felt, again to a lesser extent, in regard to indictable offences. The following table illustrates the position, *excluding Juvenile Courts* :[1]

Year.	Number found guilty of indictable offences.	Number dealt with under Probation Act 1907, including dismissal after charge proved, binding over and placing on probation.		Number dealt with by Imprisonment, Penal Servitude, or Borstal Detention.	
			%		%
1913	42,957	11,796	27·5	21,965	51·1
1923	38,787	13,111	33·8	15,091	38·9
1930	45,630	18,951	41·5	14,769	32·4
1931	47,650	19,349	40·6	14,778	31·0

These figures speak for themselves so far as concerns the effect on prison populations. It is, moreover, significant that in spite of the noticeable increase in indictable offences during the last few years the confidence of the Courts in the use of more lenient methods had not, apparently, been lessened as lately as 1930, though the figures for 1931 do suggest a check. But very curiously this check is not, as one would expect, accompanied by an increase in the percentage sent to prison—on the contrary, the reduction here continues. The explanation seems to be in an increasing

[1] The figures include the few juveniles (i.e. under 16) dealt with in Adult Summary Courts or Courts of Assize and Quarter Sessions.

disposition on the part of Summary Courts to impose fines for indictable offences.

It is unfortunate that in the absence of complete statistics for 1932 one can only speculate on the reasons for the sudden leap in the prison population of that year, which in the autumn soared beyond 13,500, and has now settled down to a steady 13,000. It is known, though figures are not yet available for publication, that the total receptions during the year increased by some 4,500, and there is reason to think that, in face of a continuing increase of indictable offences, the Courts were not only sending more people to prison but passing longer sentences—though this latter tendency was hardly noticeable in 1931.

Inferences on this subject are difficult to draw, owing to the marked variations in the practice of the Courts not only over periods of time but as between one Court and another. The Commissioners in their Annual Report for 1931 quote figures which are of considerable interest. While the general average percentage of persons over 16 sent to prison out of the total convicted of indictable offences was 31%, the figure in the Metropolitan Police District was 43% and in the rest of England 29%, while the figures for certain large towns vary from 15·7 to 58·8. It is interesting to speculate as to the effect on prison populations of any general assimilation to one or other of these widely divergent standards !

TABLE I

Receptions into Prison of Non-Criminal Prisoners in each year from 1910 to 1931.

Year ended 31st Dec.	Total for each year (excluding Surety Prisoners).	Including those committed by Summary Courts.			By County Courts.
		Under Wife Maintenance or Affiliation Orders.	In Default of Payment of Rates.	In Default of Payment of Income Tax.	
1910	17,571	4,145	2,761	No informa-tion available	7,832
1911	16,030	3,913	2,657		7,118
1912	14,197	3,816	2,465		5,824
1913	14,026	3,554	2,379		5,759
1914	11,132	3,608	1,740		3,906
1915	4,983	1,667	1,063		1,544
1916	3,750	1,381	665		1,072
1917	2,654	1,195	358	20	565
1918	1,857	931	188	50	296
1919	2,581	1,703	123	193	216
1920	4,552	3,152	209	453	234
1921	8,279	5,383	702	1,162	414
1922	12,874	No information available			
1923	12,330	7,047	1,877	1,094	1,605
1924	11,060	6,181	1,752	624	1,984
1925	11,349	6,139	1,699	355	2,625
1926	10,911	6,035	1,780	191	2,346
1927	12,312	6,759	1,926	193	2,875
1928	13,483	7,056	2,268	151	3,448
1929	12,860	6,879	2,002	84	3,381
1930	13,205	6,778	2,031	88	3,810
1931	12,969	6,563	2,345	81	3,398

PARTICULARS RELATING TO INDICTABLE OFFENCES

Year.	Indictable Offences known to Police.	Incidence of (1) per Million of Population.	Approximate numbers cleared up.		Persons proceeded against.
			Numbers.	Percentage (3) of (1).	
	(1)	(2)	(3)	(4)	(5)
1857	91,671	4,761	—	—	66,429
1870	90,532	4,023	—	—	65,173
1880	98,440	3,828	—	—	68,244
1890	81,773	2,843	—	—	60,801
1900	77,934	2,417	—	—	60,426
1905	94,654	2,785	—	—	68,747
1910	103,132	2,881	77,112	74·7	72,860
1911	97,171	2,687	74,688	76·8	68,575
1912	101,997	2,791	80,571	78·9	73,642
1913	97,933	2,653	75,934	77·5	69,265
1914	89,387	2,418	69,644	77·9	63,665
1915	77,972	2,210	64,950	83·3	59,287
1916	80,653	2,328	67,857	84·1	61,851
1917	88,864	2,599	73,462	82·6	66,016
1918	87,762	2,579	68,525	78·0	61,048
1919	87,827	2,440	64,502	73·4	57,378
1920	100,827	2,681	73,928	73·4	64,383
1921	103,258	2,726	75,734	73·3	64,276
1922	107,320	2,813	74,853	69·7	60,767
1923	110,206	2,870	76,938	69·8	59,256
1924	112,574	2,905	79,625	70·7	59,746
1925	113,986	2,931	81,815	71·7	59,993
1926	133,460	3,416	105,756	79·3	79,591
1927	125,703	3,199	94,431	75·1	65,163
1928	130,469	3,305	94,007	72·0	63,194
1929	134,581	3,398	94,908	70·5	61,723
1930	147,031	3,694	101,164	68·8	66,049
1931	159,278	3,983	107,644	67·6	68,747

a Excluding 110 transportation cases.

Notes—The figures for 1857, 1870, 1880 and 1890 relate to
Column 3—No figures are available for column 3
Column 6—For certain of the earlier years shown,
Summary Jurisdiction Act, 1879, are not

KNOWN TO POLICE. YEARS 1857 TO 1931.

Persons found guilty.	Persons dealt with under the Probation Act.	Persons sent to Penal Servitude or Imprisonment.	Persons sentenced to		Year.
			Borstal Detention.	Preventive Detention.	
(6)	(7)	(8)	(9)		
33,001	—	30,555a	—		1857
37,097	—	33,450	—		1870
42,904	—	32,999	—		1880
40,782	—	24,628	—		1890
43,711	—	22,432	—		1900
51,299	—	28,257	—		1905
58,217	18,729	26,096	490	178	1910
54,314	17,351	23,758	436	57	1911
59,289	19,716	23,994	521	89	1912
55,872	19,405	21,463	538	67	1913
51,687	18,749	18,195	462	43	1914
49,514	19,304	11,802	242	11	1915
52,935	20,110	11,027	394	21	1916
57,276	21,383	11,930	572	22	1917
52,652	19,232	11,303	632	20	1918
47,289	16,372	12,732	667	20	1919
53,086	18,531	15,518	625	44	1920
53,518	18,779	15,756	569	61	1921
50,978	19,960	15,520	523	35	1922
49,749	21,536	14,788	500	27	1923
50,643	23,594	14,132	528	38	1924
50,583	23,747	13,580	538	27	1925
68,393	29,711	14,537	616	23	1926
55,762	25,548	14,446	603	42	1927
54,514	26,386	13,726	682	31	1928
53,324	26,369	13,526	734	29	1929
56,767	28,365	14,294	774	37	1930
59,367	29,197	13,838	920	20	1931

the year ended 29th September.
until after the year 1909.
persons discharged under Section 16 (1),
included.

GRAPH A.

TOTAL ANNUAL RECEPTIONS ON CONVICTION AND DAILY AVERAGE POPULATION IN ENGLISH PRISONS FROM 1880 TO 1932.

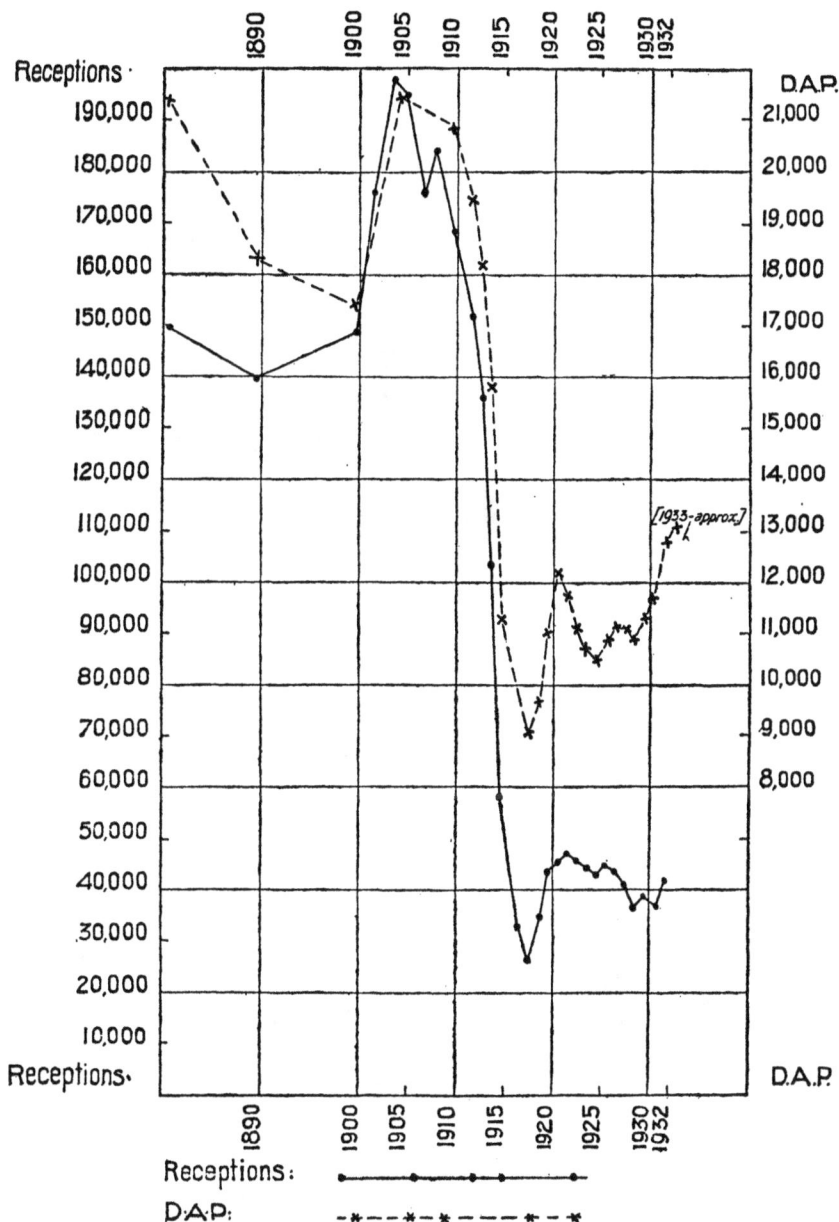

GRAPH B.

INCIDENCE OF INDICTABLE OFFENCES, AND PERCENTAGE CLEARED UP, 1857 TO 1931.

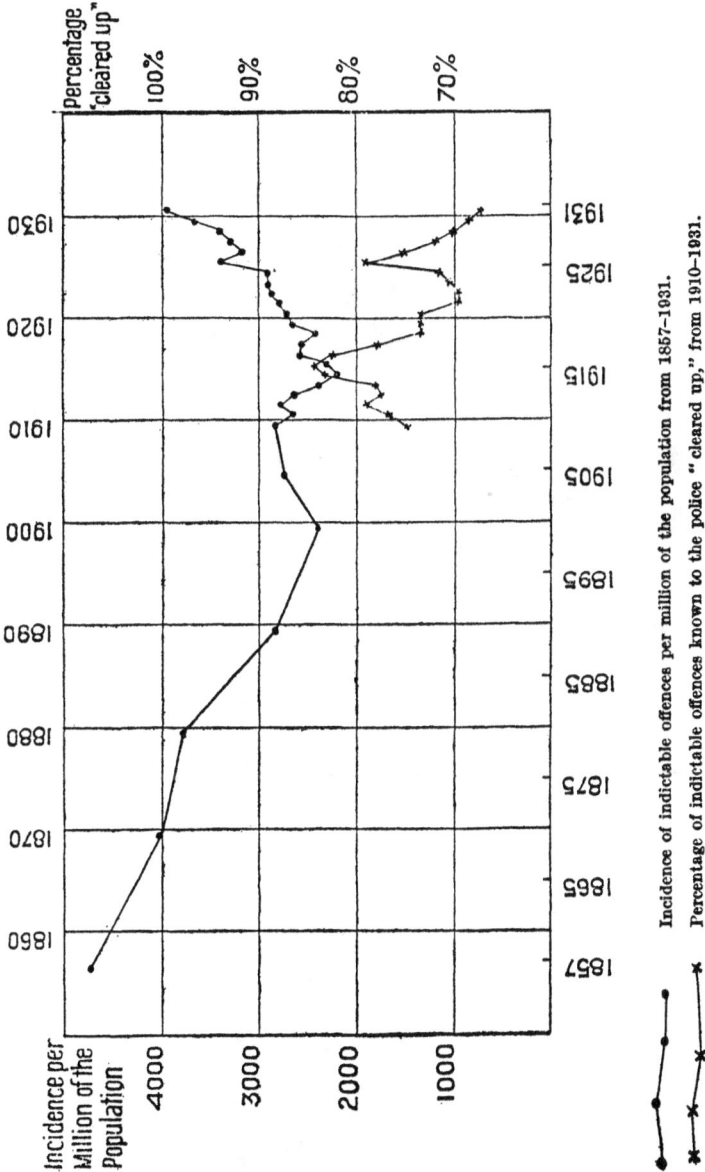

223

GRAPH C.

CRIME IMPRISONMENTS AND UNEMPLOYMENT.

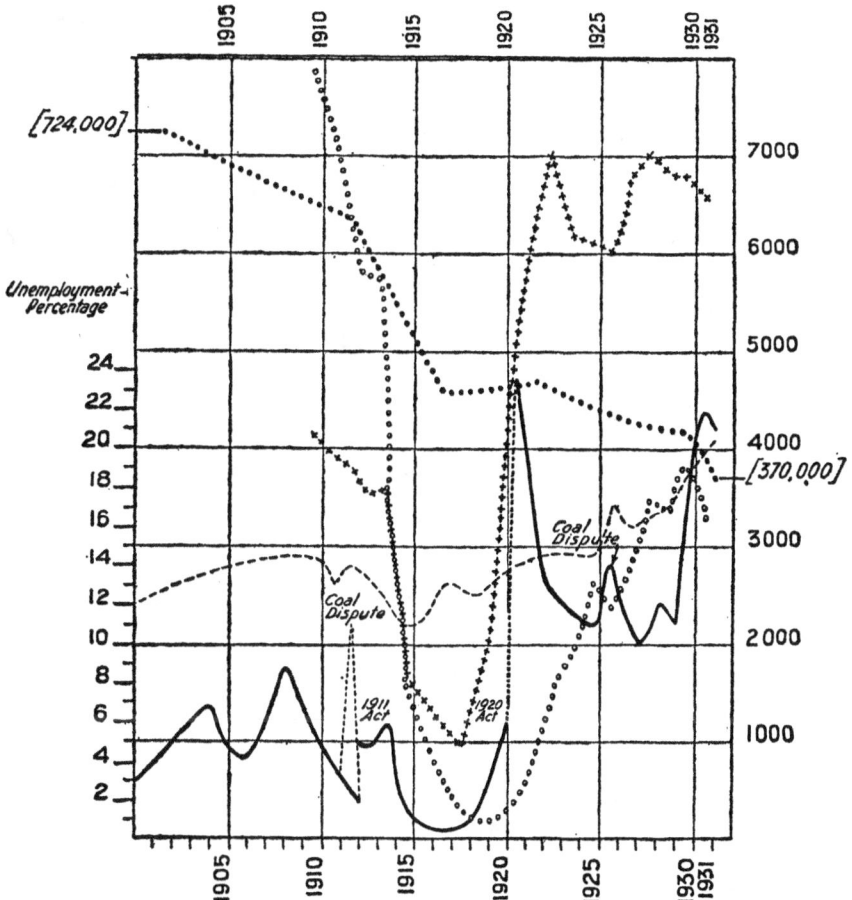

Percentages Unemployed (*Ministry of Labour Gazette*, March 1932).

Incidence of indictable offences per million of population (Graph B).

Number of persons dealt with for non-indictable offences (excepting motor car offences).

Receptions into prison under maintenance or affiliation orders.

Receptions into prison of County Court debtors.

APPENDIX A

THE PRINCIPAL STATUTES DEALING WITH IMPRISONMENT, PENAL
SERVITUDE, BORSTAL DETENTION, PREVENTIVE DETENTION AND
OTHER QUESTIONS TO WHICH REFERENCE HAS BEEN MADE

(1) *Imprisonment*

Statute.	Year.	Short Effect.
5 H. IV, cap. 10	1403	Justices may only imprison in the Common Gaol.
7 J. I, cap. 4	1609	Justices to provide a House of Correction in every County.
32 G. II, cap. 28	1758	Justices required to make rules for the government of their prisons, to be approved either by the Judge of Assize or Justices in Sessions. This act was intended primarily for relief of debtors.
14 G. III, cap. 59	1774	Laid down provisions as to overcrowding, cleanliness and sanitation, etc., in prisons. The intention was the prevention of gaol fever.
22 G. III, cap. 64	1782	*First General Prisons Act.* Provided for inspection of Houses of Correction by the Justices : separation of males and females and of felons : enforcement of " hard labour " : enacted Statutory Rules on these and other matters.

227

Statute.	Year.	Short Effect.
24 G. III, cap. 54	1784	Justices to make rules for separation of males and females, and of the different classes of prisoners, e.g. debtors, felons, misdemeanants, convicted and unconvicted.
31 G. III, cap. 46	1791	Required Justices to make rules for their prisons in accordance with the directions and provisions of Blackstone's " Hard Labour " Act of 1778 (19 G. III, cap. 74) and to inspect them regularly and report in writing to Quarter Sessions.
4 G. IV, cap. 64	1823	*Second General Prisons Act.* Revised and consolidated previous acts, and enacted the first Statutory Code of Prison Rules, some of which survive, in whole or in parts, to-day. Provided in detail for all aspects of prison administration. Based on principle of Classification rather than Separation.
5 & 6 W. IV, cap. 38	1835	Required JJ. to submit their codes of Rules for approval of S. of S., and empowered S. of S. to appoint persons to inspect prisons.
2 & 3 Vic., cap. 56	1839	*Third General Prisons Act.* Revised and amended previous acts, enacted further Statutory Rules and provided for the " individual separation of prisoners . . . during the whole or any part of his imprisonment."
5 & 6 Vic., cap. 98	1842	Miscellaneous amendments and provisions, especially as to facilities for building prisons.
7 & 8 Vic., cap. 50	1845	Authorised appointment by S. of S. of a Surveyor-General of Prisons.

Statute.	Year.	Short Effect.
25 & 26 Vic., cap. 44	1862	Recognised Discharged Prisoners Aid Societies.
26 & 27 Vic., cap. 79	1863	Provided for appointment of Prison Ministers for ministration to prisoners not of Established Church.
28 & 29 Vic., cap. 126	1865	*Fourth General Prisons Act.* Revised and amended previous Acts. Amalgamated Gaols and Houses of Correction as Local Prisons. Enacted a new code of Statutory Regulations. Defined and regulated Hard Labour.
40 & 41 Vic., cap. 21	1877	*Fifth General Prisons Act.* Transferred control of all local prisons to S. of S. Appointment of Prison Commissioners. Rules to be made by S. of S. supplementing statutory rules.
47 & 48 Vic., cap. 51	1884	Supplementary to act of 1877 as to power of S. of S. to enlarge and build prisons.
61 & 62 Vic., cap. 41	1898	*Last General Prisons Act.* Repealed Code of 1865 : all Rules to be made by S. of S. Opened way for abolition of Hard Labour. Established "Triple Division of offenders." Provided for earning of remission of sentence, and other miscellaneous matters.

(2) *Penal Servitude*

31 C. II, cap. 2	1679	Recognised the practice of pardoning felons consenting to be transported, and leaving them in gaol till they could be transported.
8 G. III, cap. 15	1768	Judges given power to order transportation of condemned felons, such orders to have effect of a conditional pardon.

Statute.	Year.	Short Effect.
16 G. III, cap. 43	1775	Prisoners who could not be transported might be put to hard labour ; imprisonment of convicted felons in hulks authorised, also in County prisons.
19 G. III, cap. 74	1778	"Blackstone's Act." Provided for building of Penitentiary Houses in which convicted felons might be confined with hard labour, which was now defined : laid down principles of "separate confinement " and " instruction."
5 G. IV, cap. 84	1824	Regulation of imprisonment in hulks, and of transportation (this having been resumed to the Australian Colonies).
9 G. IV, cap. 83	1828	Tickets-of-leave in Australia authorised. Act establishing Millbank as a " Penitentiary " of convicted felons.
1 & 2 Vic., cap. 82	1838	Act establishing Parkhurst as a Prison for Young Convicts.
5 & 6 Vic., cap. 29	1842	Act establishing Pentonville as a Prison for preliminary confinement of convicts.
13 & 14 Vic., cap. 39	1850	Power to S. of S. to appoint Directors of Convict Prisons to be directors of Millbank, Parkhurst and Pentonville Prisons and other places for the confinement of male offenders under sentence of transportation in place of the former separate governing bodies and the Superintendent of Hulks.
16 & 17 Vic., cap. 99	1853	"Penal Servitude " might be ordered by Courts in place of sentences of transportation of

Statute.	Year.	Short Effect.
		less than 14 years. Licences to be at large in the United Kingdom might be granted to convicts.
20 & 21 Vic., cap. 3	1857	Sentences of transportation abolished ; sentences of P.S. to be passed for all offences punishable by transportation.
27 & 28 Vic., cap. 47	1864	Raised minimum sentence of P.S. from 3 years to 5 years. Stricter regulation of licence-holders.
34 & 35 Vic., cap. 112 (sec. 5)	1871	" Prevention of Crimes Act "— further regulation of licence-holders.
54 & 55 Vic., cap. 69	1891	Reduced minimum sentence to 3 years.
16 & 17 G. V, cap. 58	1926	Power to sentence to penal servitude where an offender is liable to consecutive terms of imprisonment amounting to not less than 3 years.

(3) *Miscellaneous Statutes*

34 & 35 Vic., cap. 112	1871	*Prevention of Crime Act.* ss. 3–5. Regulation of convict licence-holders. s. 6. Registration and photography of prisoners. s. 8. Power to order an offender to be under police supervision.
7 Ed. VII, cap. 17	1907	*Probation of Offenders Act.* Set up probation system.
7 Ed. VII, cap. 23	1907	*Criminal Appeal Act.* Set up Court of Criminal Appeal.
8 Ed. VII, cap. 59	1908	*Prevention of Crime Act.* Part I. Set up the Borstal System. Part II. Set up Preventive Detention.

Statute.	Year.	Short Effect.
4 & 5 Geo. V, cap. 58	1914	*Criminal Justice Administration Act.* ss. 1–6. Obligation to allow time for payment of fines, and related matters. ss. 7–9. Amendments and extension of the Probation Act 1907. ss. 10, 11. Amendments of Part I of Prevention of Crime Act 1908, as to committals to B.Is. ss. 12, 13. Limitation of sentences of imprisonment to periods of 5 days or over, and power to order detention in police custody up to 4 days. ss. 16–18. Miscellaneous provisions relating to imprisonment. s. 26. Regulation of licence-holders and persons under police supervision.
15 & 16 Geo. V, cap. 86	1925	*Criminal Justice Act.* Part I. Amendment and extension of the Probation Act 1907. s. 46. Power to commit offenders to the next convenient Assizes or Quarter Sessions for Borstal sentence.
23 Geo. V, cap. 12	1933	*Children and Young Persons Act.* Revised and consolidated previous statutes dealing with children and young persons. Covers Juvenile Courts and Home Office Schools.

APPENDIX B

EXTRACTS FROM REPORT OF THE
SELECT COMMITTEE OF THE HOUSE OF LORDS
ON PRISON DISCIPLINE, 1863

(1) *Separate Confinement* (pp. v and vi)

" In all questions of prison discipline, it appears to the Committee that the principle of separation, or association, stands first for consideration. Next in importance is the question of solitary confinement.

Association, or a mixed system of association and separation, prevails, as has already been shown, in many gaols. Such anomalies, however, are, in the opinion of the Committee, very objectionable. They should be removed at the earliest practicable time ; and their present existence can only be justified by the difficulties of reconstruction, and the natural reluctance of the local authorities to incur a heavy expenditure. The Committee entertain a very decided opinion on this head, and having reference to the course of legislation now extending over many years, and the agreement in opinion and practice of the highest authorities, they consider that the system generally known as the separate system must now be accepted as the foundation of prison discipline, and that its rigid maintenance is a vital principle to the efficiency of county and borough gaols.

The Committee concur entirely in the opinion expressed by the Commissioners of Pentonville, who in their Fifth Report, dated 5 March, 1847, give the following decisive testimony in its favour :—

' We concluded our Third Report by strongly urging the advantage of the separation of one prisoner from another as the basis and great leading feature of all prison discipline.

' On reviewing this opinion, and taking advantage of further experience, we feel warranted in expressing our firm conviction

233

that the moral results of the discipline have been most encouraging, and attended with a success which we believe is without parallel in the history of prison discipline.'

And in conclusion they state as their deliberate opinion that

'The separation of one prisoner from another is the only sound basis on which a reformatory discipline can be established with any reasonable hope of success.'

It is clear that this kind of separation must depend upon the judgment and capacity of those who are locally responsible for the administration of the prison. The newest and most elaborate form of construction is an insufficient safeguard if there is any relaxation of the necessary precautions by the local authorities, whilst an old and defective gaol may in some degree, by care and proper arrangement, be adapted to the requirements of our present system.[1] Looking, however, to the ordinary arrangements which exist in most gaols, there are so many interruptions to the regularity of prison discipline, instruction is given at such various times, and the communications which pass between prisoners and other persons are so frequent, that separation, though it exists nominally in many, is really to be found in few gaols ; but where it does exist, it exercises both a reformatory and a deterrent effect. Under these circumstances, the Committee are of opinion that the principle of separation should be made to pervade the entire system of the prison, and no adequate reason has been assigned for the relaxation of the rule in school, in chapel and at exercise. It is, however, to be understood that this conclusion is not intended to limit the *cellular* and other religious instruction which the chaplain may think fit to administer to any prisoner.

[1] This appears actually to be done in the city gaol of Bristol. See Mr. Gardner's evidence. Sir J. Jebb has added his testimony to the complete success, so far as separation is concerned, which is obtained by the system that is there pursued. "I know of one prison," he says, "which is on the old construction (I speak now of the prison at Bristol), where a most effective discipline is well kept up by the Governor, with very inadequate means as regards construction : he has small cells, which are only fit for sleeping in, and cannot be certified for separate confinement ; but by dividing his treadwheel into close compartments, and letting out the prisoners from their cells at certain distances from each other, and shutting them up in the compartments of the treadwheel, and marching them back again to their cells in the same way, no two prisoners can ever see each other, and you really obtain the advantages of separate confinement without the expense which is entailed by the construction of a prison." (1207.)

The justice of this view is generally admitted, except as regards the association of prisoners in chapel. Upon this point the evidence is conflicting.

The main objections to the use of separate compartments in chapel appear to resolve themselves into two ; one moral, the other mechanical. The first is grounded upon the opinion that a gaol chapel ought to be as much as possible like a parish church ; the second arises from the belief that the compartments, from the mode of their construction, tend to facilitate rather than impede communication between the prisoners, and to induce them to deface the panels of the stalls by indecent writings or drawings. Neither of these objections seems to the Committee to be valid. With regard to the first, they conceive that the benefits which may be derived from giving a more devotional character to the chapel cannot outweigh the advantages of preventing the communication of prisoners with each other, and of rendering difficult their recognition by their fellow-prisoners on their discharge. With regard to the second objection, the Committee think that by adopting arrangements of the same nature as those which are in force in Bristol Gaol, the separation of the prisoners may be effected without difficulty. For these reasons the Committee recommend that the separate system should be carried out in the chapel as well as in every other part of the prison."

(2) *Labour* (pp. vii and viii)

" There can be little doubt that a large proportion of the discrepancies which exist in the discipline administered in different prisons is due to the different constructions placed by the local authorities upon the sentence of hard labour ordered by the Court. Committees of both Houses have repeatedly recommended, and various statutes have distinctly required, the infliction of hard labour : but it is clear from the evidence that there is the widest possible difference in the opinions held as to what constitutes hard labour. The Committee believe that, with the best intentions on the part of the local authorities, there is in many gaols a great and unfortunate misapprehension on this head, and that until some more precise definition of hard labour is assigned, the grave public inconvenience and injustice which now arise from the inequalities of penal discipline in neighbouring counties or even in parts of the same county, must continue in full force. The first step towards a better and more uniform system throughout the country, would, in the opinion of the Committee, be found in an authoritative definition, by Act of Parliament, of the term of hard labour. Nor does there seem to be in this any practical difficulty. Of the various forms which are in force in the several prisons, the treadwheel, crank and shot-drill alone appear to the Committee properly to merit this designation of hard labour. Of these, the treadwheel and the crank form the principal elements of penal discipline, and might be safely prescribed as such in any future Act of Parliament. But whenever the local authorities may think it necessary to supplement the treadwheel or crank by further hard labour, recourse may satisfactorily be had to shot-drill, and this form of hard labour may be combined with the industrial employment in the later stages of imprisonment. Industrial occupation, though it may vary in amount and character, is so much less penal, irksome and fatiguing, that it can only be classed under the head of light labour. The picking of oakum must be regarded as an intermediate form of work ; but under no circumstances, and to no class of prisoners, can industrial occupation be made an equivalent for a corresponding amount of hard labour as administered by means of the wheel, the crank or the shot-drill.

It has been alleged in the course of the evidence, that the use of the treadwheel and crank degrades, irritates and demoralises the prisoner ; but the Committee, after full consideration, see no reason for entertaining this opinion, and, under certain conditions, they highly approve of the use of both these instruments of prison discipline. Productive labour, indeed, holds out to the local authorities the hope of some profit, and is somewhat less irksome to the prisoner ; it is therefore frequently urged, that the crank and wheel, if used at all, should be confined to the pumping of water, or the grinding of corn, or some other remunerative work. The Committee cannot subscribe to this view. If the local authorities can make use of the crank or treadwheel for productive work, the Committee see no objection to such an arrangement, but they think it essential that every prisoner sentenced to hard labour should be employed upon the crank or treadwheel for a minimum period, and that in no case should the regular enforcement of this system be relinquished or impaired for the sake of making the labour remunerative.

As regards the short sentences or the earlier stages of imprisonment, the Committee believe that they are adopting a safe and a moderate standard when they recommend that every prisoner sentenced to hard labour shall, unless exempted by medical authority on grounds of health, be employed at the treadwheel or crank not less than eight hours per day the first three, and not less than six hours per day during the next three months of the first year of imprisonment."

(3) *Reformatory Influences* (pp. xii and xiv)

" The possible reformation of offenders is an object which successive Committees of both Houses have had in view. The House of Lords Committees of 1835 and 1847 both refer to it ; the House of Commons Committee of 1850 recognises its importance in marked terms. The Committee fully admits that it forms a necessary part of a sound penal system, but they are satisfied that, in the interests of society and of the criminal himself, it is essential that the other means employed for the reformation of offenders should always be accompanied by due and effective punishment. Sir W. Crofton, indeed, whose experience on this subject entitles him to much consideration, does not hesitate to go so far as to say that moral reformation of character is greatly assisted by a preliminary course of stringent punishment.[1]

They also believe that the inefficiency of the present system of administering the law in ordinary prisons is shown in the large

[1] Q. " Your view would be, that, having regard to the requirements of prison discipline, and the ultimate reformation of the prisoner, the penal element, whether it be by the treadwheel or by the crank, ought to form a constituent part of that system ?

A. " I am quite satisfied about that, and more now than ever, because nine years since we established reformatory schools at a great cost of money and time : and I think that when we do so much to prevent crime, and to train those youths up, so that they shall not pursue criminal avocations, we are bound, on the other hand, to be more stringent in the punishment of those who still pursue a course of crime in spite of what we have done for them ; and I am quite satisfied that the managers of reformatory schools would consider their hands to be strengthened by the prisoner knowing that pursuing a course of crime would lead to really stringent punishment, and other procedure externally, which I shall, I hope, point out presently.

Q. " It has been given in evidence before this Committee by some of the witnesses, that, in their opinion, the effect of the treadwheel and the crank is to create a sense of degradation in the mind of the prisoner ; is that your opinion ?

A. " I have no doubt it may do so ; but, combined with other industrial pursuits, I think it might be counteracted. I believe that the penal element is so necessary that the feeling of degradation I must place on one side altogether in my mind."

proportion of prisoners who, after undergoing a period of confinement, are again committed to prison under fresh sentences. The relapse of such prisoners is partly due to the difficulty which any one of tainted character has in finding employment. In this view, the question of rendering assistance to prisoners on discharge, as a preventive measure calculated to reduce the rate of re-convictions, appears to the Committee to be deserving of serious consideration.

2. The Committee, whilst they are compelled to admit that the reformation of individual character by any known process of prison discipline is frequently doubtful, believe that the majority of prisoners are, within certain limits, open to the influences of encouragement and reward. They therefore attach importance to the establishment, in every prison, of various gradations, which shall rise from the penal and disciplinary labour of the tread-wheel, crank or shot-drill, into the higher and less irksome stages of industrial occupation and prison employments. And with that view they would make the entire system strictly progressive throughout its several stages.

7. The Committee give full credit to both the inspectors for their wish to improve the general condition of the gaols placed under their supervision ; but they feel bound to express their dissent from many of the ruling principles of prison discipline, which they, and especially Mr. Perry, have laid down. They do not consider that the moral reformation of the offender holds the primary place in the prison system ; that mere industrial employment without wages is a sufficient punishment for many crimes ; that punishment in itself is morally prejudicial to the criminal and useless to society, or that it is desirable to abolish both the crank and treadwheel as soon as possible."

(4) *Prison Punishments* (p. xiii)

" Punishments for offences committed in prison form so important a part of prison discipline, that, under any system, they cannot be overlooked. The Committee believe that in many cases misconduct is best punished by degradation from a higher to a lower and more penal class, combined with harder labour and a more sparing diet ; in others, by the ordinary penalty of reduction of food, or by solitary confinement in dark cells—if separated by a sufficient distance from each other, and from the other parts of the prison—but that where the offender is hardened, and the offence deliberately repeated, corporal punishment is the most effective, and sometimes the only remedy. The most experienced witnesses are unanimous as to the wholesome influence of corporal punishment ; some, indeed, have stated that they have never known it ineffective ; and the Committee wish to record their opinion of its great value as one form of disciplinary correction."

(5) *State of Certain Prisons* (p. xv)

" Some of these minor prisons, such as that of Falmouth, have repeatedly been condemned in the inspectors' reports as altogether unfit for the custody and penal discipline of prisoners, and it would almost seem that the inspector in such cases has given up the fruitless duty of making his inspection, and republishing his annual censure. There is frequently an unrestrained association of untried with convicted, juvenile with adult prisoners, vagrants, misdemeanants, felons ; dormitories wholly without light or control or regulation exist, and in one case the governor admits that, in the event of a disturbance at night amongst the prisoners, the warder on duty would not be allowed to enter the room, for fear of an assault being made upon him ; occasionally two and more prisoners have been allowed to sleep in the same bed. In one instance the beds themselves have been removed, lest the prisoners should break them up and make use of the fragments, whilst in another gaol the beds form so large an element of the life of the prisoners that no less than 15 hours out of the 24 are allowed to be given to sleep. It appears that in several places the building itself is out of repair, or is overlooked by adjoining houses ; that sometimes one man alone is in charge of the gaol, and responsible for its security ; that, in one case, so little facility is there for carrying on the ordinary administration of the establishment, that the prisoners' food is supplied daily from the neighbouring inn, and the innkeeper's bill constitutes the only accounts which are kept ; that there are times of complete idleness, when neither penal labour nor light employment is given, and that amongst many other abuses communications of a contaminating and injurious tendency take place between the prisoners.

In reviewing this unsatisfactory and discreditable condition of many of the minor borough gaols, the Committee cannot conceal from themselves that it is in a great measure due to a disinclination on the part of the town councils or governing bodies to provide the necessary means for the proper administration of the prison. In one instance, where the visiting justices of the borough, as a measure of common prudence, appointed a warder to assist the governor, who is the only functionary in the gaol, the Town Council have declined to confirm this order, and the warder remains unpaid.

In the same prison no chaplain has been appointed, although the 2 & 3 Vict., c. 56, s. 15, makes this obligatory upon the authorities of every gaol."

APPENDIX C

DETAILS OF NUMBERS AND SALARIES OF STAFF IN
ENGLISH PRISON SERVICE

(As shown in Civil Estimates, Prisons England and Wales, 1933)

Grades.	Nos.	Salaries.[1]
I. HEAD OFFICE.		
Chairman of Commissioners . .	1	£1633
Commissioners	2	£1146–50–1346
Assistant Commissioners and In-spectors	4	£996–25–1146
Surveyor	1	£833–20–1043
Chief Clerk.	1	
Controller of Stores and Manu-factures	1	£668–20–833
Clerk in charge of Accounts . .	1	
Assistant Surveyor . . .	1	£446–15–622
Technical officer. . . .	1	£505–15–622
Staff Clerks	5	£505–15–622
Clerks, Higher Grade . . .	11	£388–15–505
Clerks	35	£90–329
Works Branch		
Clerk in charge	1	£388–15–505
Clerk	1	£90–329
Surveyor's Clerk . . .	1	£172–273
Clerks of Works	6	£270–388
Architectural Assistants (grade II)	1	£270–365
,, ,, (grade III)	6	£197–271
At Weekly Rates		
Shorthand Typists and Typists .	5	
Paper-keeper	1	
Messengers	2	
Cleaners	6	
	94	

[1] Salaries shown are consolidated rates inclusive of former cost-of-living bonus, to nearest pound.

Grades.	Nos.	Salaries.[1]
II. PRISONS AND BORSTAL INSTITUTIONS		
Male Staff		
Governors, Class I . . .	11	£834–25–940
Class II . . .	8	£697–20–813
Class III . . .	11	£564–20–668
Class IV . . .	21	£447–15–535
Chaplains, Established . .	8	£447–15–623
Unestablished . .	7	£380 is normal salary
Part-time . . .	23	Varying salaries from £150–240
Roman Catholic Priests . .	2	One at £535, one at £447
Medical Officers, Class I . .	12	£784–25–940
Class II . .	15	£505–20–726
Part-time . .	23	Varying salaries from £150–300
Housemasters	19	£271–10–353
Assistant Housemasters . .	26	£190
Stewards, Class I . . .	11	£447–15–505
Class II . . .	12	£359–10–417
Class III . . .	15	£271–10–353
Clerks	210	£90–329 (less 10% in provinces)
		Weekly Rates
Pharmacists	8	71/0–2/6–102/0
Farm Bailiff	1	88/0
Superintendent {Printing	1	}99/0–2/0–111/0
{Weaving	1	
Foremen of Works . . .	9	91/0–3/0–102/0
Engineers (Classes I, II, III) .	53	58/0–91/0
Chief Officers (Classes I, II) .	50	83/0–120/0
Principal Officers . . .	162	69/0–78/0
Officers (including 30 under instruction)	1776	43/0 rising to 65/0 after 20 years.
Female Staff		*Salaries.*
Governor	1	£564–20–784
Deputy Governors . . .	2	{ £388–15–476 £300–10–400

[1] Salaries shown are consolidated rates inclusive of former cost-of-living bonus, to nearest pound or shilling.

All established officers serving in prisons or B.Is. are entitled in addition to free quarters or an allowance in lieu, and subordinate officers receive uniform or an allowance in lieu. Unestablished full-time Chaplains and Assistant Housemasters are also provided with quarters.

Grades.	Nos.	Salaries.[1]
Medical Officers, full-time	2	£505–20–726
part-time	1	£288
Lady Superintendent	1	£240–10–288
Hospital Lady Superintendent	1	£240–10–288
Principal Sisters	4	£160–5–185
Nursing Sisters (grades I, II)	45	£112–148
Clerks	3	£90–246 (less 10% in provinces)
		Weekly Rates.
Chief Officers	2	76/0–2/0–83/0
Matrons (Classes I, II)	12	61/0–1/6–73/0
Principal Officers	31	56/0–1/6–60/0
Officers (including 4 under instruction)	153	36/0 rising to 54/0 (after 20 years)
Total officers of all grades	2753[2]	

[1] See footnote on page 242.

[2] N.B.—A fluctuating number of temporary officers is employed in addition, and a number (at present 29) of unestablished Civilian Instructors at varying rates of wage round about £4 a week.

APPENDIX D

PARTICULARS OF ESTABLISHMENTS IN OCCUPATION

Place.	Number of Cells.		Daily Average Numbers (in 1932).		Remarks.
	Men.	Women	Men.	Women	
LOCAL PRISONS					
Bedford . .	149		127		Y.P. Centre.
Birmingham .	495	118	413	48	Centre for "weak-minded."
Bristol . .	252		192		Y.P. Centre.
Brixton .	677		476		London "trials" and "debtors."
Cardiff . .	262	83	167	19	
Dorchester .	159		105		
Durham .	671	70	448	29	Y.P. Centre.
Exeter . .	260	36	179	14	
Gloucester .	135		106		
Holloway .		838		370	
Hull . .	312	115	213	22	
Leeds . .	594		494		
Leicester .	244		190		
Lewes . .	270		255		Centre for London district "Specials."
Lincoln . .	335		232		Centre for "weak-minded."
Liverpool .	1267	[96]	637	[63]	Y.P. Centre. Women's Prison now closed.
Manchester .	824	238	648	99	
Norwich .	166		124		
Oxford . .	147		107		
Pentonville .	1112		799		Adult recidivists.
Shrewsbury .	192		99		
Swansea .	212		113		

Place.	Number of Cells.		Daily Average Numbers (in 1932).		Remarks.
	Men.	Women	Men.	Women	
Wandsworth .	1335		981		Short - term London "Specials." Borstal Wing for "revokees." Centre for "weakminded." Adult recidivists.
Winchester .	321	[42]	251	[25]	Y.P. Centre. Women's Prison now closed.
Wormwood Scrubs	1281		1185		London "Boys' Prison" here. Stars and Second Division only.
TRAINING CENTRE Wakefield .	859		492		Selected long-term locals. Star convicts.
CONVICT PRISONS Aylesbury[1] .	—	16		5	
Chelmsford .	245		106		"Special class" convicts.
Dartmoor .	935		330		Recidivist convicts.
Maidstone .	465		255		Star and young convicts.
Parkhurst .	767		612		Recidivist and medical.
PREVENTIVE DETENTION Aylesbury[1] .	—	12		3	
Portsmouth .	162		[124]		Opened in 1932 as P.D. Prison.
BORSTAL INSTITUTIONS Aylesbury[1] .	—	352	—	122	
Borstal .			410		
Camp Hill	Accommodation		287		
Feltham	is elastic		392		
Lowdham	and varies				
Grange	from time		124		
Nottingham	to time		[85]		Opened in 1932.
Portland			448		

[1] These three establishments count as one, being within the same wall under one Governor.

APPENDIX E

PARTICULARS OF EMPLOYMENT IN PRISONS AND BORSTAL
INSTITUTIONS, WITH THE COMPUTED VALUE OF THE LABOUR,
AS SHOWN IN APPENDIX 6 OF THE ANNUAL REPORT OF THE PRISON
COMMISSIONERS FOR 1931

*Statement of the Employment and Value of the Labour of Prisoners
and Borstal Inmates for the Year ended 31st March, 1932.*

Employment.	Daily average number.	Value.		
MANUFACTURES.		£	s.	d.
Bakers	96	7,049	4	8
Basketmakers	71	2,758	11	1
Bedmakers	153	2,452	4	0
Bone pounders.	—		16	6
Bookbinders	101	8,926	7	2
Brush and Mop-makers . . .	157	4,113	13	9
Carpenters	201	9,979	4	10
Dressmakers	5	507	18	4
Glovemakers	1	10	6	0
Knitters	146	2,563	18	5
,, repairs	112	2,354	7	7
Labourers	30	1,164	17	6
Mailbag makers	3,189	112,767	17	0
Matmakers, coir	139	3,901	0	2
Matmakers, rope	30	1,200	13	11
Moulders.	10	886	19	2
Needleworkers	285	10,129	9	8
,, repairs . . .	151	5,968	13	2
Netmakers	35	905	15	2
Nosebagmakers	26	70	14	1
Oakum Pickers	31	51	19	8
Printers	30	2,687	17	6
Sackmakers	84	2,875	4	4
Sailmakers	15	230	6	0
Ship fender makers	113	3,099	1	6
Shoemakers	313	12,454	14	0

Employment.	Total.	
	Daily average number.	Value.
		£ s. d.
Smiths and Fitters	193	13,625 1 7
Stone pounders	4	156 12 4
Tailors	354	17,935 5 1
Twine and rope makers . . .	80	1,416 0 8
Washers	31	1,946 2 8
Weavers :—		
Cotton and linen . . .	119	4,475 8 7
Matting	16	1,563 3 0
Rug (on frames) . . .	39	506 19 9
Rug (on looms)	68	1,587 9 4
Sword matting	3	43 4 8
Woollen	56	2,255 16 4
Wood choppers	318	4,102 2 9
Total	6,805	248,725 1 11
Average Earnings . .	—	36 11 0
FARM.		
Attending cattle, cropping, market gardening, reclaiming land, labouring, etc.	406	14,096 7 3
Average Earnings . .	—	34 14 5
BUILDING.		
Bricklayers and Masons . . .	143	9,603 2 5
Carpenters and Joiners . . .	102	6,682 19 2
Concrete Moulders	21	1,303 12 0
Electricians	2	133 15 8
Labourers	696	32,001 1 11
Painters and Glaziers . . .	223	16,728 17 4
Plasterers	10	716 11 0
Plumbers	20	1,380 2 11
Quarrymen	20	1,068 15 0
Slaters	3	157 3 2
Smiths and Fitters	100	6,415 10 7
Stone Cutters	25	1,335 18 9
Whitewashers	42	1,802 17 11
Total	1,407	79,330 7 10
Average Earnings . .	—	56 7 8

Employment.	Total.	
	Daily average number.	Value.
DOMESTIC SERVICE.		£ s. d.
Cleaners, Jobbers and Labourers .	949	34,481 15 4
Cooks and Bakers	346	25,199 1 4
Gardeners	355	12,441 14 3
Hospital Orderlies	56	3,046 9 2
Stokers	89	4,040 2 0
Washers	294	18,268 16 0
Total	2,089	97,477 18 1
Average Earnings . .	—	46 13 3
Total (Effectives) . .	10,707	439,629 15 1
Average Earnings . .	—	41 1 2
NON-EFFECTIVES.		
Awaiting trial and appellants . .	254	—
Certified unfit for labour . . .	53	—
Not told off for labour . . .	262	—
Sick	532	—
Under punishment	24	—
Total	1,125	—
Grand Total . . .	11,832	439,629 15 1

APPENDIX F

THE following notes and rules have been drawn up primarily for the guidance of Prison Visitors and Teachers, but all Voluntary Workers in prisons are requested to read them very carefully, and at all times to regard the strict observance of so much thereof as is applicable to their own work as a necessary condition of the continuance of that work.

Visitors in particular are requested to remember that they are allowed to enter prisons on the understanding that they will strictly observe the Prison rules and orders.

1. Visitors are voluntary workers who on the invitation of the Prison Commissioners are permitted to undertake regular visitation of prisoners. Voluntary Teachers are invited by the Governor of the Prison on the recommendation of the Educational Adviser, and subject always to the general approval of the Prison Commissioners. Visitors and Teachers alike share in the work of making the best possible use of the prisoner's time, in order that he may so far as possible leave prison better fitted for citizenship in the free life of the community than before.

2. For this a vigorous training of mind and body is required. To improve character, we have to increase mental and physical health and alertness. A healthier outlook on life and human society, and a sense of responsibility towards fellow-citizens, can best be developed in the quickening mind and the sounder physique which result from making the day's work, both of hand and of brain, as strenuous and as interesting as it can be made.

To this end the prisoner receives simple but sufficient food ; the habit of work is maintained and if possible developed in him by suitable employment ; and bodily vigour is improved by physical exercises. An object of at least equal importance is that of creating and sustaining mental activity, and arousing interests which will drive out of the mind the range of selfish and sordid ideas by which it has too often been occupied, and prove an abiding gain for the prisoner's future life.

Social conversation is, however, another ingredient of ordinary life essential to most men, if they are not to lose balance and perspective. There are obvious difficulties that prevent unlimited conversation between the prisoners themselves ; topics are few and the current of talk is stagnant. People of experience, sense and sympathy, who are unconnected with the official administration of prisons, calling on prisoners in their cells, and conversing on the widest range of topics, can supply this need. Such people can also do much to alter a prisoner's outlook on life, to lessen his selfishness and to rouse in him some idea of his obligations to his fellow-citizens. Sympathy shown in the individual affairs of each prisoner will render him more responsive to the healthy influences brought to bear upon him.

It is for these purposes that the services of Visitors and Teachers are sought at every prison.

3. *Information on current topics may be imparted to prisoners, but controversial politics are to be avoided,* and it will be remembered that religious instruction, and spiritual ministration generally, are the work of the Chaplain. Considerable help can be given to a prisoner by advice as to his studies and reading. Suggestions from Visitors and Teachers as to books which may usefully be added, as funds allow, to the prison libraries, will be welcomed by the Chaplain.

4. *A Voluntary Worker should not concern himself with such questions as the justice of the convictions or the length of the sentences of those whom he visits.* He should not therefore address to the Secretary of State, to Members of Parliament, or to other prominent persons, appeals on behalf of prisoners ; nor should he in his capacity of prison worker approach the Court on behalf of a trial or remand prisoner. Prisoners will often wish to discuss such matters, but the worker should avoid such discussions. For one thing, he has no means of checking the statements of the prisoners : for another, the prisoners not only have their legal rights of appeal but they can at all times state their cases fully in petitions to the Secretary of State. Should there be brought to a worker's notice any matter which appears to deserve attention, but which there is good reason to believe the prisoner cannot present properly in a petition to the Secretary of State, the worker should communicate the point to the Governor or Chaplain of the prison, but not to any person outside.

5. Similarly, any complaints which a prisoner may make to a Worker about his treatment, or that of any other prisoner, or about the conduct of any officer, can be raised by petition or application, and if the Worker feels that he ought to take any notice of them at all, they should be referred to the Governor, who is fully responsible for everything that occurs in the prison.

6. Should a Visitor or Teacher who is interested in a prisoner's personal or family affairs desire to render him any service, the Commissioners, while welcoming such friendly offers, beg him to remember the following :—

(1) Communications with the friends of a prisoner may only be made with the consent of the Governor.

(2) Overlapping and confusion between Visitors, Teachers and the Prisoners' Aid Society are liable to result unless the Voluntary Worker before taking any action consults the Governor or Chaplain.

(3) Any offer of assistance for the prisoner's family, or of assistance for the prisoner himself after discharge should always be made through the Prisoners' Aid Society.

In particular Visitors and Teachers are earnestly requested not to spend money on prisoners in any way, except through the Prisoners' Aid Society, and with the Society's approval.

7. A matter of first importance is the re-establishment, through the Prisoners' Aid Societies, of prisoners on discharge. The recommendations and advice of Visitors, based on the knowledge acquired by them of the character, wishes, circumstances and prospects of prisoners while serving their sentences, are invaluable to the Societies when making provisions for rendering practical assistance to prisoners on discharge : *and all Visitors should regard it as a duty to help the Aid Society by giving the Society information about the prisoners whom they visit.*

Visitors have a direct interest in the working and efficiency of their Prisoners' Aid Society. It is hoped that they will become members of the committee of the Prisoners' Aid Society of their prison. Should the number of Visitors at a prison exceed fifty per cent of the elected Committee of that Society, the Visitors will be asked to nominate from amongst themselves additional members to serve on the Committee not exceeding that number. It is desirable that the Visitors at each prison should arrange for at least one of their number to attend the weekly meetings of the sub-committee of their Prisoners' Aid Society at which provision is made for the needs of prisoners due for discharge during the ensuing month.

The rehabilitation of prisoners on discharge largely depends on the efficient administration of the Prisoners' Aid Society. Generally speaking, the essential requirement is employment. The services of active agents, both paid and voluntary, are required to work throughout the whole area from which prisoners are committed to the Prison. For this purpose funds are needed and it is hoped that Visitors may find it possible to assist their committee in this direction both by suggestions and propaganda.

Those Visitors who are unable to attend the sub-committee meetings should make their recommendations by entering in the Visitors' Book or on the forms provided particulars of the help required. Such recommendations will be placed before the sub-committee of the Aid Society.

8. (1) Visitors, irrespective of creed, act under the general guidance of the Governor and Chaplain. The Visitor will only visit such prisoners as are placed on his list by the Governor. By this means, overlappings and omissions are avoided, and the greatest value is obtained from the Visitors' work.

(2) Teachers act under the general guidance of the Governor and Chaplain who select prisoners for classes and with the assistance of the Educational Adviser decide the courses of study.

Teachers are requested to report to the Governor or Chaplain on individuals whom they consider to be unsuitable for, or who are failing to profit by, their classes.

Suggestions by voluntary workers for any improvement or extension of the educational programme will always be welcomed.

9. Certain teachers find it possible, in addition to taking classes, to continue the instruction of individual members of the class, in their cells. This is a valuable addition to the teacher's work, if the teacher is able to give the time.

10. *All voluntary workers must be careful to observe the rules of the prison ; otherwise their work could not be carried on.* In any case of doubt the Governor will always be ready to advise a worker. It is the duty of the Governor and of all his officers to see that all persons obey the rules.

Particular attention is drawn to the following rules :—

(1) A voluntary worker will not write about any prison matters for publication.

(2) No letter or communication of any kind may be conveyed to or from a prisoner without the Governor's permission.

No food, drink, tobacco, books, papers or article of any kind should be given to a prisoner. Conveying articles into or out of prison contrary to the Regulations is a statutory offence.

(3) After a visit or lesson is over, the voluntary worker will always hand over the prisoner or prisoners to the charge of an officer, except when they are left locked in their cells. Prisoners must not be left in halls, classrooms, etc., without any supervision.

(4) Visits should be paid during the hours that prisoners are normally in their cells, i.e. in the evenings and at week-ends. The Governor can say which hours are most suitable.

(5) An identification card will be given to each Voluntary Worker, who is requested to bring it with him when visiting the prison, for production if necessary.

(6) If a cell key is required for the carrying out of the worker's duties it will be handed to him by the gatekeeper and should be kept on the chain, which should be attached to his clothing. It should be returned to the gatekeeper as the worker leaves the Prison.

(7) After opening a cell door the bolt should be shot double (using first the handle or button, then the key). The door can then be nearly closed, and privacy secured without fear of the door locking. When the interview is ended the door should be closed again, and double-locked.

APPENDIX G

FOR twelve months after the date of conviction the dietary is as follows :—

BREAKFAST, Daily

Bread	6 oz.	
Margarine	$\frac{1}{2}$,,	
Porridge	$\frac{1}{2}$ pint	
Tea	1 ,,	

DINNER, Daily

Bread . . . . . 2 oz.

and one of the undermentioned dinners :—

		Weight or measure.	Number of times it occurs in 28 days.
1.	Beans and Bacon . . .	28 oz.	2
2.	Beef, roast or boiled . . .	22 ,,	1
3.	Beef, and Treacle Pudding .	27 ,,	1
4.	Beef, boiled, and Dumplings .	23 ,,	1
5.	Haricot Mutton . . .	25 ,,	1
6.	Savoury Bacon Pie . . .	28 ,,	2
7.	Meat Pie	25 ,,	1
8.	Meat Pudding	21 ,,	1
9.	Mutton, boiled	22 ,,	1
	,, roast . . .	20 ,,	
10.	Sea Pie	28 ,,	4
11.	Shepherd's Pie	23 ,,	3
12.	Soup	1 pint	2
13.	Stewed Steak, and Treacle Pudding	27 oz.	2
14.	Preserved Meat	15 ,,	4
15.	Hot Pot	23 ,,	1
16.	Irish Stew	23 ,,	1

SUPPER, Daily
    Bread .   .   .   .   .   8 oz.
    Margarine   .   .   .   . $\frac{1}{2}$,,
    Cocoa .   .   .   .   .   1 pint

For the remainder of their sentence, prisoners receive the following food in addition to the dietary set out above :—

BREAKFAST, Daily .   .   .   .   .   Bread 2 oz.

DINNER, Daily .   .   .   .   .   .   Bread 2 ,,
And, with dinner No. 4. . . Fresh Vegetables 4 ,,
,, ,, ,, No. 8. . . ,,   ,,   4 ,,
,, ,, ,, No. 12 on both occasions an additional issue of Soup $\frac{1}{4}$ pint
,, ,, ,, No. 14 on two occasions in 28 days Fresh Vegetables 4 oz.
,, ,, ,, No. 14 ,, . . . Pickles 1 ,,

SUPPER, Daily .   .   .   .   .   .   Cheese 1 ,,

NOTES.

(1) Weights include gravy where applicable, and 12 oz. of potatoes and other vegetables and ingredients, which may be issued in whole or part separately.

(2) Prisoners employed on certain forms of work receive daily, in addition to the above, Margarine $\frac{1}{2}$ oz. and Porridge $\frac{1}{2}$ pint.

(3) Any prisoner who satisfies the Governor that he is a vegetarian, may, on application, be allowed a vegetarian diet. Similarly, any prisoner who has a religious scruple as to any particular article of food may apply for a substitute.

(4) Diets for women, and in convict prisons, allow slight variations from the above.

APPENDIX H

YOUTHS between the ages of 16 and 21 when remanded in custody
from any Court in or around London are sent to the Boys' Prison
at Wormwood Scrubs, and special arrangements have been made
at this prison to obtain information about the character, circumstances and history of these youths.

This information together with an indication of the effect on
the offender of the period spent in prison on remand is available
for a Court if the Court asks for a report from the Governor.

1. There is at Wormwood Scrubs a band of voluntary Women
Visitors, working under the direction and guidance of an experienced leader, who assist the Prison Authorities (a) by visiting
the young offenders in the prison, and (b) by visiting their homes
if their homes are in London or near London. The Visitor communicates to the Prison Authorities the information and impressions gained by personal interviews with the youth himself and
with his parents or guardians.

2. Special attention is given by the Medical Officers of the
Prison to the physical and mental conditions of these young
prisoners.

3. In cases where the Prison Authorities have the duty of
reporting on the suitability of the offender for Borstal training,
enquiry forms are sent to the police, to his parents or guardians,
to employers, to the Headmaster of his school, and, if the prisoner
has previously been on probation, to the Probation Officer.
Particulars are thus collected as to the general character and past
history of the prisoner.

4. These arrangements for the individual study of each young
prisoner have three main objects.

First, it is hoped in due course to compile from the data
furnished by a large number of case papers statistical and other

information bearing on the causes of crime amongst young people.

Secondly, as regards those youths who are ultimately sentenced to Borstal training, the investigation facilitates the assignment of each youth to the most appropriate Institution, and is useful to the Governor and Housemaster who are responsible for his treatment and training.

Thirdly, the Prison Authorities are in a position to supply to any Court, which asks for a report, information which may assist the Court in deciding how to deal with the offender.

Three types of reports are furnished to the Courts by the Prison Authorities.

5. GENERAL REPORTS. If a Court having remanded a youth to prison thinks that, for the purpose of considering how to deal with the offender, it may be useful to have such information as the Prison Authorities can give, it is open to Magistrates to obtain such information by endorsing the Commitment Warrant with a request for a *general* report.

The information obtainable from the Prison Authorities has no bearing on the question of guilt or innocence. The only object of a report from the Prison Authorities is to assist the Court in deciding how to deal with an offender whose offence is proved or admitted.

Usually if a general report is asked for, the report concludes with some tentative expression of opinion on such questions as whether the young offender seems likely to respond to probation, or whether he appears to need a prolonged period of training such as a Borstal sentence would afford, etc. Such expressions of opinion are offered because Magistrates sometimes find it helpful to know the impressions formed in the minds of those who have had the offender under observation while he has been in prison on remand. Any such opinions are, of course, merely submitted for the consideration of the Magistrate, with whom alone rests the responsibility of deciding what course shall be taken.

In cases where a Court decides to place an offender under the supervision of a Probation Officer a copy of the report can, if desired, be supplied for the information of the Probation Officer.

6. BORSTAL REPORTS. When a Court of Summary Jurisdiction contemplates committal of a youthful offender to Quarter Sessions with a view to a Borstal sentence, Section 10 (2) of the Criminal Justice Administration Act, 1914, provides that the

s

Court shall first consider any report or reports which may be made to it by or on behalf of the Prison Commissioners as to the suitability of the offender for Borstal detention. The usual practice is for the Courts to endorse the Commitment Warrant with a request for a report as to the suitability for Borstal training, and thereupon the Prison Authorities report to the Court as to the offender's physical and mental fitness for such training, and make any other representations that may seem desirable as to the general suitability of the case for Borstal treatment.

7. MEDICAL REPORTS. If a Court requires information as to the physical or mental condition of an offender, it is a convenient practice to endorse the Warrant of Commitment with a request for a medical or mental report. In such cases the Prison Medical Officer supplies information to the Court on the defendant's state of health or state of mind. Sometimes Magistrates find it useful to ask both for a general report and for a medical report.

(From a pamphlet issued by the Prison Commission in 1932.)

INDEX

INDEX

For Product Safety Concerns and Information please contact our EU
representative GPSR@taylorandfrancis.com
Taylor & Francis Verlag GmbH, Kaufingerstraße 24, 80331 München, Germany